TWO YEAR

PEKING

1965-1966

Living and Teaching in Mao's China

Reginald Hunt

HURUSCO BOOKS

OXFORD 2016

Copyright: Reginald Hunt 2016
Two Years in Peking 1965-1966

ISBN 978-0-9560235-1-3

Published by Hurusco Books
21 Osberton Road, Oxford, OX2 7PQ

Email: twoyearsinpeking6566@gmail.com

A CIP catalogue record of this book can be obtained from the British Library.

Front cover designed by Barry Gilbert
Pupils at the Attached School of Peking Foreign Languages Institute
Back cover
Exit visa for Hunt family to leave China by 31ˢᵗ December 1966

Book design by Holly Hunt

Printed by Wheatley Printers Ltd, Thrupp, Stroud

ABOUT THE AUTHOR

Reginald Hunt was born and bred in the City of Gloucester, and his schooling was at Tredworth Primary and the Crypt Grammar School.

He served two years National Service in the Royal Air Force, including an eight month posting to Hong Kong. After that he graduated from the School of Oriental & African Studies, University of London, with a degree in Modern Standard Chinese. He spent four years teaching English at the Attached School of the Peking Foreign Languages Institute in 1965-66 and 1974-76. He is retired and now lives in Oxford.

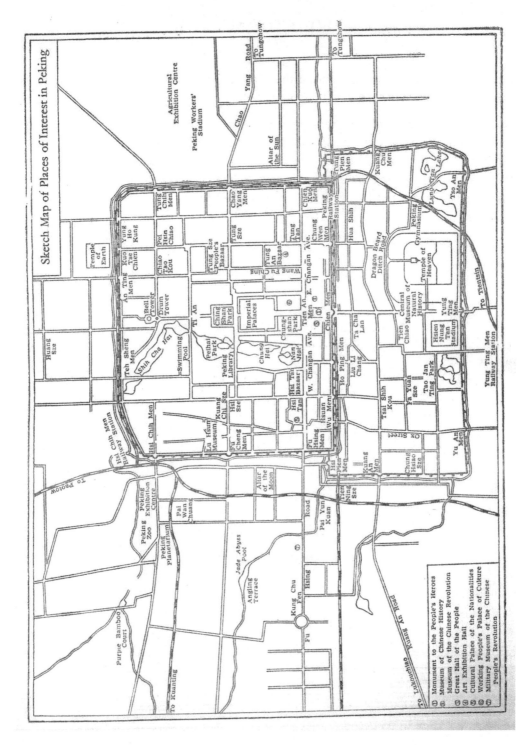

Map of Peking 1960

CONTENTS

PREAMBLE

My aim in writing this book is to record an historical glimpse of life as it was for foreigners and their families, employed by the Chinese government, and working in China in the mid-1960s. This was a mere fifteen years after the establishment of the sovereign People's Republic of China in 1949. The world that we lived in for those two years, 1965-66, has long since gone.

Memories of living in Peking, from 7 January 1965 to 20 December 1966, have brought back many feelings from that time, and I can see clearly now that my wife Waddi and I entered the unknown, when we set out for Peking with our family. We arrived there with two small sons, Tim and Matt, and we returned home to the UK with three sons, Tim, Matt and Alex, all under seven years of age. We knew nothing about Chinese society, save that it was 'communist', and we were ignorant of Marxist writings, 'dialectical materialism' and Mao's distinctive teachings; in a nutshell, we were not believers in socialism. I had studied Mandarin Chinese at university, with a little history and literature thrown into the curriculum, but no politics.

As a result of this course of study I had the incentive to go and teach in China, and see what was happening there. We were both assigned to teach English at the Attached School of the Peking Foreign Languages Institute, for the duration of our two year contracts. Then we went back to teach in Peking again, at the same Attached School, for another two years from April 1974 till April 1976. So altogether we saw the first six months of the Cultural Revolution in 1966, and the final two years of it, 1974-76. Through the year 1976, Premier Chou En-lai, Marshal Chu Teh and Chairman Mao Tse-tung all died. They were three of the main players in the history of the Communist Party, and key power figures in the leadership of the People's Republic of China from October 1949. Things were bound to change from then on.

I have made brief reference to people and events from Chinese history, wherever appropriate to my story, in order to fill out a little of the relevant background and context. All of these historical facts can be accessed online at Wikipedia, from information on the Internet, or be read in depth from the plethora of quality books on things Chinese available today. I have made a brief selection of some of these books in the bibliography, all of which are written by eye-witnesses, scholars, journalists and dedicated sinologists, some of whom have spent their careers in this field.

I have tried to give the flavour of our life and work in Peking, our reactions and responses, and our relationships with Chinese colleagues and students, with other foreigners, as well as with the formidable bureaucratic machinery watching over us. Some fifty years of hindsight have given me the opportunity to place my memories within the experiences drawn from later visits, study and thoughts on China. Good friends have advised me to stress the enormous scale of China's geo-cultural landmass, the massive population and the diversity and differences within it, in order to remind the reader that my Peking experience, even though set in the political hub of the country, does not, in any way, represent a composite reality for the whole of China.

Foreigners in Peking employed by the Chinese government, with few exceptions, were all housed in the vast Friendship Guesthouse complex, and given a comfortable standard of living there. In those early days of the People's Republic of China I can quite understand the need to look after these experts, and have them conveniently based in one place. The downside was that we were not integrated into Chinese society to any degree, and had little real contact with people outside of our work unit. Even there, our colleagues were restrained in their social contact with us, and they were the closest we could get to Chinese life and thinking.

Since we left Peking in April 1976, the buildings and streets of the city have been transformed into the dynamic, high-rise city of Bei.jing. Similarly, the Chinese people have metamorphosed, from a minimal energy output into a high-powered, manufacturing workforce, churning out countless mass-produced items for the world's consumers. Those products now include an expanding range of luxury goods and higher-quality technology. Chinese applications for patents now outstrip those from America and Japan; the number of billionaires keeps climbing.

This economic boom began from the start of the 1980s, and as they themselves describe it today, their society is now 'Socialism with Chinese Characteristics'. Notwithstanding that a Pandora's Box has opened up, revealing a host of apparently insoluble problems; such as, gross income differentials, social injustices, endemic corruption, uncontrolled development, and little protection, socially and legally, for the vast masses of society.

As this book slowly grew over the past five years, I have come to realise that all my accumulated photographs, materials and documents would require a separate book on their own. So I plan to publish two books under the title of *Two Years in Peking, 1965-66*. This is the first one, which is about our life and work during those two years. The second one will be a resource book of photos, documents and teaching materials.

I would like to thank Waddi, and sons Tim, Matt and Alex for all their memories and anecdotes of living in Peking during our four years stay there, and to the family support team of Muniya Barua, Nadine Delamillieure, Holly Hunt, Jacqui Hunt, William Hunt and Alan Rea. My great thanks to Keith Scott and David Owen, who were my two excellent editorial advisors and wise counsellors.

I greatly appreciated the help of all the following friends who found time to patiently read through drafts of my chapters, and who gave me sound feedback, and perceptive advice: Howard & Gill Allen, Alan Barr, David Blake, Adrian Brooks, Barry Gilbert, Jill Harvey, John Henty, Norman Hui, Alan Jenkins, Leslie Jones, Terence Keyms, Liz Owen, David Pettit, Gordon Purdy, Graham & Joan Russell.

For technical help on the computer in book layout and assembling the photographs and associated documents I would like to thank Barry Gilbert, Holly Hunt, Matt & Jacqui Hunt, Tim Hunt, Jonas Pollard. My thanks to Barry Gilbert for the design of the front cover, and my very special thanks to Holly Hunt for the Book Design.

All this assistance has been a great source of strength to me, and I could not have produced this book without it. In the end, as the author, the final responsibility for the contents of this book lies solely with me.

Reginald Hunt   July 2016

NOTES ON CHINESE ROMANISATION[1]

In 1965, all Chinese people, when speaking of their capital city, used the name Bei.jing, and of course it was always written as Bei.jing in Chinese characters. Yet English-speaking residents when talking about it, usually used the old name of Peking, and strangely enough, in English-language publications of the Chinese government, it was also written as Peking. In 1949 the People's Republic of China had re-named their capital Bei.jing (Northern Capital) to replace the previous name of Bei.ping (Northern Peace).

In 1958 the government had introduced a new authorised form of Romanisation for the modern standard Chinese language, called Han.yu Pin.yin[2] (Chinese-Language-Spelling). The Chinese government called it in English the 'Chinese phonetic alphabet'. This rendered the phonic sound of each Chinese character into the English alphabetic form of writing, with a diacritic mark placed over each syllable to indicate the tone. I will use this Han.yu Pin.yin system as the standard form of Romanisation in my two books, but without the diacritic markings.

This Romanisation system was crucial in the government's drive to increase literacy in China, in particular, as a faster guide and an intermediate prop to help in learning characters. So it was introduced early into Primary school teaching and adult education programmes. It took a long time in primary schooling for Chinese pupils to achieve a reasonable level of reading and writing characters, necessary to enter junior school at the age of twelve. To speed up this process they could learn by heart the English roman alphabet, just a mere twenty six symbols, which would give them the phonic sound of each character. In addition they had to know how to write each character, and the meaning. The sets of elementary character learning cards on sale in town had the character and Han.yu Pin.yin spelling on one side, and the meaning on the other side, in the form of a picture of the actual object.

My teaching colleagues at school must have learnt the old Chinese Romanisation system, derived from postal names and Wade-Giles[3], which had been in usage up till 1958, because when they were writing out the name lists of our junior and senior classes they always used that old form. The crucial difference from Wade-Giles was that it omitted the diacritic number attached to each syllable to denote the tone. The Chinese themselves refer to this system as 'Old Chinese Romanisation'.

Paradoxically, in our school in 1965, our teaching materials for the junior and senior classes still used that old Romanisation for all Chinese names and places, while at the same time the primary school classes were using the new Han.yu Pin.yin system. All primary school class lists, books and teaching materials used this new Romanisation. So it was clear that the Chinese foreign language publishing houses had not yet all adopted this new form of spelling. On the other hand, travelling around Peking, I could see all the street names were written in Chinese characters and Han.yu Pin.yin. There appeared to be no consistency.

For myself, Han.yu Pin.yin was also an initial hurdle, because it was new to me. When studying Chinese in London I had been taught the Gwoyeu Romatzyh[4] form of Romanisation, promoted by Professor Walter Simon of the School of Oriental & African Studies, University of London. So in 1965, in my teaching materials I was dealing with two contrasting Roman alphabet spellings, that is, the old Chinese Romanisation and the new Han.yu Pin.yin. Now in 2015, Han.yu Pin.yin is accepted internationally, excluding Taiwan, as the standard form of Romanisation for the transcription of Chinese names and places, and in a wider context, in the teaching of the Chinese language to foreigners.

In fact, Han.yu Pin.yin was not completely accepted in mainland publications until *Peking Review*, the weekly political magazine, finally changed its name to *Beijing Review* on 5th January 1979. So up to 1979 I am calling the city that we lived in Peking, and then, after Teng Hsiao-ping's consolidation of power at that time, I am calling it Bei.jing. I will keep all the old Romanised spellings as they occurred in our teaching materials, and in the Chinese publications. Where it is appropriate I will also give the Han.yu Pin.yin spellings in square brackets following, without the diacritic markings. Likewise, for all other names of Chinese people and places, I will present the Han.yu Pin.yin equivalents in the same way.

The Chinese spoken language is basically a syllabic language with reasonable weighting given to each character's phonic sound. Compare this with English, a stress-timed language, where the average spoken compound word has only one syllable stressed, leaving the others unstressed. To satisfy my pedagogic inclinations, and help readers distinguish between the actual Chinese syllables involved, I am trying a little experiment. When writing Chinese compound words in Han.yu Pin.yin I am inserting a single dot between each syllable, in order to define the separate syllabic sounds. As examples of this, Beijing becomes Bei.jing, and Hanyu Pinyin becomes Han.yu Pin.yin.

Chapter Notes

1. Romanization of Chinese- Wikipedia online
2. Pinyin (Hanyu Pinyin)- Wikipedia online
3. Wade-Giles- Wikipedia online
4. Gwoyeu Romatzyh- Wikipedia online

THE NATIONWIDE MOVEMENTS FROM THE FOUNDING OF THE PEOPLE'S REPUBLIC OF CHINA IN 49 TO THE YEAR OF 76 WHEN MAO DIED

1. The Land Reform Movement (1947-52)
2. The Movement to Suppress Counter Revolutionaries (50-51)
3. The Movement to Resist America and Aid Korea (50-53)
4. The First Rectification Campaign of the Party (50-53)
5. The Movement of Democracy in the Company of the People's Liberation Army (PLA) (50-51)
6. The Movement to Comb Dissidents Out (51-52)
7. The Movement to Consciously Make a Clear Confession for "Middle Ranking Cadres" (51-52)
8. The Movement to Clean Up the "Middle Ranking Cadres" (51-52)
9. The Movement of Democratic Reforms (51-54)
10. The Movement to Criticize the Film *Story of Wu Xun* and the Propagation of Wu Xun (51-52)
11. The Study of the "San Zi" Reform and the Movement of the Democratic Reform of the Christian Church (51-54)
12. The Movement of Mutual Aid and Co-operation in Agriculture (51-56)
13. The Movement of Self-Education and Self-Reform on the Cultural and Educational front and All Sorts of Educated People (51-54)
14. The Movement Against Embezzling, Waste and Bureaucracy (51-52)
15. The Movement of Ideological Remoulding on Education, Literature and Art and Science Fronts (51-52)
16. The Movement of "Five Antis": Anti-bribery, Anti-evading Taxes and Defrauding the Revenue, Anti-stealing State Property, Anti-cheating on Labour and Materials and Anti-stealing State Economic Information (52.1-52.10)
17. The Movement of Anti-Violating the Law and Discipline (53-54)
18. The Movement of Rectification and Building of the Party (54)
19. The Movement of Studies and Criticizing Hu Shi (54-55)
20. The Movements from Eliminating Hu Feng's Thinking on Literature and Art to Movement of Eliminating Hu Feng's Counter-revolutionary Clique (55-56)
21. The Movement to Eliminate Hidden Counter-revolutionaries (55-57)
22. The Rectification Campaign of the Communist Party (57.4-6)
23. The Anti-Rightists Movement (57-58)
24. The Rectification Campaign on Business Circles (57)
25. The Patriotic Health Movement with the "Killing the Four Perils" as its Central Work (The four perils: flies, mice, mosquitoes and sparrows)
26. The Movement of the Great Leap Forward (58-60)
27. The Movement of the People's Communes (58)

UNPUBLISHED MANUSCRIPT FROM CHINA SOURCE

THE POLITICAL LEADERS OF CHINA 1956-1966

Eighth Politburo Standing Committee -1956-66- of the Central Committee of the Communist Party of China

(See: 'Historical Membership of the Politburo Standing Committee' Wikipedia Online)

Old Romanisation:	**New Romanisation (Introduced 1958)**
Mao Tse-tung	Mao Ze.dong
Liu Shao-chi	Liu Shao.ji
Chou En-lai	Zhou En.lai
Chu Teh	Zhu De
Teng Hsiao-ping	Deng Xiao.ping
Chen Yun	Chen Yun
Lin Piao (Appointed 1958)	Lin Biao

THE EIGHT ELDERS (THE EIGHT 'IMMORTALS')

They were top revolutionary leaders in 1949, and through the early years of power of the Chinese Communist Party. During the Cultural Revolution they all suffered at the hands of Red Guards, but managed to survive, and they were afterwards rehabilitated, and worked with Deng Xiao.ping on the new road forward for China. None of these men are alive today, but their children, often referred to as the 'Princelings', are said to be extremely influential and rich in the China of 2015.

New Romanisation (Han.yu Pin.yin)

Bo Yi.bo
Chen Yun
Deng Xiao.ping
Li Xian.nian
Peng Zhen
Song Ren.qiong
Wang Zhen
Yang Shang.kun
(Some lists include Wan Li and Xi Zhong.xun)

CHINESE PERSONAL NAMES

(See "Jordans Mandarin Romanisation" concordance table online)

New Romanisation	Old Romanisation
Bo Yi.bo	Po I-po
Bo Xi.lai	
Chen Bo.da	Chen Po-ta
Chen Du.xiu	Chen Tu-hsui
Chen Yi	Chen Yi
Chen Yun	Chen Yun
Chen Xiao.lu	Chen Hsiao-lu
Deng Xiao.ping	Teng Hsiao-ping
Gao Li.duan	
Jiang Qing	Chiang Ching
Ke Qing.shi	
Kong Fu.zi	Confucius
Liang Heng	
Li Hong.zhang	Li Hung-chang
Li Xian.nian	Li Hsien-nien
Lin Biao	Lin Piao
Ling Ken	
Liu Shao.ji	Liu Shao-chi
Lu Ping	Lu P'ing
Mao Ze.dong	Mao Tsc-tung
Meng.zi	Mencius
Peng Zhen	P'eng Chen
Peng De.huai	P'eng Te-huai
Qiao Guan.hua	
Song Ren.qiong	
Sun Zhong.shan	Sun Yat-sen
Wang Zhen	Wang Chen
Xi Jin.ping	
Yang Shang.kun	Yang Shang-k'un
Yang Xian.yi	
Zeng Guo.fan	Tseng Kuo-fan
Zhang Han.zhi	
Zhou En.lai	Chou En-lai
Zhu De	Chu The

CHINESE PLACE NAMES

Old Romanisation	New Romanisation
Amoy	Xia.men
Antingmen	An.ding.men
Canton	Guang.zhou
Chang An	Chang.an
Changsha	Chang.sha
Chinan	Ji.nan
Chinhwangtao	Chin.huang.dao
Fukien	Fu.jian
Heilungkiang	Hei.long.jiang
Haitien	Hai.dian
Hangchow	Hang.zhou
Harbin	Ha.er.bin
Hop'ingmen	He.ping.men
Hsitan	Xi.dan
Kiangsu	Jiang.su
Liulichang	Liu.li.chang
Muhling	Mu.ling
Nanking	Nan.jing
Pei Tai Ho	Bei.dai.he
Peking	Bei.jing
Shanghai	Shang.hai
Shaoshan	Shao.shan
Sian	Xi.an
Sinkiang	Xin.jiang
Soochow	Su.zhou
Tienanmen	Tian.an.men
Tientsin	Tian.jin
Tsinan	Ji.nan
Tungan	Dong.an
Tungfeng	Dong.feng
Wangfuching	Wang.fu.jing
Wuhan	Wu.han
Yenan	Yan.an

PHOTOS by Reginald Hunt with CAPTIONS

1. Junior Three class at morning exercises- 1965
2. Morning break on school campus- 1965
3. Morning break on school campus- 1965
4. Junior Two class in Bei.hai Park- 1965
5. Waddi teaching Junior Two class in Bei.hai Park- 1965
6. Senior class excursion to Western Hills- 1965
7. Wangfuching- Wallposters on shop window- 23 August 1966
8. Wangfuching- Wallposters- August 1966
9. Red Guards in Tienanmen square- October 1966
10. Red Guard Long March squad in Tienanmen- October 1966 (Photo by Waddi Hunt)
11. Red Guard squad leaving along Chienmen- November 1966
12. Red Guard squad entering along Chienmen- November 1966
13. Great Wall at Pa Ta Ling- 1965
14. Pei Tai Ho seaside resort: Beach for foreigners- Summer 1966
15. Building clamp at Ta Tui village- November 1966
16. Rest break at Ta Tui village- November 1966
17. Host family at Ta Tui village- November 1966
18. Shanghai- Red Guard demonstration outside former Wing On Department Store - December 1966
19. Shanghai- Red Guard Long March squad- December 1966
20. Shanghai- Wall poster on The Bund "Down with Liu Shao-chi! Down with Teng Hsiao-ping!"- December 1966
21. Shanghai- Pedicab on the street- December 1966
22. Hangchow- Red Guards on Mao's 73rd Birthday- December 1966
23. Hangchow-Shanghai train- Overturned stone tortoise and stele in the country-side- December 1966
24. Hangchow- Waddi, Tim and Matt in Pedicab- December 1966

LIST OF APPENDICES

1

JOB CONTRACT IN PEKING

In 1964 I was teaching Maths to 'O' level, and assisting with Games, at Cheltenham Technical High School. My degree in Mandarin Chinese gave little hope of advancement in secondary schooling in those days, except for one particular school in Abingdon, run by Berkshire Education Committee. During the summer of that year I went to visit my old university classmate, who was teaching Mandarin Chinese at this very school, the John Mason High School. He told me the astonishing news that China was currently recruiting teachers of English language to work in their largest cities, and this was an exciting prospect for me.

My interest in China had originated in October 1955, during my two years of National Service in the Royal Air Force. Basic training had taken place at RAF Hednesford in the Midlands, and three of us from our intake had applied to join a Russian language course; and after interviews we had been accepted. Then, just before the end of our eight week 'square-bashing', we three were called in by the station Education Officer there, who asked if we wished to transfer to a RAF Chinese linguists' course starting soon. All three of us[1], standing at ease in front of him, said "Yessir" on the spot, without any time for thought, or for the future. As a result, in late September of that year, we were among the forty young National Servicemen of subordinate rank, 'aircraftsmen second-class', assembled at RAF Wythall near to Birmingham, and our one year Chinese language training got under way. We couldn't believe our luck when told that after training we would be posted to Hong Kong for the remainder of our National Service. A 'plum' posting, where we worked as radio operators on voice interception, listening in to Chinese military messages.

I was so charged up by this news of a chance to teach English in China, and to escape from being a lowly Maths teacher, that the very next day I was knocking on the side door of the Chinese Charge D'Affaires Office at 31 Portland Place in London. I had to persist in knocking until the door was opened a fraction by a suited gentleman, and marooned on the doorstep, I managed to explain in a few words that I was a teacher in a secondary school in England, could speak some Chinese, and that I would like to teach English in China. Whispered conversations went on behind that imposing door, and then I was asked who had recommended me to apply. This seemingly inconsequential question constantly recurred at later interviews, but this first time I quickly dismissed it by saying that a friend had informed me and I had taken the action myself. After further whispering I was given a name and told to write a letter to that office giving all my qualifications and background information. Then, with a slight nod, the large portal was gently closed on my first door-to-door salesman experience.

So I posted off my curriculum vitae[2] to their office, in which I recorded my two years of National Service in the RAF, but I never mentioned my linguist trade. Three weeks later I received a reply inviting me to visit them at Portland Place, and when I got there I was taken to a spacious high-ceilinged room, heavily curtained, and with large framed portraits on the wall of Liu Shao-chi and Chu Teh, but no Chairman Mao. I later noticed his painting in one of the adjoining rooms. My chat with the two Chinese gentlemen puttered along on different tracks as they tried to make me out, and see how genuine I was, but politics never once came into the conversation at all. During one pause I said that my wife Waddi would also like to teach English in China, but this, apparently, did not raise any enthusiasm on their part.

Suddenly the old question of who had recommended me to apply to their office reappeared. Although I was baffled by the irrelevance of this question, I slowly explained that John Marney, an old university classmate had told me the news. They noted his name but obviously had no idea who he was, so he was not high up on their list of crucial UK contacts. At that time I had no understanding of the power and importance of social connections (guan.xi) in greasing the wheels of career opportunities for Chinese people.

Another letter arrived two weeks later inviting me to a second meeting. The contents did not make any commitment on their side, but I realised that it was a positive step and they were interested in employing me. On that second visit Waddi came as well, so there we were sitting in the same reception room, opposite the huge painting of Liu Shao-chi, sipping Chinese tea and talking about the generalities of living in China, but never anything about politics. We had two sons under four years of age, so we wanted to know the availability of milk, dairy products and the range of food and dietary content necessary for them. They were very convincing that the milk and diet provided in China would be fine for us and our sons, and said that we would be living in a modern, fully furnished flat with central heating. In fact, when we got to Peking, the apartment was quite satisfactory, but the milk was watery and the one form of cheese quite tasteless. However, thanks to the previous Russian presence there, the Guesthouse restaurants always had nutritious yoghurt available, which fortunately the boys liked. Right at the end of our chat Waddi brought up the question of her wanting to teach English too, and they immediately became vague, and said that it would be discussed when we got to Peking; as would the contract, salaries and our place of work. In the end, we had to trust them or give up the chance of teaching in China.

The next letter took longer to come, presumably as they were waiting for confirmation from Peking about our application, and when it finally arrived it simply said that I had been accepted as a teacher of English, and could we set out for Peking within two weeks. This time I invited myself to their office to explain that I was a full-time teacher in a state secondary school, and according to my teaching contract, I had to give six weeks (half a school term) notice of leaving. That meant I couldn't finish at my school until Christmas 1964 when the autumn term ended. As we wanted to spend Christmas and New Year with our families, and we also had to vacate our rented house and pack our belongings, we wouldn't be able to depart for China until January 1965. This delay may have confused them, because after my initial enthusiasm I was now postponing our departure date.

As I discovered when I got to China, any instruction to an individual from their workplace (dan.wei) should be carried out promptly, without question. But I was a 'foreign devil', who had to be treated differently! Whatever their misgivings about this cross-cultural hiccup, the net result was that they finally agreed that we should leave at the beginning of January 1965. As proof of our intention to go to China, we filled a small metal trunk with lots of kiddie clothes, toys, tape-recorder and things, and their office

2

arranged for it to be sent by sea to Peking. We were told to address it c/o a certain Mr Tang Kai, of the Commission for Cultural Relations with Foreign Countries, a mysterious someone we never got to know, but his name has stayed painted on the battered trunk, still surviving in the garage, right up to today. And we got our visas for China. In those days my sons were registered on my passport, and their visas were too.

Our flight was originally booked for 3 January 1965, but Tim became ill just before that date so it was postponed till 7 January. On that day, Waddi's brother Roland drove us to Heathrow, his car loaded down with our luggage and children's things, and we arrived there to be met by a Chinese official from the London Office with our tickets for the afternoon Aeroflot flight to Moscow. He said that a Chinese Embassy representative would meet us at Moscow airport to guide us on the remainder of the journey. As we passed into the departure lounge I suddenly wondered what we were doing there, and just then over the tannoy system came a message of bon voyage from Rachelle, one of Waddi's sisters. It was an emotional moment, but we were so enmeshed in getting our family on board that we had no time for tears.

It was a large Tupolev aircraft furnished in a comfortable style, which I would describe as Edwardian, with little side-tables and lamps, plenty of space, and several Russian air hostesses, who were extremely attentive and helpful with the children. We saw that there were only about a dozen passengers, including us, spread around on board, so these ladies were not exactly overworked. The four hour flight passed very quickly and by the time we had finished the light meal and were more relaxed, we were able to have a short chat with our nearest neighbour, a black-haired lively young man of around twenty, who had seemed ready to talk and socialise. We exchanged superficial pleasantries, and he was quite impressed that we were going to Peking to teach English, and asked about our children and how they would cope there, and so on. He told us that he was going to take part in an International Piano Competition in Moscow, and just as we parted I wished him luck and asked his name. It was Daniel Barenboim.

After three hours waiting in the Moscow airport restaurant we finally boarded an internal Russian flight to Irkutsk. We soon became aware of the fact that our diet was already in flux, because we were served a snack of boiled eggs, yogurt and dark bread; we had to request some tea, which arrived milk-less and with a strange taste. At Irkutsk more passengers boarded there for the last leg to Peking, and I found I was sitting by a youngish Chinese man, who was dressed in good-quality dark blue Chinese jacket and trousers. When this was combined with his natural confidence I assessed him as a high official of some kind. He spoke basic Standard English, with a faint, stilted foreign accent, and when I asked which English-speaking country he had studied in he said that he had learnt his English in China, and had only been abroad as far as Moscow.

He later informed me that we were arriving over the outskirts of Peking, and looking down I was overwhelmed by the bleak, brown shades of the landscape, with some faint green lines of coniferous trees, and then little greyish clumps of hamlets and villages scattered around. It was a shock coming from green and rain-soaked England to brown and hard-frozen Peking, a city which was always short of water. There appeared to be little air traffic that day, and we landed under a beautiful blue sunny sky, but we discovered no warmth from the sun.

The airport runways and taxiways were inactive, and I could see only three other standing aircraft in the distance. The atmosphere was like a rarely-used, small regional airport in 1960s Britain, but this one could take large Russian airliners. Our almost empty Tupolev was able to park straightaway, without any hassle, near the small terminal building. We were last to disembark, and we walked down the mobile stairway on to solid land with two young sons and all our paraphernalia. They were steps into the unknown for us.

A welcoming delegation of six people was lined up on the tarmac nearby to greet us, including three future colleagues, one male and two females, and it was reassuring to hear English again, as they introduced themselves and gave us bouquets of flowers, while taking charge of our bulky luggage. That was when my first cross-cultural experience occurred. Our future male colleague tried desperately to grab the karricot that I was carrying, and I had to physically struggle to hold on to it. I had to show him that baby Matthew was asleep in this portable cot, not suitcase, before realisation hit him and he laughed nervously. Coincidentally, we discovered later that he was the only one of our colleagues who was a member of the Chinese Communist party. Nevertheless, I was touched by this reception committee meeting us.

We walked to the small terminal building, and were gently shepherded through customs and immigration without any delays, only being stopped by the health officials, who carefully checked the records of our inoculations and injections. At that time we did not realise how cold it was, and how everyone was wrapped in well-padded clothing. For some reason one of the female colleagues noticed my socks, and was shocked when I told her that I was wearing only a pair of normal trousers, without any under-layers. I was dressed for the average cold and wet English winter, but was not really prepared for the dry, insinuating cold of the Peking climate. She instructed me forcefully that my family and I should all be wearing padded clothing from now on. We did heed her advice, and on our first trip into town after settling in we bought cotton-padded clothing for the boys, and then padded overcoats for ourselves. To illustrate the extreme coldness of Peking, all lakes, canals, and standing water, including the Imperial City moat, were frozen solid from roughly mid-November to mid-February.

Within minutes we were ensconced in the back of a warm, capacious black limousine belonging to our institute, and we were off into town at a slow stately speed of somewhere around 20 mph. The Dean of the Foreign Languages of the Institute, and our School Head, took the front seats, while the two women colleagues sat with us. The others followed behind in a much smaller car, with all our luggage in. In this short space of time, we were hit by another cultural practice, which proved to be the most irritating of all, and that was the regular use of the car horn, which constantly interrupted our conversations. In fact, the driver had every right to use the horn in this way, even though he only drove at a slow speed; in the event of a road accident, especially one involving pedestrians, he would be held solely responsible for any injuries or worse.

We were told that we would have a little tour through central Peking on the way to our home in the Friendship Guesthouse [You.yi Bin.guan]. Passing through the countryside outskirts seemed to take a long time before we reached the eastern end of Chang An [Chang.an] boulevard, which was the pivotal east-west axis running directly through the centre of Peking. It was very broad without much traffic, only a few official cars, fac-

4

tory trucks, lorries, and then within the city environs, various single decker trolley-buses and red buses. In the curb-side lanes there were a mass of bicycles and a range of pedicarts transporting an array of goods. At that time no donkey, oxen or horse-drawn carts were permitted to travel on this central avenue, so they had to go by circui-tous routes, and you could always see them on the side roads.

Our colleagues pointed out famous places, including the Observatory of Ancient Astro-nomical Instruments, established during the Ming dynasty 1368-1644, and situated on a part of the old city wall that was still standing. Reaching Tienanmen [Tian.an.men] square we saw the famous rostrum on the main gate where the Chinese leaders stood on celebration days, and then on the sides were the Great Hall of the People, built in ten months in 1958, and the Museum of the Revolution. As we drove westwards, our col-leagues proudly pointed out the few new buildings erected since 1949, all of which were large and imposing, and stood out in comparison to the generally low skyline of buildings in Peking; one memorable building being Peking Radio and Broadcasting.

We left Chang An boulevard and started the long drive north, eventually passing the Zoo and the Purple Bamboo Park, before ending up at the Friendship Guesthouse. It had very imposing solid stone, main buildings, flanked by blocks of flats that stretched back into the distance. A huge self-contained complex, it had been originally built for the Russian experts and their families who had come in large numbers during the 1950s. The Russian name was Druzhba, and foreigners still sometimes used that name when referring to it. We entered one of the blocks, and immediately several white-jacketed service personnel appeared and carried all our bags and baggage up to the third floor and into our solid and comfortable centrally-heated flat, with varnished wooden floors and thick Chinese carpets. The lounge and our bedroom contained huge thermos flasks, and our colleagues explained that this was hot boiled water for drinking, as we should not drink water from any taps. The bathroom was functional with a bath and shower, and a western-style toilet. We were advised that water, especially hot water, was ra-tioned, and we were told the times that it was available daily. Strong assurances were given that there would be hot water for us that evening.

So all six of our welcoming delegation were inspecting our flat with us, and we eventu-ally reached the kitchen. It was a small room with stone floor, completely bare except for a small stone sink and one cold tap. My heart sank on seeing it, and Waddi broke into tears. Her reaction prompted a rapid dispersal of the delegation, and a thick enve-lope containing four hundred yuan[3] (£57), in five yuan notes, was quickly thrust into my hand, before they all disappeared. In actual fact, although our kitchen was a disas-ter area, we never had to use it for the next two years, and always ate in one of the com-munal dining halls. So we were spared all the associated chores of food shopping and cooking every day. The chief function of our kitchen was as the home of a small elec-tric ring and kettle, which we used to make coffee or tea for breakfast.

We were left to survey our apartment and organise the children, before dinner was served in the main dining hall at 6 p.m. And to ponder that such emotions as crying seemed to present problems for our Chinese colleagues. When we had settled in, the only tangible problem facing us was the old-fashioned cot on four legs, with wooden bars, that was going to be Matthew's bed that night. On closer examination it was very grimy, and although the service staff gave it a cursory clean, after they had left, we gave it a thorough scrubbing ourselves. Around six o'clock we wandered over to the large restaurant, situated in the main building, and there met my old college friend Giorgio Zucchetti, who had studied Chinese with me at London University. He ordered our meal, made some introductions, and generally briefed us on things about our new residence. So ended our first day in China.

Postscript

Over the following months we had several meetings with Lao Han, the tall Deputy-Head of our school, and asked him about signing our contracts, but were usually told that it would happen later. Right from the beginning the Institute paid our salaries of 420 yuan per month for me, and 270 yuan for Waddi. I didn't sign my contract until September 1965, and my monthly salary was then raised to 460 yuan. Waddi, after a year of meetings and negotiations on her contract, during which time she had shown the school her capabilities and success in teaching English, finally signed hers in January 1966, and was granted 'foreign expert' status. To take on Chinese bureaucracy, and to go from low status foreign wife to become a 'foreign expert' in her own right, was an outstanding achievement. As a result her salary increased to 340 yuan per month. The Chinese currency was the ren.min.bi (people's currency), which foreigners referred to as the 'yuan', and the rate of exchange was seven yuan to the pound sterling. For our two year stay in China, all financial transactions were carried out in paper money and cash, and all calculations carried out on the ubiquitous abacus. The nearest we got to a bank account was the savings bank in a small room within the Druzhba, where all our deposits and withdrawals were carefully recorded in a little notebook, by the person on duty.

I understood that in western terms, a simple contract consisted of an offer, an acceptance and an exchange of consideration between the two parties, and all these basic conditions had been met on both sides, but here in China, before signing it, more negotiations seemed perfectly acceptable. Obviously we were in a weak position, and everything was laid down by the Chinese side. I felt, instinctively, that the Chinese needed to assess us before signing contracts, and anyway we were being treated according to the vague agenda outlined in London. Contrast this with the UK, where all teaching contracts had to be signed by teachers well in advance, before they could take up their new post.

Chapter Notes:
1. Ten years later, one of us was lecturing in Chinese at Leeds University, another lecturing in Chinese at Sydney University, while I was teaching English in Peking. We are still in touch.
2. Curriculum vitae- details of qualifications and work experience.
3. Chinese Yuan- Wikipedia online

2

POTTED HISTORY OF OUR SCHOOL

In the 1940s, an embryo foreign affairs school was set up in the communist-controlled areas of China, and after their victory in the civil war in 1949, it was established as the Foreign Languages Institute, situated in the north-west district of Peking. Two of the first foreign teachers at that time were David[1] and Isabel[2] Crook, who had joined the Foreign Affairs School in a village near Shih Chia Chuang [Shi.jia.zhuang] in 1948. They were well-respected lecturers in English at the Institute, when we arrived in January 1965.

During the years 1959 to 1964, Premier Chou En-lai and Minister of Foreign Affairs Chen Yi had established foreign language schools in the largest cities of China. In 1959 our school was the first one to be set up, and it was titled the Foreign Languages Attached Middle School [Wai.yu Fu.zhong] of the Peking Foreign Languages Institute. It admitted students aged from 12 to 18: Junior Middle School was for three years from 12-15, and Senior Middle from 16-18. In 1963 it had begun to admit Primary age pupils from 9-12, so the name was modified to Attached School [Wai.yu Fu.xiao]. All the pupils boarded there, and they could leave school from Saturday afternoon till Sunday evening, if their homes were close enough. The four languages taught then, were English, French, Spanish and Russian. In later years German and Japanese were added.

When we started teaching the school was situated just outside the Peace Gate [He.ping.men], not so far from Tienanmen [Tian.an.men] Square, in a former Normal Teachers Training College. Some of the nearby ancient walls of Peking were still standing, but were under serious and gradual demolition. Waddi and I had a half hour journey by taxi from the Friendship Guesthouse to school every morning for our ten minutes past eight start. The Central Telecommunications building along Chang An (Eternal Peace) boulevard would invariably be relaying the dulcet tones of the "East is Red" as we passed it on the hour. When returning from school at midday we were always 30 minutes late into the restaurant, which opened at 12 noon on the dot, if not earlier, and any popular dishes went like hot cakes, so frustratingly, we missed them. It was a powerful feature of Peking life that lunch was always at mid-day. Even on any organised local visits for foreigners, meetings would miraculously end just before noon.

The school essentially provided an elite education, with the focus on foreign languages, for children from the vast strata of top cadre families, who made up all the government officialdom and functionaries living in Peking. We were told that it came under the organisational umbrella of the Ministry of Foreign Affairs, and also the watchful eye of Premier Chou En-lai. That was very comforting for us to know, because as time passed we realised that our teaching colleagues placed great faith in him, and always spoke respectfully of him. As for the pupils, we were not informed of the family status and background of any of them, but somehow we heard a rumour that a nephew or niece of Chairman Mao was a pupil there. It stayed a rumour, and we never took it too seriously, as we could not possibly identify any such pupils anyway. Neither of us was concerned about the background of our students, and it was only years later that I really comprehended that we were teaching the offspring of the cream of China's top administration [gao.di de gan.bu]. We were never asked to participate in any of the entrance examinations held by the School, so we knew nothing about the families of our students, and where in China they might come from.

Senior students who graduated from the school could be transferred to the Institute itself for higher studies, or be allocated to other lesser academic or vocational work areas, according to their abilities. We gleaned from our colleagues that the future careers of all graduating students lay in the hands of the school and institute's leadership. Always bearing in mind, that high-ranking parents within the Chinese Communist Party might help lift some students to move directly into desirable positions of work, regardless of their capabilities. In effect, we were teaching children of some of the leading cadres of China, and those male offspring of the very top families are sometimes referred to as 'Princelings'[3], who hold considerable power today.

Somehow I'm glad that we taught in China then, in a period when low bands of wages and salaries applied in the cities, and everyday things were very cheap. I felt that our work in teaching English was much appreciated, although this was never expressed, and with my salary at £65 (460 yuan) per month, we obviously weren't there to make money. That was the time of food rationing, and standards of living were very low, and it reminded me of the wartime years of my childhood. Looking back it was a genuine time of struggle for the Chinese people, and with little disposable urban incomes, it was a survival society, not a consumer society. This was another world, well before China's financial growth had rocketed families to the current levels of wealth and status. For the greatest prestige nowadays, top family pupils are often educated abroad, as can be seen from the numbers of Chinese students present in the British boarding school system; not to mention the vast number of Chinese students from the middle classes, who are studying at universities in the UK, and all over the world.

The pick of the Institute's graduates would be selected and groomed for the field of international relations. They would work in the hierarchy of the Ministry of Foreign Affairs, and then the top ones might take on responsible work overseas at Chinese Embassies around the world. Others might move into teaching posts at universities, institutes and schools, and the host of other jobs available to the educated classes. In effect those young people did not have to make choices about their careers, because it was all done for them. The only choice they had was to refuse the work offered to them, but this was surely a rare, un-socialist attitude to exhibit, and could be a black mark against them. I was intrigued to know how much flexibility was in play in this process, but after two years of living in China I never found anything out. Then in 2015 I saw the career patterns of some of my junior classes. Many of the more able had had successful careers, but the lesser academic pupils had had to forge their own lives in the labour market, with jobs such as primary school teachers, clerical workers, and taxi and lorry drivers.

It reminded me of my National Service days in the R.A.F. in the 1950s, where during our basic training we were asked to select five 'trades', in order of preference, that we would like to follow during our two years' service to Queen and Country. You can imagine that not everyone was satisfied with their final postings, but a fledgling aircraftsman second class, just one little atom at the bottom of such a huge organisation, would have no chance of reversing these decisions; except perhaps for public schoolboys with Old School Tie connections.   In this field, the Chinese are masters at nepotism, and pulling strings to help their family members, while in my limited experience, I would say that we are mere amateurs in comparison.

In the 1960s Attached Schools became part of the educational scene in the largest Chinese cities, and were always available as a specially designed route to higher education and good positions, for the privileged cadre children. Most of the top higher institutions in Peking had Attached Schools, such as at Peking, Tsinghua [Qing.hua] and People's [Ren.min] Universities, and at our Foreign Languages Institute.   In addition to this elitist stream for career advancement, quite a few of the standard Middle Schools in Peking had notable academic repute.   Some of the top ones were Nos 4, 8, 28, 31, 101, plus No 1 Girls, Coal Hill Girls, June 1st, August 1st and October 1st schools.

It was quite ironic that when the Cultural Revolution unleashed this young educated generation from their traditional shackles, and gave them the power to assault the organisational structures established by the older generation, students from the elite schools were virtually attacking the power base of their parents, with its associated status and better standard of living.   According to Mao's instructions, things had to change in urban society, but it was a formidable dilemma for the children of the top families, because lack of commitment to the great cause on their part, would leave them open to criticism and pressure from their peers.   In old China and its Confucian social value system, youngsters only had duties and responsibilities towards their elders, with little in the way of individual rights.   They were trapped into family subordination, by the established filial piety concept of looking after their parents, obeying both their elders, and the Emperor.

One spin-off effect of the Cultural Revolution on the youth was that they were being granted this freedom of greater individuality. This must have some effect on the traditional relationships in the family, because it could be difficult for the young generation to ever go back to the old status quo. Youthful rebellion had happened before on a smaller scale, during the Republic of China period, 1912-1949, such as in the May the Fourth Movement[4] of 1919, when Peking students had demonstrated spontaneously on the streets, against the settlement of the Treaty of Versailles, which had permitted former German concessions in Shantung [Shan.dong] province to be taken over by the Japanese.

The Cultural Revolution was yet another stage in the gradual emancipation of China's youth away from the family constraints of traditional China. Bertrand Russell[5], writing in his 1922 book, *The Problem of China*, is very critical of the Chinese family system:

"It is useless to deny that the Chinese have brought these troubles upon themselves, by their inability to produce capable and honest officials. This inability has its roots in Chinese ethics, which lay stress upon a man's duty to his family, rather than to the public. An official is expected to keep all his relations supplied with funds, and therefore can only be honest at the expense of filial piety. The decay of the family system is a vital condition of progress in China."

Our school was closed down in 1988, for reasons unexplained and hard to fathom, much against the wishes of many of the past and present generations. Even my old colleagues can't offer any good reasons for this closure. Then, in 2002, it was resurrected as the Beijing Foreign Languages School[6], on a new campus, with the motto 'united-alert-tolerant-rigorous', and a learning atmosphere of 'meticulousness, studiousness and striving for excellence'. It seems to be expanding and thriving, and there is now a small cohort of international students. Others of the old original Attached Schools have survived successfully, one good example being at Tsinghua University[7].

Chapter Notes
1. David Crook- Wikipedia online
2. Isabel Crook- www.isabelcrook.com
3. Princelings- Wikipedia online
4. May Fourth Movement 1919- Wikipedia online
5. Bertrand Russell- Wikipedia online
6. Beijing Foreign Languages School- information online
7. High School attached to Tsinghua University- Wikipedia online

3

THE FRIENDSHIP GUESTHOUSE, Part I

Accommodation for our two year stay in Peking was at the Friendship Guesthouse [You.yi Bin.guan], often referred to as the Druzhba, the old Russian name that still lingered on from the 1950s. Another name used was the 'Youyi'. After living there a while and adjusting to the reality of their separation from Chinese life, some of the younger foreigners often called it the 'Goldfish Bowl'. A rarer term for it was the 'Golden Ghetto'. We soon met the one remaining Russian in situ, and that was the middle-aged female doctor in the resident clinic, married to a Chinese man. Not knowing anything about the quality of Chinese medicine and treatment, I was quite reassured to have a Caucasian person treating our sons' ailments. She did not appear happy with her lot, but she did a good job for us. The clinic could deal with common everyday problems such as fever [gan.mao], or anything requiring antibiotic injections into the buttocks, but serious medical cases were immediately sent to the Hsieh Ho [Xie.he] Hospital, also known as the Peking Union Medical College[1] (PUMC), or to the Children's Hospital in town.

On my first gan.mao visit to the clinic I was prescribed a huge, brown sticky ball, reminding me of an oversized aniseed ball, a large sweet from my childhood, and I had to store it in a safe place in the bathroom, while seeking help on how to use it. The answer was to use my fingers to take a small lump of the substance, roll this into a small ball and swallow at regular intervals. However, I recovered so quickly that this brown mass was left, virtually untouched, in the bathroom cabinet, and I could only ponder the merits of traditional Chinese medicine.

As soon as we had arrived, several veteran residents had advised us to open an account with Watsons the Chemists in Hong Kong, and we did this, settling the account regularly with cheques from my bank in the UK. We ordered all sorts of minor medicines, such as aspirin, antiseptic cream, skin cream, kaopectate 'liquid cement', and even a blue plastic potty for baby Matthew. Opening the regular parcels from Watsons became a source of great excitement to all of us; they were extremely reliable and never let us down. Eventually I started ordering French Gauloise cigarettes, and on receipt I would pass them round after the evening meal, so that the main restaurant would have a distinctly Parisian aroma wafting around. Smoking restrictions were unknown in those days. As far as we could see in our everyday life, the range of cigarettes on sale to the urban public was enormous, all without filters, and quite cheap, topped by the famous 'China' Chunghwa [Zhong.hua] brand, made in Shanghai, that Chairman Mao was reputed to smoke; and this did have a filtered version. Even a brand of Turkish type Albanian cigarettes was on sale, but they were extremely rough.

The Druzhba was a huge complex of buildings, comprising all sizes of rooms, flats and apartments, with two main restaurants, swimming-pool, theatre-cum-cinema, recreation club, tennis courts, football pitch, hairdresser, basic grocers, butcher's and various shops, and Post Office. For outdoor recreation in the winter, a thin strip of earth, about a foot high, was built around the football pitch which was then flooded, and the water froze rapidly, so creating an immediate ice-skating rink. Tucked away in a little room we found a savings bank, and I started depositing miniscule sums of money there. It was nothing like a western bank, and there were no cheque books or bank statements; just a mini-notebook in which everything was faithfully recorded and signed for.

Incidentally, all of our money transactions in China were by paper money and cash only, and everything was computed on an abacus[2], a primitive form of counting frame, at a breath-taking speed. When we transferred a third of our joint salaries home, we would hand over the paper money to the accountant in our school office, and with delicate fingers she would play on the abacus for an incredibly short time, before passing to a colleague for checking. Several days later we would receive a receipt for the amount of sterling paid into my bank account.

I would estimate that the number of foreigners living there in 1965-66 was in the several hundreds, and Anne-Marie Brady in her book *Making the Foreign Serve China* makes a roughly similar estimate for experts and their families. Of course it was a fluid situation with a regular flow of arrivals and departures. This large international cohort was easily absorbed into the section south of the imposing main block buildings. That was where all the shops and facilities were based. We rarely went to the northern section where the bulk of the Chinese service personnel and PLA (People's Liberation Army) soldiers lived. The recreation club [ji.lou.bu] in the main building was a popular haunt of the younger foreigners, and had ping pong and pool tables, with a little bar where you could get lemonade, beer or even stronger stuff. It had the mandatory shiny metal spittoon standing hidden away in a corner, which you tended not to see after being in China for some time. The Peking climate being so dry, clearing the throat and spitting was commonplace everywhere.

The whole complex was surrounded by a medium height wall, unadorned by barbed wire or equivalent, easily surmountable, and the main entrance was guarded by unarmed PLA soldiers around the clock. One of the rules for foreigners was that they should dismount from their bicycles when passing through the entrance gates. However, many foreigners ignored this edict, especially after their mandatory settling-in period of adapting to Chinese bureaucracy, and would smile and cycle past the helpless PLA soldiers on duty, who, in turn, would make futile arm gestures to stop this violation of the rules, alas in vain. We could never detect the inner reactions of these soldiers, whose faces would usually remain impassive, or with a faint frown. On the other hand, I was grateful for their presence, and the feeling of security they gave; the PLA were a fixed part of our existence, and often we would see little coveys of soldiers jogging along or marching in step around the place.

The architecture was solid, functional soviet-style, but the main central buildings had a more Chinese flavour with a topping of beautifully tiled roofs. And hidden up there was a roof garden, open in the summer, that was extremely popular in the hot weather. With regard to capacity, I didn't know how many people the Druzhba could accommodate, but at that time I felt that it could easily cope with double, or even triple our numbers. On checking the internet for the Friendship Hotel in 2015, various websites quote the number of rooms as between 1,800 to 2,000, with a total area of around 335,000 square metres, so it was indeed a huge complex, and more than a hotel.

We lived in a block, three storeys high, with two spacious apartments, which could, if required, be modified to three smaller ones, on each floor. Chinese service personnel occupied the ground floor, and with access only through one central staircase they were able to monitor everyone's movements. There were lifts in all the main buildings, but none in the adjacent blocks of flats like ours. Situated on the top floor, our apartment had a main bedroom, comfortable lounge and a smaller bedroom all with wooden strip floors and ample, luxurious Chinese carpets. The bathroom-cum-toilet and the kitchen had stone floors. The two main rooms each had an old style ceiling fan and these were gratefully used in the summer, but not at night because they did generate some noise. In the end we relied on a large, standing electric fan in each room, and to help with sleeping in the overnight heat we bought rattan cane mats, which were cooler to lie on.

Wooden 'French window' doors in the lounge opened on to a small balcony, and an additional pair of metal, fine mesh doors was in situ for the summer season, to stop insects, mosquitoes and cicadas coming in. A few mosquitoes did infiltrate these defences, so in the evenings we would light incense coils to combat them. Whether this worked or not, mosquitoes were never a problem for us. In the winter the balcony doors were locked tight and all the cracks very carefully sealed over in order to keep out the Gobi desert dust and the bitterly cold north winds. All the windows received the same treatment, like a kind of primitive double-glazing, which worked remarkably well.

Every morning, several Chinese cleaners, strolling at a slow and relaxed 'peasant pace', appeared in the flat, armed with large damp mops and sundry equipment, which did not include any electrical devices, to give it a cursory once over. The two huge vacuum flasks of hot water that came with the flat were re-filled daily, and once we had adjusted to them they proved invaluable, even making a bearable cup of tea. Our Chinese colleagues were constantly advising us to drink plenty of hot water, because of the dryness of the winter climate, and gradually I acquired some taste for hot water, but not if a cup of tea was available. We soon bought a small kettle for our single electric ring, and with Lipton tea and powdered milk, we were able to make a proper cup of tea.

From the beginning we had been warned never to drink tap-water or eat raw fruit and salads, but only drink water from the flasks and eat cooked food. Water was in short supply in Peking, and hot water for baths and showers was only available at limited times during the week. That water would often look suspiciously cloudy and impure, so we had to take care when bathing the boys. This was quite different to home in the UK where water was plentiful, and could be drunk from the tap; and tap water would be used on the garden, and to wash the car.

The toilets in the Druzhba, to satisfy foreign habits, were the western-style sitting type, rather than the traditional Chinese hole in the floor; However, going out on official visits, particularly to factories and communes, foreigners requiring the toilet might suddenly be confronted by the hole in the floor, and have to negotiate their position accordingly. Waddi and I had experienced such conditions when camping on the Continent, and we knew all about unpredictable flushing systems, but some older experts must have had problems bending their joints for this form of sanitation. Of course that topic rarely figured in our mealtime discussions, but there was a general consensus that the Chinese, by upbringing, were much better at squatting on their haunches than the foreigner. In fact on any trip into town you could usually see a few Chinese having a rest in this way along the pavements.

In our block, the head of the team of cleaners was middle-aged Old Li, and he was always chatting away to us and making helpful suggestions or issuing polite sanctions. In fact he worked hard at learning some English with Waddi, and helped her to quickly acquire a survival level of spoken Chinese. Our early relationship, however, was marred by a fractious drama over the question of the two single beds in our bedroom. It had originally contained two separate single beds with ornate metal frames, rather like those of our grandparents' generation. We immediately removed the upright frames, fixed the two beds together, and rested them on piles of thick straw mats bought from the Handicrafts shop in town. This was out of order, and Old Li's face became strained, as he filled the air with "Bu xing! Bu xing!" (Won't do, won't do!); the stand-off lasted several days until realisation set in that we were not going to yield on this point. And presumably higher authority was not on his side either, as we received no letter from the Experts Bureau about it, so the matter just died away.

All in all he and his squad did a good job and we always appreciated their morning cleaning visit, and the faintest disinfectant smell that lingered on after they had left. During our two years stay we never heard of any foreign possessions being lost from any of the flats, and I just took for granted this high level of honesty and behaviour from our service personnel. The cleaners also performed the valuable job of taking away our dirty laundry, and returning it pristine clean several days later, for less than a pound. Every item of clothing had our flat number sewn on in red thread to make sure nothing was mislaid or lost.

A new shock for me occurred once, when I got up in the middle of a night for some reason, and went into the kitchen. When I turned on the light there was a scurry of cockroaches rushing back to their boltholes. I had never seen so many cockroaches before in my life, and was worried about their effect on the health of my family. The next day Waddi and I accosted Old Li and asked if something could be done about it, but he immediately replied that they were Russian cockroaches that had come into the flat hidden within the luggage of the previous Soviet experts. We both burst into laughter, thereby devaluing the gravitas of our negotiating position, while at the same time causing him to go pale, and lose some face in front of his cleaning team. That ended the first and last round of discussions on roaches.

In the dining hall we questioned other residents about cockroaches, and discovered that flats with a kitchen had them. We were advised to buy some special DDT[3] type powder downtown, and spread it around the kitchen, and we informed Old Li of our plan, so that the cleaners would know what was happening. But with the two boys around I was not keen on this chemical powder, so I only used it once and kept the kitchen door locked for a couple of days. For some reason the roaches restricted themselves to the bathroom and kitchen, the only two rooms with stone floors, and they never appeared in our living areas which had varnished wooden flooring. I would like to think that the disinfectant smell in the cleaning mops had some reductive effect on the roaches, but we had to live with them like everyone else, and I never made any midnight incursions into the kitchen again.

The main dining hall was enormous and could accommodate hundreds, and because of its 'international menu' it was the one used by most foreigners. Breakfast was 07.00-08.30, lunch 12.00-13.30 and dinner 18.00-19.30. But the Chinese, unlike the British, were not hidebound by official timetables, and I would go there around 06.30 every morning to collect our breakfast, and carry it back in a set of four aluminium panniers held together in a metal brace with carrying handle.   Usually it was boiled milk, boiled eggs, yogurt, white bread toast, ersatz butter, jam, and sometimes several thin strips of bacon.   Porridge and rice congee also figured, when the boys had decided that they liked them.   Waddi and I would make our own tea or powdered coffee.   Then, around seven o'clock Wongyi, the faithful young Auntie [Ai.yi] and reliable child nurse, would arrive. She had started off in the household as Wang Ai.yi, but Tim modified this to Wongyi and that name stuck.   She would take charge of baby Matthew for the rest of the day up to dinner-time, especially if we were teaching after lunch.

We would rush off around seven thirty to get our delegated taxi to school in central Peking, and then Wongyi would take Tim to the Guesthouse kindergarten right next to our block, where he would spend the morning and have lunch, and we would collect him when we returned home.   As the summer progressed our afternoon teaching timetable became lighter, and when the swimming pool opened the boys would be brought home earlier and we'd take them to the pool, and sometimes Wongyi would come along to help us.   She was another provider of basic spoken Mandarin Chinese, as we asked her daily about our boys, and of any problems over food and their health.

Tim spent the whole of 1965 at the Guesthouse kindergarten and became proficient in Chinese, correcting both of us at times.   He taught us the popular children's song "Big Red Flower" [Da hong hua], which I learnt and then reproduced on social occasions at school whenever a party piece was needed; and it was always well received.   Although we used English at home, by the end of our two years, Tim's spoken English had slowly been influenced by Chinese, now his 'temporary' co-mother-tongue, and he sounded like the pupils at our school.   Matthew could understand basic English, but only spoke 'baby' Chinese.   The Guesthouse had a school for older foreign children up to junior school level, taught by Chinese teachers.   Other parents sent their children to the Catholic Convent in central Peking, but those numbers were small and didn't even half fill the small-sized bus that took them every day.

Wongyi's days with Matthew were very long, including giving him his daily lunch, and he still likes a bowl of boiled rice to this day.   Anyway, she was a blessing with both of us teaching, and would always be available to babysit in the evenings, without any hassle. With an average monthly pay of around 45 yuan, that is, £6, she was comparatively well off, and for babysitting she got overtime pay.   I later discovered that in 1965 all my teaching colleagues at school, most of whom had started teaching around 1959 or after, were classified as assistant teachers, and their pay scale was 56 to 89 yuan per month. With the exception of the older scholarly male, all of our colleagues were paid 56 yuan, and it remained at this figure until 1978, meaning that they had been on that fixed salary grade for around eighteen years.   There were always graded pay scales in force, and I was told that senior professors at the Institute were getting three times that amount or more, that is, over 150 yuan per month.   That was a comfortable salary in those days.

We were told that all the Auntie child-nurses and their little foreign charges, stayed together throughout the day within the Guesthouse, and this was heartening news for us, because although Wongyi didn't have any children of her own, the group of older Aunties would provide a repository of sound, experienced advice on Chinese baby-rearing. Several young western women had babies or small children at the time, and the well-thumbed book on childcare going the rounds, was the famous one by Dr Benjamin Spock, entitled *Baby & Childcare*.

In the shops the array of children's toys was limited, and of simple designs; they seemed similar to the ones of my childhood memories. All were made of wood or cardboard, and no plastic. In particular they had boxes of fascinating wooden building blocks that Tim really liked, so we bought two of them. One book series for the young generation that impressed me was titled *100,000 'Why's'* [Shi Wan Wei.shen.me], and it dealt with a huge range of basic scientific and everyday practical questions. The profusion of children's books were written in characters, but with the emphasis on primary literacy there was a sizeable selection using the new Romanisation of Han.yu pin.yin, and also sets of cards for learning characters. As well as such books, the boys were well supplied with toys and English books by the two Grandmothers, in the parcels that they sent us, as well as second-hand items bought from foreigners departing the Druzhba and going home.

Chapter Notes
1.   Peking Union Medical College- Wikipedia online
2.   Abacus- Wikipedia online
3.   DDT- Wikipedia online

4

THE FRIENDSHIP GUESTHOUSE, Part II

The dining room daily menus were printed by typewriter in English and Spanish, with a Chinese translation done by hand, and each table had a salt cellar and little pot of soy sauce, with a tray of toothpicks, paper napkins and a choice of cutlery or chopsticks. The lunch and dinner menus consisted of three to four main meat dishes loosely based on European, Indian subcontinent and Latin American cuisine, plus other lists of side dishes, such as eggs, chips, fried rice, steamed cornflour bread rolls [man.tou], vegetables, noodles, thin white toast, red caviar, and the one and only form of Chinese-produced soft cheese. Several Chinese dishes were always available as the home contribution to the international flavour, and the menus always finished off with one pudding, and the regular ice-cream.   Family favourite dishes included fried noodles with pork, fried eggs both sides and chips, fried rice cakes, and bread pudding.

Seasonal delights in the summer were strawberries, and then the delicious Hami watermelons from Sinkiang[1] [Xin.jiang Uyghur Autonomous Region]. A reasonable cup of coffee was available after the meal, which I'm sure was not filtered a la current mode, but most of the Brits were not seasoned coffee drinkers, so we were happy to go with it. We realised early on that the French residents, and most continentals brought up on good coffee, made their own proper coffee in their flats. The restaurant ambiance was relaxed, and the cooks would always try to produce what the foreigners ordered, though when the main dishes were sold out, that was that.   We were served mainly by young Chinese girls wearing white jackets and blue trousers, the majority with two long plaits down to their waist, and ordering was done in Chinese or by pointing at the menu. Some of them did attempt to learn English, but only spasmodically, and not to survival levels.

Fortunately for our health, portions were not large, but we could order as many dishes as we liked, or as our budget allowed.   Large sized portions of steak or other meat did not appear on our plates, just small pieces of pork and chicken, while mutton figured mainly in curries and Arabic dishes. A small Moslem restaurant inside the Druzhba served that community well, and for those of us in need of more lamb, we could go to any Hui[2] minority (Moslem) restaurant in town.   The most famous of these was the Dong Lai Shun in Tungan [Dong.an] market where everyone went to have Mongolian mutton hotpot.   I can't remember any foreigners being excessively fat, although some of the older ones and some Old China Hands were stout and overweight, but nothing like the gross obesity situation that holds in the western world today.   Most of the new intake of foreigners were all young and active, and not plump.

Two makes of bottled beer were served. The Ts'ing Tao (Qing.dao) beer from the former German concession city of Ching Tao was excellent, while the Peking Five Star brand was not far behind.   Interestingly, the Ts'ing Tao brand name has never been changed to the modernised form of Qing.dao, and can still be seen in any supermarket today, with its slightly modified 'Tsingtao' label. The only lemonade [qi.shui], in small bottles, was orange flavoured.   In town you could buy orange ice lollies (called 'popsicles' in American English) from street vendors, although I shudder to think now of the low level of hygiene involved.   And in the autumn there were toffee crab-apples on sticks. The little grocer's shop in the Guesthouse introduced us to varieties of fruit that we didn't know the names of, and had not tasted before, such as lychees, kumquats, persimmon, Hami water melons and apples tasting like bananas.

The Chinese wine industry was then in its early days, way before technical exchanges with the French viniculture-ists and wine producers, and the red wine on offer was just a ghastly sweet drink, and not really wine. It was very entertaining to watch young French newcomers in the dining room taking their first sip of Chinese 'wine' or 'brandy'. On the other hand China was much stronger in the spirits section, and in the Druzhba shop we could buy bottles of traditional colourless spirits [bai jiu[3]], made from sorghum, grain or rice, such as 'Moutai', 'Kaoliang', 'Wuliangye', and the cheapest and most popular brand, 'Erguotou'. There was even a type of gin, called 'Jinjiu', which was quite bearable when mixed with a soft drink. Since those days the status of 'Moutai' (Maotai)[4] has gone through the roof, and the price has rocketed up, so that nowadays it's more of a luxury drink for the rich. French brandy is another celebratory drink nowadays, probably influenced by Hong Kong, where it became very popular with the young nouveau riche Chinese businessmen in the decades before 1997.

The Guesthouse complex had a profusion of trees along the boundary walls and inside it, but there was very little birdlife inhabiting them, just a few scrawny sparrows flitting nervously about, and definitely no dawn chorus or any form of birdsong, such as we were used to in the UK. The poor sparrows had suffered considerably during the Patri-otic Health Campaign against the Four Pests (flies, mice, mosquitoes, sparrows) of 1957-58, and they must have been prime targets for a small meal on the table in the bad harvest years of 1959-61. By 1960 the ecological disaster created by this campaign had been realised, and sparrows were removed from the list and replaced by bedbugs. Even when we visited the Western Hills on outings, few birds were around, but on a longer day trip to the Great Wall and Ming Tombs we could see some magpies, and sometimes they appeared in the suburbs too. Peking was not a good city for wild birds, which were rare on the ground. The only other bird of note was the Peking duck, which you might manage to see on a visit to a local commune, or when presented by the chef at a banquet in the famous Duck restaurant, Chuan Ju De [Quan.ju.de],in town, where tradition required the guests to proclaim it 'piao.liang' (beautiful), as a preliminary to the feast itself.

Very few pets could be seen either. Regulations issued to foreign residents in the Guest-house stipulated that pets could not be kept in our flats, and I cannot recall any foreign-er having a pet. The cleaners would have spotted them anyway. Sometimes, if you walked through some of the hidden lanes of old Peking, you might see old men with a tiny singing bird, or even a cicada, in a cage, but you never saw cats or dogs; only on a trip to a village would you see a dog. On the other hand, donkeys, small ponies and horses, mostly of mangy appearance, were the pack animals of transportation, and they were ever present on the streets. Oxen could also be seen pulling carts of the night-soil collectors around.

However, in the early summer of 1974, during our second two year stay, our sons were given a couple of one day old Peking ducks, and somehow we kept them as pets, alt-hough they stayed outside our block, never in our flat. Whenever the boys went out of the door of the block the little ducklings would immediately appear from under their bush home, and tag along behind them. Titch and Quackers survived all the summer, and were getting quite big and problematic, so we eventually handed them over to the care of the school farm. By coincidence, during the following New Year celebrations, the school organised a Peking duck banquet for all the foreign staff.

In the summer months everything changed from around mid-May, as an incessant clicking and screeching of cicadas filled the heat of the days, and we often saw them mid-flight in the guesthouse grounds. In the spring of 1965 when trawling the antique shops we had seen these beautifully-made little wooden cages for housing cicadas, an insect unknown to us in the UK, although we had heard them on holidays in France, and now we knew what the Chinese ones looked like.

Chinese-made bicycles, which filled the roads of Peking throughout the day, were a key means of transport for the Chinese people. The price range varied from 125-145 yuan, and one of the favourite brands was the 'Flying Pigeon', a well-made model which could easily take the weight of plump foreigners. Many able-bodied foreigners would buy a bicycle, and take to the roads, especially at weekends to get away from it all. Popular venues were the nearby Summer Palace, the remains of the old Yuan Ming Yu-an Summer Palace that had been destroyed by Anglo-French forces in 1860, and the longer ride to the Western Hills.

On a bicycle foreigners were able to roam around Peking, and enjoy some freedom of movement in their lives, and in a way get a little closer to the Chinese people. And for repairs, a little bicycle shop opposite the guesthouse entrance could sort out any problem for a paltry sum. Of course, some parts of Peking, containing military camps, airfields or security areas, were closed to foreigners, and if you happened to intrude into these out of bounds districts then you were told firmly by the security guards on duty to turn round and go back. Foreigners were restricted to the confines of Peking, and needed an exit permit from the local public security office to travel outside of the city.

Inmates of the Druzhba came from all over the world, although for political reasons, Americans, Russians and Indians (Sino-Indian border war 1962) were thin on the ground. As a result of the US hostility to Communist China, there was no American diplomatic presence in China, although the USSR and India did have established embassies in Peking. So English-speaking foreign experts from the UK and Commonwealth countries were recruited to work in China, instead of Americans. We were the unlikely beneficiaries of the so-called US 'Domino Theory'[5] foreign policy. In fact, from the 1950s right up to 1978, when full diplomatic relations were finally established between the US and China, the Americans had maintained an embassy in Taiwan.

Many of the foreign experts came from Portuguese or Spanish-speaking countries in Latin-America and elsewhere, and they constituted the largest language grouping, while the French[6], now in the second year of their cultural exchanges with China, were the next largest. The French seemed to come on one year contracts, especially students, as compared to our two year contracts, so there was a regular turnover of faces in the Dining Hall. Other residents were from African states, either newly independent or on the way there, while others were 'freedom fighters' trying to overthrow their governments. Some countries only sent one person to Peking, always male, maybe with their family if they had one, and we met solitary people or families like this from such countries as Afghanistan, Albania, Burma, Cambodia, Egypt, Hungary, Indonesia, Poland, Romania and Sudan. The highest prestige fell to Albania, as being China's main mouthpiece ally in Europe, and the Albanian family always had their embassy to help them out, as well as some of their students studying Chinese at the No 2 Foreign Languages Institute.

The main languages in use by adults in the Druzhba were English, French and Spanish, while for all the foreign children Chinese became their lingua franca. In the restaurants, your language, and your political hat helped you to decide who to sit with at meals. The 'English-speaking' group, included all the northern Europeans of Belgium, Germany, Holland, Scandinavia and the UK, with the addition of various Commonwealth personnel, so we always had an interesting circle of people to share meals with. Sometimes there would be newly-arrived foreigners passing through, on their way to work in another city. These mealtimes constituted relaxing interludes, where we were away from our daily Chinese teaching environment, and it was a relief to converse in your own language in the evenings. We rarely talked about our own countries, although the BBC World service on radio, and the international daily Hsinhua [Xin.hua] news agency reports kept us vaguely in touch with home. The Druzhba was like a spontaneous 'research institute' which focused solely on all things Chinese, where the inmates daily compared notes, exchanged rumours and gossip, and talked about their latest findings.

Social life revolved around the mealtimes, and evening visits to the flats of people we got on with, or sometimes going out for a meal together. Regular visits downtown were organised to see performances by visiting foreign cultural groups. I well remember in 1965 we went to the Capitol Theatre to see a rousing performance by the Red Army Choir and Cossack dancers. The choir was huge and they filled the stage with their Caucasian faces. Another occasion was a French ballet group, and from my seat at the back of the stalls all the female ballerinas with their long mousey-blond pony tails looked the same to me. I noted at the time that I was beginning to see life through Chinese eyes. During all such visits the mainly Chinese audience chatted away regardless, and chewed melon and sunflower seeds, and other little snacks. Chinese productions were on the menu too, and one striking performance was the 'Red Detachment of Women', a Chinese-style, revolutionary modern ballet. Another ballet was the 'White Haired Girl', with some haunting Chinese-cum-western musical backing.

Within the Druzhba we had the weekly films and newsreels, plus special variety performances in the guest-house theatre at the celebratory times of the New Year, May Day and National Day on October the 1st. We could sign up for the organised trips to nearby factories, schools, universities, or communes. And twice a day the Isuzu bus, with its grinding gears and noisy engine would slowly wheeze its way for over 30 minutes to No 19, the Friendship Store, in central Peking in Tunganmen (Eastern Peace Gate) street. The Friendship Store was open to foreigners only, and had a wondrous array of the top quality manufactured goods, and arts and crafts products made in China. We spent a lot of time browsing there. As well as the bus, a Warszawa[7] taxi was always available for hire in the guesthouse at very reasonable costs.

In the summer afternoons the swimming pool was a great attraction, and foreign children could learn or improve their swimming skills. After a few days the numbers in the pool would fall because the water hadn't been changed and looked quite unhealthy, but after the re-filling of the pool happened everyone surged back in to enjoy the colder water, until that cycle of events recurred.

But the artificial life in the Druzhba did have its problems. It was an unnatural environment where everything was done for us. We didn't have to worry about the everyday
living costs of rent, mortgage, insurances, transport, food shopping and cooking, etc.
On the other hand we had left behind our social and emotional support system of family, friends and workplace. We did have a phone in our flat and could use this for calling anyone within Peking, but we couldn't phone home.   To make a telephone call
home we were told that we would have to go to the main communications building on
central Chang An boulevard, so in the end we renounced the telephone and relied on
letter-writing to our families; these letters proved to be an invaluable record of our life
there. At school we had good colleagues, although limited in friendship terms, and we
had to create a new set of social relationships within the Guesthouse community.

Some foreign couples might arrive, and the wife might not have a job, so the Druzhba
veterans would strongly advise the woman to get a job, even part-time, as it was too
mind-numbing to stay in the complex all day on your own.   That is, unless you were
single-minded and had a personal project to work on.   Another aspect of this synthetic
atmosphere was the large number of single young males in residence compared to the
number of females.   The sexual pressure so created by this environment could often
mean the break-up of couples soon after their arrival, and this would only became clear
to all by the behavioural patterns at mealtimes on the days after the nights before. This
sedate Guesthouse had a clandestine nightlife of its own.

One bearded Cape Verde Islander, whom I shall call Oliviera, was a charismatic guitar-
playing personality, well-liked by both men and women, and he was said to have
worked his way with many women, single or coupled or married, and then effortlessly
moved on.   It was possible to chart his progress by watching who he sat with for the
evening meals. One night, when for some reason our sons weren't eating with us, I was
unnerved to see him coming towards our table, and he asked to join us. He was as
charming as expected, and I introduced myself and Waddi, with underlying mixed feelings. During the meal he was good company, but for some reason he didn't approach
us again after that. Maybe we had given him some subliminal messages.

On the streets the Chinese people viewed foreigners carefully without getting involved,
and if you did stop for a while on Wangfuching street, then you were soon surrounded
at a distance by a circle of staring Chinese, whose faces showed no feelings, except perhaps bemusement at seeing a new species of humankind. In the winter, if you dressed
in the blue Chinese padded overcoats you could often escape instant detection. On the
pavements the Chinese walked slowly and solidly, and unlike the British, they made no
effort to avoid body contact with passers-by. I suppose that when covered by winter
padding you would hardly notice bumping into others along the way. We would always
see a few old ladies with bound feet, and they would be bobbing along the streets with
that strange gait caused by walking on their heels. They seemed to dart around faster
than the usual 'peasant pace' pedestrians.

In the warmer months, while walking around central Peking with our two small sons,
old ladies would suddenly come up and gently prod them, and enquire about their age
and sex, before asking if we were Russian.   When we replied that we were British,
there was no recognition or interest on their faces as they quickly moved on.   Talking
to foreigners was a suspect business, and many pairs of eyes were watching.   Personal-

ly I never felt any degree of danger on the streets of Peking that were frequented by the foreign community, but we rarely ventured into the backstreets.

One or two foreigners invited to China were possibly too mentally vulnerable before they arrived, so they couldn't take the strain of being gawped at by groups of Chinese whenever they went outside the Druzhba; and should they ask to leave China early, then they had months of paperwork and waiting before finally being given an exit visa. There was the rare story of one young Swiss male, who accidentally discovered a faster route. His wife was pregnant, and one night he got over-amorous while in one of the lifts in the main building, and allegedly attempted to kiss, unsuccessfully according to the grapevine, the Chinese female lift attendant. The Chinese authorities took umbrage at this unacceptable insult to their womanhood, and he was expelled from China within thirty six hours. In a similar vein, on one or two occasions over the two years we heard rumours of groups of African college students, being involved in fights with Chinese men, because of their efforts to get to know Chinese girl students. These happenings were never reported in Hsinhua News Agency, and remained hush-hush, in order to avoid the negative publicity of diplomatic incidents with emerging African countries.

It was necessary for foreign adults in China, to have an identity card, and this was supplied by your work unit [dan.wei]. And our family were all given medical cards by the Clinic in the Druzhba, as soon as we arrived. Westerners could not blend into Chinese society because of their physiological features, and much more effectively than any ID card, you could always be spotted and tracked down by the Chinese populace, wherever you went. Under the wing of the Foreign Experts Bureau or our own work unit or at a hospital, we were always well-looked after and given priority treatment over the ordinary Chinese people, and I certainly appreciated this favourable practice.

However, outside of that protection, if you decided to risk going home from town on a No 32 bendy bus, you first had to participate in a mass melee in order to get onto the packed bus, and then probably stand all the way to the local stop at Wei.gong.cun. Each half of the bendy bus had a conductress to collect the cash fares, and they always seemed to be fighting their way through a thick scrum of customers to do their job. The prevailing olfactory aroma on the buses was a not unpleasant garlic flavour. I learnt that the western equivalent was described as rancid butter; all dairy products being distasteful to the Han Chinese.

The special status and treatment of foreigners, appears now to be an inverted form of racialism, but it may have been the only practical answer for the Chinese in controlling and looking after foreigners. At that time, it seemed quite normal and convenient, and we soon took it for granted. Looking back at the China of the 1960s, and the previous Chinese history, perhaps their way of dealing with foreigners was the best solution to a potentially problematic scenario of those times.

Chapter Notes

1. Xinjiang Uyghur Autonomous Region- Wikipedia online
2. Hui minority- Wikipedia online
3. Baijiu- Wikipedia online
4. Maotai- Wikipedia online
5. US Domino Theory- Wikipedia online
6. China-France relations- Wikipedia online
7. FSO Warszawa cars- Wikipedia online

5

MR CHI PAI-SHIH [Qi Bai.shi] [1]

Letter to Mr. Chi Pai-shih   *5 October 1952*

*I thank you heartily for the gift of your scroll painting 'Pu tian tong
ching'* [Joyous Celebration for All in Heaven] *which I have received. I would
like to express my gratitude to your co-creators of the masterpiece.*
                                                        Chairman Mao

Having arrived in Peking in the January, and with the Chinese New Year[2], that is,
Spring Festival [Chun.jie], looming up on 2nd February 1965, we didn't start teaching
until a week after that. We were based at the Attached School, of the Peking No 1 Foreign Languages Institute, which was situated just south of the Peace Gate
[He.Ping.men] along the old Tartar city wall. Parts of the old walls were still standing
in 1965, but were being slowly and systematically demolished in order to prepare for
the building of an underground line, with a wide, modern highway above it. Looking
at an underground map of the city today you can see that the Inner Circle route roughly
follows the line of those old city walls. At that time the huge Gates in the city walls
were all still standing, but most were in desperate need of care and restoration.

By sheer chance, the old Teachers College buildings that we worked in, where Lu Hsun
[Lu Xun], the famous Chinese writer, had once given a public lecture in the 1930s, was
close to Liu Li Ch'ang [Liu.li.chang][3] street of antiquities. It was just a line of dilapi-
dated and rundown one or two-storey buildings, which housed the collections of Chinese paintings, art, scrolls and old furniture that were currently on sale. The only new
building, partly two-storey, was Jung Pao Chai [Rong Bao Zhai][4] which catered for
budding artists and calligraphers, and where we could buy new scrolls with modern
prints, and old Chinese rubbings too. We once bought an old tattered scroll from a
nearby shop, and gave it to them for restoration, which they carried out very well, over
a period of months.

Today I see the Peking of 1965 as being a veritable treasure trove of old Chinese arts
and antiques at knockdown prices, just waiting to be discovered by knowledgeable foreigners. Alas, I was not to be one of them! For a few months I started collecting Chinese teapots, until I realised that transporting them to Britain would be a huge undertaking. I should have collected the small snuff bottles, readily available and quite cheap,
which would have been much easier to package along with our family goods, and which
are currently of considerable value. A colourful genre, that I didn't pay much attention
to, was the new art form of propaganda posters, pure socialist realism[5], right in front of
my eyes. Lots of them were on sale, printed on thin, inadequate paper, and very cheap.
It would have been easy to take a collection back to the UK.

Of course, many foreign visitors to Peking were taken to Liu Li Ch'ang, and we later
discovered that it was a favoured haunt for the Ladies of the Diplomatic Corps during
their shopping sweeps through the city. The list of places open to foreign consumers
was extremely limited in scope, and reflected the political and economic stringencies of
the times, but it included all the 'treasure houses' on offer in Peking then; several sec-

ond-hand shops and old emporiums, the chinaware store south of Chien Men gate, the adjacent Ta Sha Lan alleys, and in Wangfuching street, the handicraft shop, Big Store and Tung An market; and the dear old Friendship Store, commonly known as No 19, and open only to foreigners. Going north up Wangfuching, and taking the first turning west, it was in Tung An Men street; and that was the terminus stop for our daily coaches into town from the Friendship Guesthouse.

My weekly teaching schedule included several free periods, so following the practice in my UK school-teaching experience, during those breaks, I often went out of school and took short walks around the locality, usually down to Liu Li Ch'ang to look in the scroll shops and soak up the art scene. Going in the other direction I would often stop and watch through an open window a cook standing there, effortlessly and nonchalantly throwing multi-strands of noodles from a large lump of dough. He was an absolute master at it, and I could only stand and marvel at his performance before waving good-bye and wandering off.

After several weeks of spending free periods off-site, I gradually became aware, by means of loaded questions and comments from my Chinese colleagues, that my actions were out of order. One or two of them even looked embarrassed as we talked about it. Whether measured by socialist standards or traditional Chinese practice, my behaviour was not acceptable. None of my Chinese colleagues would dream of doing this, and they certainly wouldn't be permitted to behave like this by the school powers that be. It was one of the many instances of cross-cultural disparities that I encountered in our early days in Peking. I must have presented a dilemma for the school leadership, because I seemed unaware of their school conventions, and did not appear to have a dedicated 'socialist' attitude to my work, although carrying out all my teaching responsibilities correctly. The school leadership did not officially advise me of my transgression, but eventually my free periods were whittled away and converted into teaching sessions with my Chinese colleagues. A perfectly harmonious solution.

In retrospect, I would argue that this issue revolved around traditional Chinese values and educational practice, and was only partly due to the veneer of socialism that stretched over the Old China society that I could view around me. Social control over the individual in China seemed very tight, and that was undoubtedly due to the bureaucratic machinery in place, controlled effectively by the communist party cadres. Within my workplace, socialism seemed to demand complete commitment from an individual in job output, thought and effort, and generally mantled an extra layer of pressure onto a person's life. I sensed that some heaviness was present in everyday life at school, with few days of any relaxed atmosphere. As an example of these, the sports days were light -hearted occasions with a holiday atmosphere. At other times, morning classes were suspended, as the teachers took all the pupils out to line the main streets, and greet a foreign head of state.

Two such leaders I remember, were President Julius Nyerere from Tanzania, in February 1965, and President Kwame Nkrumah from Ghana, a year later. On those days, a huge portrait of the foreign leader would be erected on West Chang An boulevard just where our taxis turned north to take us home, and hundreds of his country's flags would be hung around Tienanmen and along the central highway. Whenever classes were suspended we were never informed in advance, and we foreign teachers would arrive at school around eight o'clock to find the whole campus eerily silent and empty, and we would be given a free morning. The first time it happened, I was rather peeved that we hadn't been told, but I quickly adjusted to the reality, and most of us got back into our taxis and returned to the Druzhba, to work at home on preparing and recording materials. As a postscript, Nyerere's visit saw the beginning of his country's co-operation with China on building the Tanzam railway[6]. Unusually, Nkrumah's portrait stayed up for several weeks, because his stay in Peking was extended much longer than expected. He had lost power to a military coup at home in Ghana, and then became an exile in Guinea for the rest of his life.

But my story is about Mr Chi Pai-shih. While on a visit to Liu Li Ch'ang, in a small dingy single-storey building, one of the well-padded up, lethargic old men produced several dusty old scrolls for me to view. I liked the small one with two blobs of colour, one orange the other aubergine, maybe they were fruit, I can't remember, and the painting couldn't have been more than two feet in height and lesser breadth. He said it was by someone called Chi Pai-shih, and it cost three hundred yuan (foreign term for the ren.min.bi Chinese currency)[7]. At that time with the exchange rate at seven yuan to the pound, it came to about £42 sterling. My monthly salary was only four hundred and twenty yuan, so I said that I would think about it. I never ever thought that it might be a reproduction, rather than an original.

When home that evening in the Friendship Guesthouse I talked it over with Waddi. Our policy was to convert one third of all our earned income into pounds sterling, as permitted by the Chinese authorities, so we were on a tight budget. And we had already bought a cheaper modern scroll showing peach blossom over a canal in Soochow [Su.zhou]. The clinching point came from our Italian friend Giorgio Zucchetti, who was scheduled to leave for home soon. One of his possessions was a lovely classical guitar that he played beautifully, and he had decided to sell it. Yes, he wanted three hundred yuan.

To us it was no contest. A guitar would be much more valuable to our family than a small painting. Waddi could play the guitar a little, and maybe our sons would be able to play it when they grew up. There was no thought of buying both the guitar and the painting; that would have strained our budget and may have caused us to borrow money. I could not think laterally, regretfully, and I was not used to buying beautiful objects just for self-indulgent reasons. In a word, I was not mentally able to lift myself out of the straitjacket of my thinking, and the need not to owe money to anyone. So we bought the guitar only.

We were able to exploit it, for the rest of our stay, at school functions and parties, when Waddi would play guitar and I would sing. Popular English language songs among foreign residents in those days were Pete Seeger's 'We Shall Overcome' and 'Barbara Allen', plus others such as 'Frankie and Johnny', 'Take this Hammer', 'It Takes a Worried Man' , 'John Henry', 'Click go the Shears', 'Widdecombe Fair', 'A Bomber above her'. Songs about working-class history included 'Fourpence a Day', 'Four Loom Weaver', 'Gresford Disaster' and the American ballad 'Joe Hill'. Our Chinese audiences were always very attentive, and fascinated by the guitar instrument, and they all enjoyed the communal singing of 'Auld Lang Syne' that we insisted on at the end.

I often think about that painting, and wonder if any of the Ladies of the Diplomatic Corps bought it, and where it rests now. In summer 2011, a painting by Chi Pai-shih was sold for sixty six million US dollars, an astounding amount of money. However, we had that old guitar, and we faithfully carried it around with us on all our travels afterwards. One of our sons played it classical style at school, but in his teens he moved onto the modern guitars of the pop scene, playing in a small group.

Sometimes I find myself dreaming about that luxury villa on the Riviera where we could have stayed if I had had any knowledge of Chinese art in 1965, or had taken the slight risk of borrowing a small amount of money; after all it was only £42. Or if I had known that Chi Pai-shih was on Chairman Mao's mailing list. A salutary story for anyone thinking of buying an original painting! Since 1965 I have acquired several paintings at humble prices, mainly by friends, and I am hoarding them while they appreciate in value. I have a Chi Pai-shih reproduction hanging in the lounge.

Chapter Notes
1. Qi Bai.shi- Wikipedia online
2. Chinese New Year- Wikipedia online
3. Liu Li Chang- Wikipedia online
4. Rong Bao Zhai- Wikipedia online
5. Socialist realism- Wikipedia online
6. Tanzam Railway- Wikipedia online

6

LEARN FROM COMRADE LEI FENG

One of the outstanding characters of 1965, at the forefront of the socialist dictum of 'Serve the People', was the young soldier Lei Feng[1], who had been stationed somewhere in the north of China. This was the year before the Cultural Revolution took off. One of the first Chinese slogans that we encountered in January 1965 was 'Learn from Comrade Lei Feng' [Xiang Lei Feng tong.zhi xue.xi]. A young PLA soldier from a peasant background, he had died in a pointless accident two years previously. Now he was held up as a people's hero, who ceaselessly and unselfishly helped other needy or vulnerable members of the public, wherever he encountered them in his daily life. In our school materials he appeared in all the cyclostyled textbooks, produced by the teachers for the primary, junior middle and senior pupils. Our primary school was four years from age 9 to 12, junior middle school was three years from age 13-16, and senior middle was for three years up to age 18-19 years, very similar to our sixth form pattern. Each booklet would be written at a language level appropriate to the pupils' age and reading ability in English. Every story had a simple socialist code, and they were political parables for the young generation to absorb.

During my first weeks I spent some time with two of my Chinese colleagues translating one of the many storybooks about Lei Feng's life and times that were readily available on sale in town. My colleagues would give me the stilted English translations direct from the Chinese text, in what we teachers of English came to term 'Chinglish'[2], and then I had to 'polish' and improve their words into a more reasonable form of living English. 'Chinglish' was Sinicised English, and it was always grammatically correct and understandable, but not always connected to the living English forms that we native speakers used in 1965. For example, the articles of the English language political weekly, *Peking Review*[3], were couched in classic 'Chinglish' style. Although 'Chinglish' did not read well to native speakers, this strange written English had to be quite advanced in vocabulary and grammatical structures, in order to satisfy an adult and sophisticated readership, however small, throughout the world. I always think of the term 'Chinglish' as describing *Peking Review* English. *Peking Review* was set up on 4 March 1958, and was published in English, French, Spanish and Russian. Presumably the same linguistic phenomenon must have occurred in those languages too, but I can't recall any mention of it from our French and Spanish speaking colleagues at school, or in the Friendship Guesthouse.

Nevertheless our brief was to produce teaching material for young learners at school and I couldn't deviate much from my colleagues' input, because any contemporary English usage, with which they could often be seriously unfamiliar, might have confused the learners and warped the true essence of the story. It had to be expressed in a plain and direct style, using only the basic words and structures of English, and definitely not containing any strange idioms or sayings. On looking back, it seems reasonable for the teachers to work within the confines of their own English language level, and then simplify the vocabulary content to suit the needs of their pupils.

One spin-off effect was that my colleagues took me to the administration block, and I met some of the ladies involved in producing the reams of cyclostyled teaching materials required weekly throughout our school. I was told that the full school complement was about one thousand pupils and students, and the foreign languages taught were English, French, Spanish and Russian; in later years, German and Japanese languages were added to the curriculum. In one of the printing rooms I came across a Chinese typewriter[4]. It was much larger than any western typewriter, and looked more like a small printing machine with long typewriting arms. The lady operator showed me how it worked and explained that it had a basic font of around three thousand characters. She had to locate the required characters from memory, extract them and then type them efficiently. Quite a slow process, but she seemed to be master of the machine, and must have been a pivotal member of the printing team.

In effect, Lei Feng was one of the leading aspirational heroes offered to the younger generation growing up at that time, as a role model to follow in the building of the New Socialist China. The People's Republic was only established in 1949, so that anyone in 1965 under 15 years of age would have been born after that date and would know nothing of the 'bad old days'. In order to focus on these young minds and try to inculcate a new philosophy for the future society, there were many stories for children and teenagers written about Lei Feng, as well as songs and even a film of his life. In 1965 however it was all valedictory, as he had died sometime previously in 1962 from an accident, while on humdrum army duties. The truth of his life story became a frustrating question for cynical foreigners, as to what was fact or fiction, and how much had been grafted on to reality by propaganda experts. No one, to my knowledge, ever got an answer.

Books, songs, radio and film were the main media forms used in this period of intensive political propaganda for the masses. For the younger generation, children's books, posters and songs provided a ready means of influencing the mental outlook of the youth of China. Materials for every school subject were permeated with socialist attitudes and thinking, as far as was possible. Questions in Maths had to be framed within the underlying political context and vocabulary. Even on sports day at our school, students ran obstacle races with knapsacks on their backs and carrying wooden rifles. Another contest was throwing the 'replica' hand grenade, a small piece of shaped wood, weighted by a thin metal band. Quite a difference to my own schooldays, when we threw the cricket ball.

Most primary-level reading and picture books available in the shops were dominated by socialist characters and deeds, rather than by the traditional folktales and stories of 'ghosts, monsters and demons' of the old days. However, adapted short stories and picture books about Monkey King, Pigsy and others, were still on sale in town, but needless to say they never figured in our teaching materials, and were never mentioned by colleagues or pupils. That sector of old, mythologised folk literature did not fit in with the thinking and practice of socialist reality. I wonder if this 'socialist' generation of young Chinese may have missed out to some degree on absorbing the traditional stories that are intrinsically part and parcel of primary school life and learning. In our school, all the students were boarders, and according to their daily timetables they had little free time, and what with sleeping in large dormitories, hardly any privacy. Of course they could always read such books at home outside of school. It's interesting to see that Lin Piao in his speech at the First Mass Red Guard Rally on 18 August 1966 made a brief allusion to this inherited culture of superstition:

"We will strike down those in authority who are taking the capitalist road, strike down the reactionary bourgeois authorities, strike down all bourgeois royalists, oppose any act to suppress the revolution, and strike down all ghosts and monsters"

Nearly three months earlier, on the first of June 1966, the editorial headline in the *People's Daily* had been 'Sweep Away All Monsters and Demons'. In 2015 in Bei.jing I talked over old times with three of my Chinese teaching colleagues, and I happened to mention the ghosts and monsters of fifty years ago. They all agreed that the level of superstition in Chinese society now was considerably less than in those old days, which they thought resulted from the increasing affluence in living standards, and rising levels of education. Of course, this was just an opinion from educated urbanites, who only knew city life, and it could not be taken as a generalised truth for the whole of China, and for the masses still occupying the countryside.

After some weeks of teaching about Lei Feng, his character and activities began to pall, and his earnest, smug selflessness created a wilful reaction from me. His assured innocence seemed to form a Candide-like[5] image in my mind. Of course the stories were meant for a young primary and teenage audience, as well as uneducated adults, but the underlying simplicity of the storylines was incredibly naïve, and would not have been acceptable at equivalent secondary school level in the UK. I was quite irritated by one particular story; on this occasion just as it was about to rain, he noticed a few bags of cement lying outside a building, so he ran and threw his greatcoat over them for protection.

At my next session with some of the Chinese teachers I pointed out that anyone with any knowledge of the effect of water on cement, that is, by implication, anyone with a practical upbringing, would not have left bags of this building material uncovered and open to the elements. They smilingly said that this issue was not crucial to the story, that my critical analysis came from an irrelevant standpoint of 'capitalist society' thinking, and anyway it didn't rain so much in north China. This vigorous defence against my criticism indicated that a balanced discussion was not on the agenda. I could cede their first point, but the other comments were not so logical to me. And the one on rainfall rankled with me because the locations of his stories were rarely mentioned. Thus I had the first inkling that my mind-set and applied approach were not quite the same as theirs, and that my western 'common sense' may not be so relevant or valid in China, and was possibly too culture-specific. It looked as though I had a more 'industrialised' background and outlook on life than them. I felt that I would be able to tackle some of the practical problems in the home, whereas my colleagues would be unable to deal with such situations, and would call in the school electrician, carpenter or boiler man. They had the collective umbrella of their unit looking after them.

For moral questions they could turn to the Party and Mao Tse-tung Thought for the answers. It seemed as if they were more 'moralistic' in their daily life than I was, and could argue their corner on any political points relating to the merits of socialism, even if they were only mouthing the propaganda churned out by the press and radio. They were not so much discussing and arguing a case for and against, as merely parroting the correct formula laid down by the Party. In fact, pragmatism did not seem to be a required instrument in socialist theory and practice, because the Party decided everything in the end. I remember on one occasion I asked a group of teachers if Psychology was a subject taught at university level, and they looked askance at my simple question! *(We have the Party, stupid!)* Their answer was that the Communist Party would deal with all such matters in society, with the implication that it was not necessary to study this subject. Interestingly, the Chinese for 'psychology' is 'heart-inside-study' (xin.li.xue), while westerners regard psychology as being the study of the mind.

Yet over my two years stay I was struck by the considerable efforts that the government put into expressing the essential elements of China's political slogans and policies, and how they were presented to the populace. Serious intellectual input was invested in the written words of the socialist philosophy, and in the arguments underpinning the campaigns. So there was a vast amount of explanation offered for every movement. The Chinese masses knew there was no alternative to the socialist objectives, and everyone had to follow the party line, but at least some degree of clarification was entailed, and this was restated day in day out. You only have to read the *Peking Review*s for 1966 to appreciate and understand the surging flood of words necessary to introduce and sustain the beginnings of the Cultural Revolution movement.

Anyway, I moved on to my next point, which related to why Chinese university graduates could not be accurately described as 'intellectuals' in current English usage. In translation work, my Chinese colleagues automatically talked about themselves and university graduates in general as 'intellectuals', and I had a long struggle to explain to them that 'intellectual' had a more precise meaning in British society, and was never used to describe the mass of university graduates. In China, pupils who attended middle school until 16 were described as educated youth, so to continue their education and graduate from senior middle school, and then tertiary education raised the stakes and status pretty high. Such students of higher education could be labelled as college or university graduates in the UK, rather than intellectuals, but the Chinese term for intellectual was zhi.shi fen.zi, and had to be translated as that. Although accepting my explanation, the Chinese teachers never did adjust their terminology; it didn't fit in with their experience, and for me it was yet another cultural-linguistic difference to add to my list. Many years later I discovered that Premier Chou En-lai had faced up to this same question, and in speeches he had used the Chinese term 'higher-level intellectuals' to denote the group that in English we would call 'intellectuals'.

At mealtimes in the Friendship Guesthouse, I discovered that some of the other western teachers of English also reacted against Lei Feng's ingenuous attitude, no matter how commendable his actions were. However there were teachers and teachers! Westerners with a strong Leftist background would find little fault with him and his exploits, while teachers with little political consciousness, like myself, would have no socialist belief system with which to support him, and therefore were more questioning. Other foreign expert teachers, several of whom were practising Roman Catholics, seemed to be searching for some signs of humble Christian values in the practice of New China, and they were also loath to criticise the man. Lei Feng's attitude, along with the many other emulatory heroes of the times, could be seen as a source of encouragement to any foreigner seeking to find some superficial similarities between socialist and Christian theory and practice.

In one of our mealtime discussions a heresy was voiced that the propaganda campaign of emulatory heroes was actually introducing a set of improved social mores into Chinese culture; or at least a level of caring for others outside of the family that was not so visible in traditional thinking and practice. That is, notwithstanding the array of plausible old Confucian virtues[6] that still receive public acceptance, and a modicum of respect, in Chinese communities outside of mainland China. Nevertheless our heretical proposition seemed to have merit, and would have made a worthwhile project to research, but none of us had time. It ties in with comments made by Bertrand Russell in his book, *The Problem of China*, published in 1922, when he offered callousness as a negative trait of the Chinese.

> *"The callousness of the Chinese is bound to strike every Anglo-Saxon. They have none of that humanitarian impulse which leads us to devote one percent of our energy to mitigating the evils wrought by the other ninety nine percent."*

Lei Feng was a model of anti-callousness. In his diary he had set out his ideals as:

- Be warm as Spring towards your comrades
- Be enthusiastic and conscientious in your work like Summer
- Sweep away all selfishness like the Autumn winds
- Be as merciless towards your class enemies as the harsh Winter

Maybe the first three aims could be acceptable in Christian thinking, but the last one was the sting in the Chinese tail, as no feeling of compromise was revealed in his stated attitude towards class enemies. And during the worst horrors of the Cultural Revolution, 1966-68, this mental approach was put into practice on a national country-wide scale, leading to the suffering and deaths of large numbers of fellow Chinese, at the hands of China's youth. No statistics on this are available to date, and there is no record of whether the Chinese people see this as a blot on their history. Only a few years earlier, millions had died in the famines of the three bad years, 1959-61, and maybe the Chinese were inured to the mega-sized loss of life that had occurred regularly in their recent century of history. Bertrand Russell, writing in 1922, looked at this Chinese lack of humanity towards each other:

> *"A great deal of Chinese callousness is due to a perception of the vastness of the problems facing them. But there remains a residue which can not be so explained...the spectacle of suffering does not of itself raise any sympathetic pain in the average Chinaman."*

It remains to be seen whether the recent meteoric rise in living standards, combined with the new parental-infant bonding arising from the 'one-child policy'[7] of 1980, which was aimed mainly at the urban population and not the peasantry, has had any effect on this question. In 2015 the Chinese media announced the decision to abolish the 'one-child policy', and this would become law in 2016.

In those days of 1965, a year before the Cultural Revolution, there was a temporary lull in new mass political movements, yet Peking streets were always awash with political slogans. We did not understand this hiatus at the time. But during our second stay in Peking in 1974-76, the last years of the Cultural Revolution and the Gang of Four[8], we were always prepared for the possibility of a pendulum swing in the thrust of political movements, according to the balance of power in the Standing Committee. When Mao was ascendant, the stress was always on 'politics in control', at the expense of economics, while during any waning of his power, the emphasis became more inclusive of economic issues.

When we arrived in 1965, the Socialist Education movement was coming to an end, and the overall emphasis was on 'Serve the People', as exemplified by the Lei Feng campaign. Sino-Soviet relations were abysmally low, after the exodus of all Russian experts in 1960, and the relevant anti-Russian slogans were all critical of the Revisionist road (code words for the Soviet Union policies). On this Chinese side of the Pacific Ocean, the growing Vietnam war took centre stage, with the main slogans being 'Down with American Imperialism', and 'Defend the Motherland'. The unresolved, contentious matter of control of Formosa manifested itself in the warning slogan of 'We shall certainly liberate Taiwan'. Coincidentally, Britain maintained a consular office in Taiwan, and this was a crucial bone of contention between the two countries.

That year saw an increasing number of foreigners arriving at the Friendship Guesthouse. General de Gaulle had established full diplomatic relations with China in 1964, and consequently there was an influx of French experts and students. However, Britain's diplomatic status was still at the level of Charge D'Affaires representation, as it had been from 1950. A smaller intake of English-speaking experts arrived in 1964-66 too, and we all indulged in the diverting game of placing newcomers into political categories. Some of the English-speaking Old China Hands, who frequented the Friendship Guesthouse, seemed to have a watching brief to check out this inflow of foreigners. They soon assessed whether incomers were politically acceptable 'party line' folk, who had come to help the Chinese revolution, or whether they were politically naïve 'bourgeois opportunists', who had come to China, only to further their own careers. I found myself cast in this latter group. On the benchmark spectrum between these two poles of party liners versus opportunists stood a collection of foreign friends of varying hues of grey. This did not appear to bother our Chinese employers, who assessed people on whether they could do a good job of work, irrespective of their political leanings. Pro-Chinese line foreigners were presumably preferable, and probably caused them less hassle. Shades of Teng Hsiao-ping's attributed comment that it didn't matter if a cat was white or black, as long as it could catch mice.

In 1965 a new film entitled 'Girl Divers', extolling the virtues of Lei Feng, had been made, and in the autumn Waddi and other English-speaking ladies were invited to the Peking Film studios to help dub the soundtrack into English. They made many visits there, and all said it was a great experience. The film was released before the Cultural Revolution started, and we saw it several times trying to identify the mixture of British and Commonwealth voices in the film, especially when they sang the catchy Lei Feng song that was one of the top hits of 1965. Like all the Chinese feature films that we saw in those days, it was a heavily-weighted piece of black & white propaganda, aimed at inspiring the mass audience of newly-educated youthful urbanites and the huge proportion of peasantry throughout China, still engaged in the slow and laborious process of gaining some literacy.

The storylines of Chinese films in that era were always extremely simplistic and, more often than not, were concerned with the struggles of the recent civil war before 1949; either it was the Eighth Route Army defeating the 'puppet' Chiang Kai-shek troops or just countryside struggles of the Chinese peasantry versus the landlords. A few might be on the sufferings that the Japanese invading armies inflicted on the Chinese people, and the guerrilla warfare carried out against them by the Chinese communist forces. To me, these films were all reminders of the old American cowboy films of good guy versus bad guy, but for the mass of unsophisticated Chinese having these films available must have been a treat.

One day when talking about Lei Feng with a senior class, I tentatively broached the question of the uncovered bags of cement lying in the open, as being defective management and un-socialist, and I was given short shrift by my students. This was anathema to them and also a stimulating trigger to speak English; and they showed more aggrieved feelings in discussion than did my Chinese teaching colleagues. Then, one day in a junior class, I suddenly realised that Lei Feng was being eclipsed in the emulatory stakes. The students were reading aloud a story about the latest posthumous Army hero, Ouyang Hai[9], and some girls in particular, were reduced to tears. In all my previous classes, when reading Lei Feng stories, none of the students had ever cried.

Dear old Lei Feng, along with a host of other emulatory heroes of New China, disappeared from view in the Cultural Revolution. They had all become redundant within this violent and disturbing society of continual class struggle. Attempts to re-introduce Lei Feng and his social values, have been made since the Cultural Revolution, most recently in 2008 in Chong.qing by Party chief, Bo Xi.lai[10], but without success. He initiated a 'Red Culture' movement in a series of Maoist-style campaigns to revive the public morality of the Lei Feng period, and to protect China from the 'spiritual pollution' of the West. It was not well received, and his critics labelled him 'Little Mao'. Then, because of a personal scandal he was investigated and found to have committed transgressions of the impenetrable code of the Communist Party, and sentenced to life imprisonment. His father was Bo Yi.bo[11], one of the 'Eight Immortals'. This term is used to describe eight of the foremost old party revolutionaries, who suffered in the Cultural Revolution and were then rehabilitated after Mao died in 1976. As a 'princeling' of one of those leading families Bo Xi.lai seemed destined for very high office, but it was not to be.

Lei Feng was a man of his socialist times, and his standard of moral behaviour seems hardly relevant in Chinese society today, where money is God, and all the emphasis is on the acquisition of wealth.

Chapter Notes
1. Lei Feng- Wikipedia online
2. Chinglish- Wikipedia online
3. Beijing Review- Wikipedia online
4. Chinese typewriter- Wikipedia online
5. Candide- Wikipedia online
6. Confucianism- Wikipedia online
7. One child policy- Wikipedia online
8. Gang of Four- Wikipedia online
9. Ouyang Hai- Wikipedia online
10. Bo Xilai- Wikipedia online
11. Bo Yibo- Wikipedia online

7

SCHOOL LIFE- WELL BEGUN, HALF DONE

"Well begun, half done!" I had never heard this English saying until Little Liu used it during one of my sessions with a small group of the teachers at School, and I took to it. Waddi and I both had time with colleagues allocated on our timetables, and we did this regularly each week.   We tried to do language work with them that they themselves requested, but often we would give a talk or lead a discussion on certain topics that had been approved by our head of English, maybe even relating to the materials that they themselves were teaching.   Their attendance was varied and inconsistent, because of the pressures on their timetable, and sometimes they were tired and just wanted to listen to us; maybe some of them were more concerned with improving their English than others, so it was hard to know what their motivation was.   Judging by the range of topics covered in these sessions, I would say that there was little interest in subjects outside of China.

We soon became aware of the need to teach simple, basic English to the pupils, and heed the fact that very few idioms and sayings could be safely introduced into the elementary classes.   Our colleagues did know a minimal range of the most common English sayings and proverbs, and these figured more regularly in the advanced levels of the senior classes.   Early on, we had an example of idiom-deficiency during one of our mid-morning 'tea breaks'.   With a group of our colleagues, I joked that Waddi was 'pulling my leg' over something, and immediately everyone went quiet; they didn't know this saying, and one of them told me afterwards that they thought it had sexual connotations.   I had to quickly explain the meaning, and then everything returned to relaxed normality, and the conversation revived.

Right from the start, I couldn't resist making testing remarks to the teachers that after all, Waddi and I, as Westerners, were 'big noses' and 'foreign devils'.   This would elicit some embarrassed smiles and laughter, and I would be firmly told that such terms didn't apply in New China.   My efforts to further my study of Chinese were not so successful.   The school leadership had agreed that I could have some Chinese classes, which were added to my timetable in the afternoons after lunch, but this extra burden was not popular with the colleagues who would be delegated to come along in their free time, rather drowsily, following their post-lunch nap, and I soon gave up on these. Instead, I asked if any of the teachers could help me translate some classical Chinese texts that I had brought with me, and was told rather sheepishly that they had not studied the classics during their schooling.

I felt that this was a Chinese way of saying no, because I knew that one of our older male colleagues, who looked everything like an ancient scholar, and sometimes even wore a traditional long gown, had probably studied the Chinese classics before 1949. He later suffered very badly at the hands of the school's Red Guards (his own students) in the Cultural Revolution.   He had a few long wispy hairs on his chin, like a number of the old men that we saw in the streets. As for the rest of my other male colleagues, they did not apparently need to shave regularly.   In fact I never saw a fully-grown beard in Peking, except on the huge portraits of Marx and Engels that were erected around Tiananmen Square on special occasions during the year.   Then, in April 1971, on a visit to the Revolution Museum in Yenan [Yan.an], I did see a photo of a much younger Chou En-lai, on horseback, sporting a full, black beard. Such a contrast, when compared to his distinguished bearing in 1965.

On 8 March 1965 we suddenly discovered International Women's Day, an event that we had never heard of before. Waddi had the day off and went with several women colleagues to the Great Hall of the People for a grand lunch, with speeches by top women officials. She was quite impressed, and it raised her awareness of the emphasis on Chinese women in society, who, as Chairman Mao said, "Hold up half the sky". On the other hand the Chinese treatment of foreign women was an irritating and vexing matter for those married ones who were not 'foreign experts'. In any official communications they were designated as 'fu.ren' (wife), and their personal names were not used. Some of the European women were incensed by this practice, and complained to their work units, but nothing changed in this respect during our stay.

One of our Chinese teaching colleagues, who was comparatively outspoken, would often talk about the pride and euphoria that the young educated generation felt in the positive achievements of the 1950s and the early days of the Great Leap Forward[1], and he mentioned especially the new buildings that went up in Peking in 1958. However none of them ever mentioned the Korean War, or indeed the three Bad Years of starvation, 1959-1961. I asked colleagues if they were affected by the 'Let a Hundred Flowers Blossom'[2] movement of 1956, in which the Chinese people were permitted to give their feedback on the government. This led to such a flood of disapproval from the educated classes and intellectuals that the leadership responded by initiating an Anti-Rightist campaign, to close down any forms of criticism of the Party and government. Most colleagues told me that they were still studying at college during the 'Hundred Flowers', and were not involved. They would never say anything negative about their country.

Right from the beginning several male colleagues invited me to stay for lunch in the school canteen, and I did realise that this was a friendly gesture, and maybe a desire to get me more involved in school life. I hesitated and stalled for a couple of weeks, and then did it several times. As soon as the lunchtime bell had sounded, everybody rushed off to the canteen to join the lengthening queue. Most people were standing and eating and talking, but my three male colleagues grabbed one of the small tables around, went to the front of the queue and got me some hot food. Each time it was some form of large, semi-unleavened buns, made from the available grain, usually corn flour, which gave them a dark yellowy-brown colour, filled with a little sauce, either meat or vegetable. I only managed one bun very slowly, and felt really full, but my colleagues could manage two buns easily, as well as side dishes of salted turnips, other vegetables, and soya beancurd tofu [dou.fu].

Most people were drinking the hot water, readily available in a large urn, and there were no alcoholic or soft drinks available. One day they got me a small bowl of noodle soup, and that was good. They did serve rice regularly in order to satisfy the needs of the southern Chinese on the staff, but in the north a bowl of noodles was the most common dish. I knew that rice, grain, meat, eggs and cooking oil were all rationed, but I was shielded from those grim realities of food coupons. This was not a new experience for me, because growing up in wartime I had been used to food rationing as part of my young life.

36

At one of those lunches I mentioned that I was missing cheese in my diet, and they immediately recommended that I try fermented soya beancurd called 'stinking bean curd'[chou dou.fu]. I managed to track some down in the Guesthouse restaurant, although not on the menu, and it was the closest taste to strong cheese that I discovered in China. I liked it, but in small portions only. Our lunch was over in twenty minutes and everyone went to have a nap before afternoon school, while I got the waiting car to take me back to the oasis of the Friendship Guesthouse. Years later, an old colleague told me that during this time when meat was in short supply, a common saying was that "Soya bean is China's meat".

Although everyone was wearing padded winter clothing in the school, I could see that my colleagues all seemed finely-boned, and could hardly be said to be carrying any surplus fat. They were from the urban educated class, and their diet appeared to be mainly carbo-hydrates, with minimal nutritional value, except for the soya bean curd. This applied to all that generation, and older, of the Chinese that I saw in the streets, and on my travels. They were all of average Chinese height, with Northerners being the tallest, but without the bulk of most western people of their age. However some of the junior and senior students at our school were much taller and stronger than their teachers, so maybe a better diet in their early years was making the difference.

We once discussed the question of Chinese youngsters learning to read and write, and how much time this consumed when compared with the literacy learning of British primary school children. Hackles were raised when I mildly suggested that it was much easier and quicker to learn the twenty six symbols of the English Roman alphabet, than the years of constant rote-learning that was required in the reading and writing of thousands of Chinese characters. For good measure I added that the English alphabet could also provide endless permutations and combinations for future expansion of the word base. My colleagues immediately outlined the great emphasis on adult and primary school literacy, initiated in the educational field in the 1950s, including a whole raft of new simplified characters, modern language teaching methods and books, and the introduction of standard Han.yu Pin.yin (Chinese-language-spelling) Romanisation to help in the learning process. There was never any mention that roman letters might possibly replace Chinese characters in the future. Even to me that seemed unthinkable.

Our differing stands were eventually resolved by the diplomacy of one male colleague, Old Yang, who challenged me to a simple speed-writing test of one sentence, with roughly the same number of written strokes in each language. We were closely watched by colleagues, and finished our sentences at the same time; both sentences were then pronounced legible, so honours were even. Later on, several colleagues privately admitted to me that English was an easy language for them to learn in the initial stages, especially reading and writing, but became more demanding at later levels.

In terms of phonology, most of the northern Chinese were able to reproduce English phonetics without problems, even the two differing 'th' sounds represented in 'the' and 'three'; both of which necessitated the forward movement of the tongue between the upper and lower front teeth, or at least to the upper front palate. I can't think of any spoken syllables in Chinese phonology that require this action. Some of our female colleagues were not so happy about revealing their tongues, and they managed these sounds with minimal effort. In laughing, some of them would often cover their mouth with their hand. Nevertheless, the teachers were well ahead of us in the study of phonetics, because they all knew the International Phonetic Alphabet.

However, when interpreting for us, one problem they all had in common was the correct use of the personal pronouns 'he' and 'she', because the Chinese language used 'ta' to denote both the male and female person. Another constant challenge for them was translating large numbers from Chinese into English or vice versa, because the Chinese used 10,000 [wan] as their large unit of counting, while we used both one thousand and one million. So for them, 100,000 was ten 'wan' 10 x 10,000 [shi wan]. 1,000,000 was a hundred 'wan' 100 x 10,000 [bai wan]. This 'wan' occurs in the famous saying "Mao zhu.xi wan sui" (Long Live Chairman Mao), where 'wan sui' (10,000 years) becomes 'Long Live'. Even the most proficient English speakers that I met during my time in Peking, had difficulties with numbers.

Another time, for one of my teachers' groups, I took in a small tape spool with several of the early Beatles songs on from 1964, but there was little interest and I had to turn off the tape quite quickly; it was another stage in my learning curve. I explained that the Beatles were an up and coming pop band at home, and they played guitars, but sitting in that little bare room talking about the musical scene in Britain, I felt that the two worlds were on different planets. Their feedback was that it sounded like a repetitive and monotonous rhythm, and they couldn't understand the words anyway. By chance, soon after that I went to see the 'Yang Family', my first traditional Peking Opera, and I had similar sentiments on exposure to its high-pitched vocals. However the stylised postures, movements, and vivid make-up were quite entertaining on that initial visit. Chinese characters telling the story were thrown on to the walls adjoining the stage, by some primitive cinematic projector, and the English translation had to come from our interpreter colleague.

One day I asked several colleagues about their ability to hear and recognise different western European languages, and was surprised by the general consensus that they all sounded similar, and that they contained a lot of 's' and 'sh' sibilants. I understood that this similarity was possible for the north European languages, which came from Germanic roots, but I had thought that the Romance languages sounded somewhat different phonologically. Then I asked them if they could distinguish between different European nationalities by looks, and they said that we all looked the same. I ploughed on and asked about the differing hair and eye-colouring of Europeans, and they responded that this didn't matter, because we all had 'big noses', and 'round eyes', as one of the ladies laughingly added, 'like monkeys'. Our sessions may well have taken place in an amiable atmosphere, but colleagues could give as good as they got. This is the pot calling the kettle black!

Another of these exchanges occurred when Waddi and I had a joint session with colleagues. At some stage I asked them how the basic character 'qing', as in the compound qing.nian (youth), could be translated as blue or green or black (as per Matthew's Chinese-English dictionary). I came from a country full of greenery, with a rich lexicon containing many ways of describing shades of green, and to me green was always green. Then we got onto the topic of black hair, and they declared that all Chinese people had black hair. I disagreed because two of them, one female and one male, had what I regarded as dark brown hair. Waddi actually had very black hair, but they would not concede this fact, and unanimously asserted that it was dark brown, while they themselves all had black hair.   In several of her classes, Waddi's pupils said that her hair was 'brown'.   It seemed that Chinese people were sensitive about this matter, and it was not up for debate; black hair was part of the Han Chinese identity, full stop.

We got to know our teaching colleagues very well over our two year stay, and relations were always amiable and respectful.   Their humour came mainly from recounting amusing stories and situations from real life, and I never heard any of them tell a Chinese joke.   Equally, I never told an English joke either, but I did introduce some banter into our meetings, and could get them smiling or laughing.   At school parties, Waddi played the guitar while I sang songs.   Once I briefly mimicked the stylised, operatic actions of a modern revolutionary hero, frowning fiercely at his enemies, and everyone laughed.   As for the Chinese laughing at themselves, I can't recall any such occasions.

At celebratory times of the year there would always be some special programme of variety acts at the Friendship Guesthouse theatre, and one outstanding performer was a male maestro of the Chinese fiddle [er.hu].   We twice saw bamboo clapper talk [kuai.ban] [3] acts, between two men.   It consisted of rhythmic, fast monologues or dialogues, and the Chinese section of the audience was soon in fits of laughter.   Our interpreter, Old Chang [Zhang], said that it would take him too long to translate and explain, even for just a few of the jokes, so we missed out on that.   Later on, he did say that a lot of the humour was based on the large pool of homophones present in the Chinese language, which could easily be misinterpreted and confused, and give rise to ambiguous, double meanings.   Several times in town I would see another instance of the homophones syndrome, when one person in conversation with another would suddenly use a finger to scribble a character in mid-air, in order to clarify which meaning was intended for the spoken syllable.

Chinese politeness from our colleagues was never an issue for us, as they could be smilingly direct when aroused.   In the beginning, their range of facial expressions seemed more limited than we were used to, but later on they relaxed, and revealed more of their feelings, although I never saw any of them show any signs of anger or annoyance, apart from a mild frown.   This form of expression for showing displeasure, was a commonly used technique on stage or screen, where an assortment of frowns would be used by the revolutionary heroes when confronting their enemies.   There were always enemies in every storyline, with the degree of frown being calibrated according to the situational context.

Those colleagues of ours had a heavy workload, with few days of rest, but they never complained to us.   As well as the inherited polite barriers to keep us at a distance, they had instructions from above on not becoming too familiar with foreigners, regardless of any spontaneous combustion of friendship that might occur.   From a small core of colleagues, one of them, selected by some mysterious process that we were never privy to, would act as our oral interpreter for any meetings at school or on any extramural visits. English standards varied amongst the teachers, mainly in terms of information omitted when translating, and we soon realised the range of competences involved.   We were always able to get the main meat of the talk from their translations, and could ask them to fill in any gaps afterwards.   This may have been good practice for their language proficiency and vocabulary usage, but it was a gruelling experience for them, and, in retrospect, I can only thank them for all their efforts.

Our head of English, Old Chang, was the most gifted one, and in 1975, during our second tour in Peking, he was sent to work as an interpreter at the United Nations in New York for several months. This was high prestige for him. When he came back he said that it was the most mentally exhausting work he had ever done, with each one of the Chinese interpreters working for twenty minute bursts, on a rota schedule. Further recognition came his way, when he was appointed Education Counsellor at the Chinese Embassy in London in 1979.

Some of our colleagues would consult with us on teaching materials, and we tape-recorded reading texts for their classes or special pronunciation exercises, at the speed requested. They would sometimes show us the materials they used to supplement our 'direct method' classes, and we discovered that singing songs was popular with the pupils. However, there was much rote-learning and repetition chanting, and basically it was the good old grammar-translation method of teaching. On the whole though, throughout our contract, there seemed to be a reluctance by colleagues to impose too much on us, in seeking our help in English language teaching. We even brought this up several times at meetings with the school leadership, who unexpectedly admitted that they were aware of this situation, but nothing much changed.

Chapter Notes
1. Great Leap Forward- Wikipedia online
2. Hundred Flowers Campaign- Wikipedia online
3. Kuaiban -Wikipedia online

8

OUR COLLEAGUES AND STUDENTS AT SCHOOL

As well as the leaders from our school and institute, we had been met by three teaching colleagues on our arrival at Peking airport in January 1965. They were friendly and concerned, with strong advice from the two ladies on wearing warmer clothing, and adjusting to the dry Peking climate by drinking lots of hot water, that was always available in the ubiquitous thermos flasks wherever you went. After several recovery days in our new home in the Friendship Guesthouse we were taken to school, a half hour's car journey into town to the Ho P'ing (Peace Gate) district, to meet the leadership for an introductory briefing, and get to know our teaching colleagues. They seemed pleased to see us and have the chance to practice their English, and all this was on top of their heavy workloads. They were already preparing materials for the second term of the academic year, which started after the Chinese New Year holiday and ran until the summer. Foreign experts employed by the Chinese government to teach their native language were rare on the ground in those days, and now two English-speaking teachers were coming to work in their school. This emphasised the status of the school, and the importance of their work.

We were completely surprised to find that we had another English colleague already in place; Mr Harry Chandler, a cheerful, chatty and dapper Englishman who had never taught in his life, and had then started a new career of teaching at our school in September 1964. He was a retired engineer, who told us vaguely that travelling somewhere in South East Asia he had visited a Chinese Embassy and had been recruited to teach English on a one year contract. Aged about 70, he was always immaculately dressed with tie, blazer, creased trousers and polished shoes. Every morning his face shone from his daily shave.

He had a full head of white hair, with blue eyes and smiling face, and he spoke good, clear English with little accent. Truly a veritable 'foreign devil' confronting all those young Chinese pupils, who had probably never seen anyone like this before. Our colleagues told us that the junior school classes were fascinated by him. They also ruefully admitted that he talked non-stop and rarely paused for the essential bookwork, reading exercises or questions. One Chinese colleague who attended all his classes would have given him teaching plans and relevant teaching materials to cover, but after paying lip service to these, he was away. So it was mainly the pupils' listening skills that could benefit from his teaching work.

He seemed not to be politically aware, and he did not get involved in any political cliques in the Druzhba. The clearest evidence of this came one day in a junior class when he committed an inexcusable lapse. Trying to illustrate the meaning of the verb 'to shock', he made up a sentence: 'If you hear the news that Chairman Mao has died, you will be shocked'. The young pupils were indeed shocked and angry to hear this statement, and the class ended early. He was gently eased out of teaching the junior classes, and was restricted to teaching the senior classes, and then later was transferred to the institute itself, where the older college students were perfectly capable of engaging him in any arguments in English. He was always punctual and never missed a class.

In our first year we had charming French colleagues, a husband and wife team, Michel and Marie-France Duverger, and in our second year four more French teachers, including Suzanne Fromont from the Alliance Francaise in Paris. Our regular Spanish colleague was Jose, nicknamed Pepe, a grizzled veteran from the Spanish Civil War, who had been exiled in Paris for many years before moving to Peking. From time to time he had female teaching colleagues from Latin America, but he was always the mainstay and lode star of the Spanish section.

In January 1965 it was coming up to the Spring Festival break(Chinese New Year), with that subdued air of expectation and excitement, combined with an end of term feeling, just like Christmas at home. Colleagues gave us next term's teaching books and materials for each of our classes, explained the levels of English involved, and advised us on what we should teach. For a starter we both did some recording of English language material on the school's utility tape recorders, which we found to be manufactured in China. In fact, we had a good three weeks of preparation time before the term started. What's more, we had three books on teaching English as a Foreign Language, which I had bought from a local bookshop just before departure, and we had brought them in our suitcases. One of them was a classic book by E. Frank Candlin, on teaching English to foreign students.

During the New Year celebrations we were invited to school for the Wedding Reception of Old Jin, one of our male colleagues, and it made a great impression on us. I vividly remember snatches of it, and whenever I go back to Peking, I usually see him and remind him of that day. It was a crowded, jostling party atmosphere with tea, lemonade , just a few bottles of beer and lots of snacks, but I didn't see anyone the worse for wear, and it was restrained and good-natured with plenty of banter about the newly-weds. The head of our English section was Old Chang [Zhang], and we saw that after drinking a little beer his cheeks blushed red. He was extremely sensitive about this, and explained that it was something to do with enzymes and his stomach. I can't recall this happening on later social occasions, so he must have stopped drinking beer at the few banquets and social occasions when alcohol was available. I never did find out whether Chinese white spirits had a similar blushing effect on his cheeks, or if he had the enzymes to cope.

Then we were invited by the Institute to attend a Grand Banquet-Party, and all the foreign teachers were there. We played games, such as the egg and spoon race, where Michel and I became very competitive, and some of our colleagues were unwillingly pressed into action too. Meanwhile, I had been accosted by old Comrade Ma, a Long March veteran, now retired, and on the periphery of the school leadership, who insisted that we have a friendship toast, with two very small stem glasses holding a colourless white spirit called 'Moutai' (Maotai[1]). We had to empty our glasses on the spot, turn them upside down and say 'gan bei'(empty cup). This was my first meeting with 'Moutai' spirit. Coming from a machismo rugby-playing and beer-drinking background in Gloucester, I was not going to be awed by this old veteran and his little glass. I sort of sensed that my 'face' was being tested and measured. So we drank to his friendship toast, and then I proposed my toast to world peace. This was the only safe topic that came to mind at the time, but I later acquired the standard, acceptable toast to 'the friendship between the British and Chinese peoples'. I had now drunk two small glasses of 'Moutai' spirit on an empty stomach; it was not a good beginning.

The adjacent banqueting tables were full of an amazing assortment of cold dishes, including the famous dish of 'hundred day old eggs', so I went over and started picking and eating, with one or two other foreigners. Most people were standing around politely waiting for the senior host to start things moving according to the correct Chinese protocol. Then, suddenly Old Ma appeared again with another toast and more 'Moutai'. I can't remember my counter toast, but that was now four glasses in total. Waddi said my face was going red, just like Old Chang, so I obviously did not have the enzymes to cope with 'Moutai'.

The next shock was that all those cold dishes, most of them barely touched, were removed and a succession of delicious hot dishes started to appear. This was the solid substance that my stomach had needed to absorb the 'Moutai', but they arrived four glasses too late and made little impact. Things became blurred, but again that smiling old veteran Ma materialised at my elbow with two glasses, and I stubbornly took on his challenge. No matter what happened, my motivation not to lose 'face' was reaching Chinese proportions. Soon after that Waddi escorted me to a waiting taxi and we went home early, and as a result I missed the golden opportunity to socialise and meet with the various leaders of the institute and the school. The following day several Chinese colleagues came to visit us and check me out, and Teacher Hu whispered to me that Old Ma had had to leave the party early too, just after me. A little pittance of satisfaction for me, because I had left first and lost face, but I now knew the potency of 'Moutai', which should undoubtedly be seen as China's secret diplomatic weapon; and I never succumbed again. My view seems to be confirmed by an alleged comment made by Henry Kissinger to Deng Xiao.ping, who was on a visit to the US in 1979, to the effect that "I think if we drank enough 'Moutai' we can solve anything."

Another social event organised over New Year by the institute was a dance party in the Friendship Guesthouse, especially for their foreign students, who consisted of four French and two British, one of whom was female. Several school teachers were there as well as some of the institute leadership, and western-style waltz music was being played on a gramophone. The party guests seemed to be mainly male, and I was invited to dance by the Assistant Dean from the Institute, a spry man dressed in top quality winter overcoat, and still wearing his woollen Mao cap. This was one culture shock too far for my flexibility of outlook, and I politely declined. Regretfully, this was yet another lost opportunity for me to meet one of the top men, but he was soon gliding around the dance floor with another male.

When the real teaching started in February our timetables included five classes. Mine were spread over the junior middle and senior middle classes, covering ages 12-18, while Waddi was given primary and junior middle classes, covering ages 9-16. We were also allocated time with small groups of our colleagues. It was a six day week, with morning classes between 8 a.m. and noon, but thankfully, only two afternoons, so we totalled around twenty teaching hours a week, plus four hours with the teachers. All our preparation time was in addition to this schedule.

For every group that we taught, we worked with a Chinese colleague, who was responsible for that class, and who sat in for each of our lessons, at the back of the room; and they were instrumental in getting our teaching plans and materials primed at just about the right level for their class. In the beginning we had to be very adaptable and listen to our colleagues' suggestions and advice, and as time passed things settled down fairly smoothly. As we had never taught English before, we didn't have any fixed ideas on how to teach our mother-tongue, so we relied a lot on various teaching books, and on our initiative.

My co-teachers gave me a list of the pupils' names, always in old Chinese Romanisation, and where they sat in class. When talking in class, it seemed perfectly normal to use the full Chinese names of our pupils, and we followed this practice over our two year stay. There was never any mention of using English names for the students or teachers. In return, my Chinese surname was 'Han', and so I was called, Han lao.shi (Teacher Han), while Waddi was called Teacher Waddi. Outside class our colleagues called us Reg and Waddi, while in return we used their complete names, with one exception. That was for a lively and diminutive female teacher, who had the English nickname of 'Shorty'. The only other nickname I ever used was for one of the Chinese teachers of Spanish, and it was 'Wo.tou' (Corn bread). Apparently, during a previous stint of manual work in the countryside he had complained everyday about all the cornbread in their diet, and his colleagues had named him accordingly. Outside school when talking to Chinese people in the Guesthouse, or in town, we would always use the term tong.zhi (comrade). This was the accepted word in general usage by the Chinese people amongst themselves. It is not used anymore.

On entering each class the pupils would stand up and say "Lao.shi hao" (Hello, teacher) while I would respond with "Hello, class". Sometimes with the senior classes, an alternative greeting would be "Tong.xue.men hao" (Hello, fellow students). Only then could I start the class by saying "Shang ke", and end the class when I said "Xia ke". We had been requested to focus on spoken English in class, so we took to the 'direct method' style of language teaching and worked hard on preparing interesting exercises for each class, and trying to involve every pupil. I'm sure that I started off talking a lot, and I always tried to explain the meanings in simple English as I went along. Now and again I used a Chinese word in class, but with advice from colleagues I gradually reduced that to a minimum. It took time for me to involve the pupils more regularly, and get them talking, and I was definitely too teacher-centred in the beginning. Of course, this was the old traditional way of teaching in China too, so nothing new about that.

But as we warmed to the direct method approach, the atmosphere slowly changed and our colleagues said that the pupils looked forward to our oral/aural classes, because we introduced action exercises, played language games and got them speaking. Nevertheless some of our Chinese colleagues frowned at the notion that playing games could be regarded as 'proper' language teaching. For our part, we never heard any negative comments from the school leadership, so we must have been doing something right. The pupils, on the whole, were very keen and a delight to teach, and were always well-behaved, with absolutely no disciplinary problems. Non-motivated pupils, who were difficult to spot and apparently few in number, had to be on their best behaviour in front of their classmates! In one of Waddi's primary classes there was a boy who was a talented artist, but wasn't into English, so she always got him to draw pictures on the blackboard relating to their class-work.

To complement this approach, our Chinese colleagues would see the class later every day and would concentrate on the grammatical points being covered. They would drill the class on all the vocabulary and structures, often by chanting and rote learning, as

well as by teaching them simple songs or poems. Over the two years we often suggested to colleagues that they develop more direct method techniques in their teaching, but
it was a serious hurdle for them to handle as non-native speakers, and it was certainly
outside of their own learning experience. I must admit that in those early days, a really
big advantage for us was living communally in the Guesthouse, where some of the pool
of foreign teachers of English would often sit together at mealtimes, compare notes and
talk shop. That was a godsend to us from the start.

Some of the older classes, who I saw less frequently, were more like conversation sessions, with reading exercises intermixed, and I had to rely on materials supplied by my
co-teacher of the texts or topics chosen for that day. I went along with this, but it was
more difficult to engage with the students and the sessions were not so satisfying for
me, and presumably for them too, although the students had plenty of aural practice.
Such classes encouraged my propensity for digression. In the second term with my
Junior Three class, once or twice my co-teacher did not come, and one day I found myself explaining how the British National Health System, of which I was very proud,
functioned. This was a case of me leaving the beaten track, because up to then I had
always stuck to the school's teaching materials and curriculum requirements, and had
never talked about my country. I knew that anything I said could be construed as disap-
proving propaganda.

The Chinese health system was free to everyone, but you had to pay for food consumed
during a stay in hospital, and also for medication, yet I was saying to them that UK hos-
pitals were also free, and you didn't have to pay for food and medicine. I tried to explain that we all paid taxes every week or every month towards these health costs. I
am not sure that those young pupils understood the word 'taxes' anyway, and how
could they understand and accept my story that this was a reality in a 'capitalist' country such as Britain. Socialism was the correct way forward for China, and they were
told that capitalist countries were the enemies of socialism. Chinese people with capitalist tendencies were castigated as the lowest of the low. I slowly realised that the
class was motionless and freezing up on me, so I stopped and asked them what they
thought. There was an icy silence before one of the girls in the front row said "We
don't believe you".

Years later I was told that that front row of four girls all came from high-ranking families, and the one who had spoken was the youngest daughter of Marshal Chen Yi[2], the
then Minister of Foreign Affairs. Another one was the daughter of Liao Cheng-chih
(Liao Cheng.zhi)[3], a high official in Sino-Japanese relations. I had chosen a top lineage
class to digress to. Not knowing their family backgrounds at the time, I can see now
that the front row was the prerogative of the highest status students. In 2013, Chen
Xiao.lu, eldest son of Marshal Chen Yi, publicly apologised to his old teachers for his
behaviour as a Red Guard in 1966, at his No. 8 Middle School in Peking. Such apolo-
gies, especially from a 'princeling' like Chen, are not encouraged by China's leadership
today, who do not want wide discussion on the horrors of the Cultural Revolution.

On other occasions I overreacted with my colleagues, when the teaching materials included short extracts from the novels of Charles Dickens, touching on the dreadful social conditions of the British working-class a hundred years beforehand. By default
and omission of dates the texts appeared to be about England today. I would argue with
them that he was a great writer, but he lived in the nineteenth century, and his work

should not be taught as reflecting life in 1960s Britain, and I was not willing to do that. Fortunately, these texts were contained in the reading materials books, which my Chinese colleagues taught.

Students didn't wear uniform of any kind, except in the summer when the junior and primary classes, with few exceptions, wore blue cotton trousers, and white blouses or shirts. They also had a red scarf around their neck to indicate that they were Young Pioneers, a system based on the Soviet model for schooling. Surprisingly, we were told that one of the junior boys had refused to join the Young Pioneers, but without having an explanation of his background, we couldn't assess the significance of this. In the winter, everybody was encased in thick cotton or wool-padded clothing to protect against the freezing temperatures, and the general colour scheme of our students was a massed blur of blue, grey, green or khaki. They probably had their red scarves on underneath too. All classrooms had a metal stove in the middle, fed by coal or coal balls, which provided a comfortable heat.

Morning break was for twenty minutes, and the dreaded broadcast relay system would swing into action with the 'exercises' music. All the classes would assemble on the cramped campus grounds, and start performing a fixed routine of gentle calisthenics, which they knew by heart. I participated once or twice, but my uncoordinated arm-swinging tended to distract nearby students, and raise smiles. I can still hum this music at the drop of a hat, and it would definitely be on my reserve list of Desert Island discs. Ten minutes of action would be followed by a couple of minutes of eye exercises, where the students carefully massaged the areas around their eyes. I never ever saw students or anyone else practising 'T'ai chi ch'uan' [Tai.ji.quan[4]] exercises on the school campus, but I could see older people doing the slow motion version in all the parks in Peking. At that stage in my life I thought it too laid back, and dismissed it without a second thought.

After the exercises students had some free time, and they congregated in groups or played games, just like students anywhere in the world. The most popular games for the boys were ping-pong and basketball, which was the only team game that I saw. There was little interest in football, although there were tattered old footballs and one set of posts around. Other activities included a form of hopscotch, keeping up a small feather shuttlecock, and the diabolo, while the junior girls excelled at skipping the thick rubber band together. In the summer months, there would be more emphasis on athletics, and students would be preparing for the sports meet by using the gymnastic parallel bars, throwing the hand-grenade, putting the shot and so on. During such events we were able to see that some of the senior boys were well-muscled and quite strong. Games such as tennis or squash, which required a larger area of land or special buildings, did not exist. Open air badminton would be played on the school grounds during the warmer months.

The school had eight ping-pong tables, standing side by side, made of huge concrete slabs, with a line of bricks for the nets, and this area was always crowded and full of boys, as few girls seemed to participate. I ventured my hand against some small primary boys and got beaten hands down; they all laughed at my handshake grip, and were supremely confident in their penholder grip. This was the time when Japanese supremacy at the international ping-pong scene in the 1950s had passed, and China took over after Chuang Tse-tung [Zhuang Ze.dong][5] became world table tennis singles champion in 1961, and retained his title in 1963 and 1965. He used the penholder grip with ease, and it was a delight to watch him in action on the newsreels. Here was an emulatory national sports hero for the Chinese youth to look up to and enjoy, and as far as I could see the boys at school did just that.

Chapter Notes
1. Maotai- Wikipedia online
2. Chen Yi (marshal)- Wikipedia online
3. Liao Chengzhi- Wikipedia online
4. Tai chi- Wikipedia online
5. Zhuang Zedong-Wikipedia online

9

DICTATORSHIP OF THE PROLETARIAT

"The People's Republic of China is a socialist state of the dictatorship of the proletariat[1], led by the working-class and based on the alliance of workers and peasants." Article 1 of the Chinese Constitution adopted on 17 January 1975

The Foreign Experts Bureau, who were responsible for the life and times of all the foreigners employed by the Chinese government living in the Friendship Guesthouse, maintained a steady schedule of group recreational activities and local visits. It was a good way to entertain them, and also to inform them on the latest developments in building socialist China. In a word, to keep them reasonably occupied and satisfied. So there were trips to a prison, factories, urban communes, schools, higher education institutes and an army unit; some were well outside Peking, such as two separate one day visits, to Tientsin [Tian.jin] Docks, and to 196 Division of the People's Liberation Army, based near to Tientsin. All of them were fascinating insights into aspects of Chinese society after fifteen years of socialist government. The anchor-man for the Foreign Experts Bureau, based in the Guesthouse, was Mr Gao Li.duan, a much put-upon individual, who bore the brunt of foreigners discontent face to face, with a benign smile and a thick skin. I think that, all in all, he and his colleagues did a good job.

On every such trip, once we foreigners had arrived at the venue and were seated around the room, each with a porcelain mug of Chinese tea with their little lids, then the leading host would welcome the 'foreign friends'. They would give a standard introduction of their unit, of the historical background, workers' living conditions, increased production figures, current successes and so on. The preamble had to include a comparative simplistic analysis of the terrible days pre-Liberation before 1949, and the much improved conditions post-Liberation, showing the betterment of life for the Chinese people since 1949. Incredibly, on our second contract in Peking in 1974-76, this simple assessment was surprisingly turned upside-down, when host officials in their introductions to groups of Guesthouse foreigners, proclaimed that the situation in the first years of New China, 1949-1966, had been bad, but was now much better. So much for the flexibility of thinking required by Chinese officialdom, when 'politics' is in command, but I do not think that it was a problematic dilemma for them to swallow. They were saying, in so many words, that during the 1949-1966 period Mao did not have full control, but now in the Cultural Revolution he was in charge, and the situation was much better.

After the host presentations, there would usually be a questions and answers session, with them handling an array of questions from the group of foreign, but sympathetic, barbarians. Question time was often seen as just a polite formality, with no awkward questions being asked. Some foreign experts felt that grilling our hosts in depth could be regarded as being unfriendly to China, and that their own political stance would be judged by others, according to the line of their questioning. In my experience of this 'unfriendly question' syndrome, the Chinese were always quite capable of looking after themselves in this respect, and did not need any such patronising help from over-sensitive foreigners.

It was during these organised visits that I first heard the term 'Dictatorship of the Proletariat' used, an expression that I initially found quite baffling. When visiting factories we would see the workers at their benches or their machines churning out quotas of some product, and carrying out their ten hour days and six day weeks. I couldn't relate those factory workers to the Politburo Standing Committee or any form of dictatorship. My knowledge of this terminology was sadly lacking, yet it was a familiar expression for anyone who had studied some Marxist political science. It had originated from the writings of Marx and Engels in the Communist Manifesto[2] published in German in 1848, and over time had developed as an integral component of socialist theory, before arriving in practice in China in 1949.

When my unpoliticised western mind was confronted by the phrase 'dictatorship of the proletariat', I could only think of the British parliamentary representative model. I just could not see how the Chinese working-class held any form of dictatorship in their hands. That is, unless there was some kind of democratic electoral system of selecting delegates, which allowed the proletariat to have their interests expressed at the top table. This was not the reality in 1965. The National People's Congress, and the State Council, the highest organs of state control, led by Premier Chou En-lai, were the pseudo-democratic bodies meant to fulfil that role, and give some voice to the masses.

The answer to my problem was that the Chinese Communist Party, the vanguard of the workers and peasants, was representing their interests, and was leading the dictatorship of the proletariat. Whenever I asked my school colleagues this question, they would uneasily protest that the Communist Party acted on behalf of the needs and aspirations of the workers and peasants. Several of the more confident ones would explain that this was now a transitional period of socialism, when the state power was in the hands of the people, but most of them would quickly change the subject.

I soon discovered that the workers and peasants had no say in the selection of the Politburo of the Central Committee of the Chinese Communist Party, and that the election of the members to the National People's Congress involved no genuine democratic process. It seemed to me that the reality of the governance of China was the 'Dictatorship of the Chinese Communist Party', which for the everyday life of the Chinese masses meant a 'dictatorship of the bureaucracy', with strict government control of people's lives. This question about party power had been raised before. In fact, Rosa Luxemburg[3], the famous Polish political activist, who died in 1921, had made exactly this point in the early days of the Bolsheviks rise to power in Russia.

So the period of transition of power in China after 1949, to the new state control by the masses, was called the 'Dictatorship of the Proletariat'. It was the intermediate stage of socialism that was the necessary path to follow, in order to reach the theoretical goal of communism. Lenin and Stalin spoke and wrote extensively on this topic. In March 1922, at the Eleventh Party Congress of the Soviet Communist Party, Lenin summarised the situation as: "Among the people, we communists are as a drop in the ocean, and we can administer only when we properly express what the people are conscious of. Unless we do this the communist party will not lead the proletariat, the proletariat will not lead the masses and the whole machine will collapse."

It may be said that the Chinese Communist party was not accountable to anyone, but in effect, in those early years of the 1950s they had a sort of unspoken rapport, a modern

49

version of the Mandate of Heaven[4], with the Chinese people. As well as removing the foreign presence from their shores, the communist party had given China a stable economy, social order and currency, with the implicit aims of building a reconstructed form of society, and thus improving the status and living of the people. Such ideals would have been quite unthinkable barely forty years previously, at the end of the Qing dynasty in 1911. The Constitution of the People's Republic of China of 1954 stated all this in writing. It was the blueprint for the future of China. When we arrived in 1965, the most powerful men in the Chinese Communist Party, putting this blueprint into practice, were the Politburo Standing Committee of the Central Committee, made up of seven veterans of the party's historical struggles: Mao Tse-tung, Liu Shao-chi, Chou En-lai, Chu Teh, Chen Yun, Teng Hsiao-ping, and Lin Piao.

The fundamental rights and duties of Chinese citizens were covered by Articles 85-103 of the Chinese Constitution (1961: Revised Translation of First Edition 1954); Article 91 states:

"Citizens of the People's Republic of China have the right to work. To ensure that citizens can enjoy this right, the state, by planned development of the national economy, gradually provides more employment, improves working conditions and increases wages, amenities and benefits."

Article 92 followed on, in two sentences, by briefly proclaiming the right of workers to rest and leisure. Soon after arriving I had asked colleagues how long holidays they had per year, thinking of my twelve week vacations in the UK school system, and they replied fifty two days, which puzzled me, until they explained that meant every Sunday.

Those two Articles 91 and 92, enshrined the principles of giving the Chinese people more respect and status in developing their country's future, and promising them a better standard of life tomorrow. To my mind, for the common people, this was the main meat on the bone that could be extracted from the term 'Dictatorship of the Proletariat'. Yet these two articles were only theoretical statements that would require immense efforts by the government to fully implement and put into practice. I did not doubt that living and working conditions had been improved for the workers in the fifteen years since 1949, as was borne out by what we saw and heard during all our organised factory visits. Working in three Gloucester factories during my student vacations in the 1950s, I found an entrenched 'them and us' mentality between management and workers, with confrontation being the more prevailing approach than co-operation, much to the future detriment of British industry. On factory visits in Peking, everything seemed calm on the surface and I could not tell if there was a 'them and us' attitude among the workers. They seemed to be on their best behaviour for us.

We learnt that trades unions were benign agencies intent on improving conditions in factories and workers homes; and were definitely not instruments of political struggle for fighting management over money or hours of work. The benefits that the Peking workers enjoyed in New China were small family rooms, or dormitories for the unmarried, with basic electric lighting, coal or wood-burning stoves for heating and cooking facilities, and if they were lucky, recreational amenities, with an attached local medical clinic, usually dealing in traditional Chinese medicine. Treatment in hospital was free, but patients had to pay for prescriptions, and any food consumed. There was no such thing as an ambulance service, and families had to arrange for the transport of relatives to hospital, even if only a pedicart, as I saw several times. Most factories had a canteen to meet the daily needs of the workers and staff.

The Chinese Communist Party had imposed itself on the Chinese people in 1949 in time-honoured fashion, by the power of the gun, without any embedded process of representation for the people or agreement by the people. Then on 20 September 1954, it sought to legitimise itself by formulating a Chinese Constitution, which stated in one hundred and six articles, the structure of the country's administration and governance. The key body, that was repeatedly mentioned, was the National People's Congress, which notionally represented the voice of the Chinese masses. Its status is contained in Article 21: "The National People's Congress of the People's Republic of China is the highest organ of state power." Strikingly, in all those one hundred and six articles, the Chinese Communist Party was never mentioned once, and the term 'Dictatorship of the Proletariat' was also conspicuously absent.

That all changed completely in the new-look Constitution adopted on 17 January 1975; that is, twenty one years on from the first Constitution. Article 1, in which the 'Dictatorship of the Proletariat' is mentioned, is the quotation at the head of this chapter. Article 2 boldly stated:

> *"The Communist Party of China is the core of leadership of the whole Chinese people. The working class exercises leadership over the state through its vanguard, the Communist Party of China. Marxism-Leninism-Mao Tsetung Thought is the theoretical basis guiding the thinking of our nation."*

So the reality of China's governance, which the Chinese people had well understood since 1949, was finally committed into writing in 1975. Yet such were the eddies and currents of the political scene that five years later, Teng Hsiao-ping [Deng Xiao.ping] was back in supreme power at the top, and was taking China along a divergent road with new goals and priorities. The philosophy of this new direction, in so many words, was to focus on economics and manufacturing, rather than on politics. This meant that it was acceptable to acquire individual wealth, and in this way release the energies of the Chinese people. Over the past thirty five years it has evolved as a hybrid form of capitalist-socialism, that the Chinese call 'Socialism with Chinese Characteristics'[5]. As for the 'Dictatorship of the Proletariat', this term is no longer relevant in 2015, and languishes as an obsolete, historical concept in the annals and archives of Mao's socialist China, 1949 to 1976.

Chapter Notes
1. Dictatorship of the Proletariat- Wikipedia online
2. The Communist Manifesto- Wikipedia online
3. Rosa Luxemburg- Wikipedia online
4. Mandate of Heaven- Wikipedia online
5. Socialism with Chinese Characteristics- Wikipedia online

10

PEI TAI HO-FOREIGN EXPERTS HEALTH RESORT

Our school came under the umbrella of the Foreign Languages Institute, so we were always invited to any social events organised by them for their staff of foreign experts. One day in May 1965, our classes were cancelled and all the foreign teachers were transported by coach to Tiananmen Square, where there was a huge demonstration taking place against the Vietnam War. Speeches over the broadcast relay system were given by several leading figures, including P'eng Chen [Peng Zhen], the Mayor of Peking, and also by representatives from Vietnam.

I happened to be sitting with a staff member of the Institute, and he had passable English. He looked at me and repeated the constant slogan "Down with U.S. Imperialism", and then he added in a censuring manner "and their running dogs". I knew what he meant, and I didn't like it. Britain was usually cast as the chief ally of America, and I made the forceful response that Britain had not sent any armed forces to take part in the Vietnam War[1]. But his blood was up, and my words were not acknowledged. I was surprised to see a mild red mist appearing in his eyes, and he ended our conversation by hissing "The Chinese people and the Vietnamese people are as close as lips and teeth". It was an unexpected and irritating experience for me. Ten years later, on a trip to Hanoi during the Spring Holiday of 1975, I discovered that the Vietnamese did not entirely reciprocate these sentiments.

Our first term at school, from February to July 1965 stretched out a long time, and in June we were pleased to hear that the Institute had organised a three week summer tour of Chinese cities for their foreign teachers. While this was taking place, the wives and families could spend their holidays at Pei Tai Ho [Bei.dai.he], a small coastal town on the Bohai Sea, very close to the port of Chinhwangtao [Qin.huang.dao]. Fortunately, all of these options were included in the contracts that we had not yet signed, and were free of charge. The continuous summer heat of Peking was building up, and a seaside holiday was very appealing, especially with the small children. So we arranged with our school that Waddi and the boys would go to Pei Tai Ho around the beginning of August, while I would go on the Institute tour. When our teaching ended around mid-July I set off on the tour.

There were nine foreign experts in the tour group, with interpreters for English, French, Spanish and Japanese. Three older administrators, all from the Institute staff, came along too. The English language interpreter was a charming young woman called Zhang Han.zhi[3], and she was extremely proficient, so much so that she rarely made a mistake, or was lost for the right word, and her pronunciation was pretty faultless. She was undoubtedly the best English speaker that I met in my two years in Peking. We three English speakers in the group were fortunate to have her as interpreter, and she was a great source of information on our tour venues. As we got to know her we chatted a lot, and she touched on her recent experiences in the countryside in the Socialist Education[4] movement. It was nothing political, just an anecdote about coping with bedbugs there. Years later, I learned that during the Cultural Revolution she had been an occasional tutor to Chairman Mao in the rudiments of English; very high status indeed.

Our first stop was Nanking [Nan.jing] and during our stay we made day visits to Muh Ling village, Dr Sun Yat-sen's[5] mausoleum and to the Hall of the Kingdom of Heavenly Peace, 1850-64 [Tai.ping Tian.guo][6]. Zhang told us that Nanking was one of the 'Three Ovens' of China[7], and walking the darkened streets one evening we saw this at first hand. All the population seemed to be resting or sleeping in the open, on rattan mats, cane chairs and beds, trestle tables and the like. The next day we had a short river trip on the Yangtse River [Chang Jiang], before ending up in the town of Wusih [Wu.xi], where we visited a small handicrafts factory, and then had a day at nearby Lake Tai [Tai.hu]. All the day trips were well-organised and conducted at a leisurely pace, and it was proving to be a relaxing holiday.

From Wusih we travelled to Shanghai by train, and by then we had already spent nine days on the tour, with the schedule still including visits to Hangchow [Hang.zhou], Soochow [Su.zhou] and Sian [Xi.an]. However I spoke to the senior leader of our group and explained that I would like to return to my wife and family, and join them on the trip to Pei Tai Ho. He understood my wishes and raised no objections, and the very next day I was on a Vickers Viscount internal flight to Peking. I never saw Miss Zhang Han.zhi again, until February 1972, when watching TV coverage of President Nixon's visit to China, she suddenly appeared as an official interpreter between the President and Chairman Mao. In the following year 1973, she married Ch'iao Kuan-hua [Qiao Guan.hua][8], who was China's Foreign Minister 1974-76.

The school leadership were very flexible when I told them of my change of plans, and I got the travel permit to Pei Tai Ho very quickly. We were all ready for our holiday, and we set off on our journey, with a contingent of other foreigners, all arrangements made efficiently by the Foreign Experts Bureau. First by bus to Peking Railway Station, and then on to the train and placed in comfortable four berth soft sleepers, with an adjacent dining car. The almost five hour trip, via Tientsin [Tian.jin], was conducted at a gentle speed. When we reached Pei Tai Ho station a small bus was waiting to carry us to the delightful Health Resort, where we were registered, given explanatory notes, and then taken to our rooms in the array of two-storey, stone block buildings, nestling among the trees and beautiful flower gardens. Our beds all had mosquito nets, even a small one for baby Matthew's cot, but they weren't really necessary because north China was malaria-free.

We soon made our way through the peanut field down to the sandy beach, which had shaded areas of straw matting, a small building for drinks and toilets, and best of all, comfortable loungers made of bamboo cane. The large swimming area was enclosed by a safety net, and a small wooden 'rescue' boat, with several crew, was on permanent duty. We immediately recognised some of the foreigners on the beach by sight, and it was like a home from home, a mini-Druzhba by the sea.

During our two weeks holiday, we had daily visits to the beach, followed by delicious lunches and suppers in the resort restaurant, where sea food figured prominently, and fried rice with crab and lobster was a favourite. At breakfast we discovered millet porridge, a new dish which the boys liked. After supper people would tend to congregate in the recreational club, where there were games facilities for the young ones. Various outside visits were organised, and we went to a small factory, a nearby village of Korean minority families, the port of Chinhwangtao, and to Shan Hai Guan[9] (First Pass Under Heaven), the famous gate at the end of the Great Wall. The small bus would run to town three times a week, and resort taxis were available, but several times we pushed the pram into the little township to do some shopping, and have a look around. Little traffic passed along that road, except for the occasional large, sleek black car gliding by. They had curtained windows, which were clear indicators of the proximity of top leaders.

On our first foray into town we soon found the excellent Kieslings cake and ice-cream shop, a famous attraction for foreigners, and it became a regular stop for us whenever in town. The first bakery had been established in Tientsin by an Austrian family, way back during the heyday of the foreign powers in China, and it had survived up to 1965; probably, because of its renown and reputation, and the high quality products. Disappointingly, it did not have a similar outlet in Peking.

On our travels, other new sights for us were the ripened maize harvest towering over us, as well as the crops of millet and kaoliang [gao.liang], a sorghum grain. I had never seen maize growing in English fields up to 1965, while millet seed was only available as canary food. In the local countryside we saw many western-style bungalows blending into the low lying hillsides, relics from the old days of the foreign presence. They were now all being fully utilised by the Chinese leadership and elite cadres who, it was said, retreated to Pei Tai Ho every August. We also learnt that small sanatoria for workers had been built there since 1949.

Pei Tai Ho was a relaxing break for us, and we came back again in the summer of 1966 for another two weeks. That was a memorable stay because one day on the beach our colleague Pepe, who had an excellent portable radio, came over to say that England had just won the Football World Cup. I hadn't even realised that the World Cup was on that year.

Chapter Notes
1. Vietnam War: British involvement- information online
2. Beidaihe District- Wikipedia online
3. Zhang Hanzhi- Wikipedia online
4. Socialist Education Movement- Wikipedia online
5. Sun Yat-sen- Wikipedia online
6. Tai Ping Tian Guo- Wikipedia online
7. Qiao Guanhua- Wikipedia online
8. Three Furnaces- Wikipedia online
9. Shan Hai Pass- Wikipedia online

11

OLD CHINA HANDS, Part I

After arrival in Peking we slowly became aware of a hidden set of long time foreign residents, the 'Old China Hands', who usually lived outside the Friendship Guesthouse in their specially granted flats and accommodation, sometimes in their work unit. A fascinating group of people with amazing life stories, and some of them had lived in China from well before 1949. We might only see them together at their distant, and high-placed tables, on the occasion of the huge celebratory banquets for May Day and National Day in the Great Hall of the People, to which the foreign experts were invited. Needless to say, to a varying degree, they were all adherents and advocates of the socialist way, and presented a united front in their championing of China's road.

As a result, some of the new intake of younger English-speakers in the 1960s, began to refer to them as the 'Three Hundred Percenters' or 'Sunshiners'. Thinking back, I don't feel these labels to be malicious in any way, but they definitely expressed our assessment of their sympathetic mind-set in following the Chinese line. They had a degree of certainty in their belief in the Chinese road to socialism that was remarkably solid, and they never seemed to admit any serious shortcomings in Chinese policies, in their conversation, public discourse or in writing. Of course we didn't know much about their early days of coming to China in the 1920s, 1930s and 1940s, when the chaos and disastrous instability of those times must have tuned in to their social conscience, and the desire to help the Chinese people. Another factor that I had not realised was the strict discipline imposed on communist party members; a basic requirement within the structure of this organisation. Members followed the official party line in public, regardless of any misgivings or discord.

However we did appreciate that some of the Old Hands, working in the medical field, in teaching, in writing and in the media, had also provided a valuable international service to China for many years, by presenting their picture of New China to the world. They had the confidence of the Chinese leadership in this particular field of work. That was the key difference between the Old China Hands and the short-stay foreigners. We were merely 'experts' employed to do a job of work over a short time span, while they had acquired a degree of Chinese trust over many years. From our superficial viewpoint, it was as if they had committed themselves to the Chinese cause, and were not going to rock that political boat. Understandably, they were initially careful in their discussions with the younger foreign experts.

On a related theme, Paul Hollander, an American academic, in his fascinating book, *Political Pilgrims: Travels of Western Intellectuals to the Soviet Union, China and Cuba,1928-78*[1], published in 1981, looks at the positive reactions of certain western intellectuals, Americans and western Europeans, when on short visits to socialist countries. By the time the paperback edition of his book came out in 1997, the subtitle had become 'Western Intellectuals in Search of the Good Society', a more accurate description of the writer's theme. He felt that many of these intellectuals had experienced some degree of alienation or estrangement within their own societies, and were opposed to certain actions of their governments, such as the Vietnam War for example, and the associated anti-China anti-communist policies of the US. A combination of alienation at home, and suspension of the critical faculties when abroad, led these intellectuals to be more susceptible to the appeals of alternative societies. He offers the proposition that as long as a degree of alienation persists, then it is possible that emotional input may overpower or neutralise the intellect to some degree.

It is also conceivable that the responses of these intellectuals may have been triggered by diverse psychological factors in the individual, which remain hidden and cannot be evaluated. Yet it seems apparent that Hollander's thesis on the behaviour of this discrete, small pool of intellectuals, is not a phenomenon exclusive to that group, but has a blanket application to mankind in general. He makes the point that although they publicly approved of or were sympathetic to these socialist countries, they were not inclined to live in them, but remained domiciled in their own countries.

However in Peking in 1965, in contrast to any visiting western intellectuals, the Old China Hands had committed themselves to living in China, some of them for several decades already. On the surface, whatever their differences, they always presented a coalescent body of similar views. They were ideal persons to talk to foreign intellectuals passing through, and to give their succinct impressions on China's progress and policies, to try and offset the negative ideas and images prevailing in the West. This was quite an important part of their value to their country of residence. Certain of them did mix with and talk to the incoming younger foreigners, all the way through right up to the beginning of the Cultural Revolution in Summer 1966. Some of them, high up in the hierarchy, were not so readily involved, and therefore we did not meet quite a number of significant, long time foreign residents.

I felt that most of the young, native English-speaking foreign experts, who had arrived in 1964-66, whatever their motives, had a genuine and sympathetic desire to try and understand China, and what was going on there. Most realised that China did not get a good press in the West. When, in May1965, we heard that an organisation, called the Society for Anglo-Chinese Understanding (SACU), had been set up in London[2], we and many of the younger, newly-arrived Brits joined up on the spot, regardless of any compromising implications that might arise in the future. The Chairman was Dr Joseph Needham[3], and Deputy Chairman was Professor Joan Robinson[4], both academics at Cambridge University. The publicly expressed aim of SACU was to spread knowledge, dispel misconceptions and counter misrepresentations of China. And the target market was meant to include any members of the great British public who might be interested. In theory it was intended to be a broad-based grouping that would appeal to the moderates, and get mainstream backing. In actual reality there was intermittent friction over the political role of SACU, and its small membership fluctuated accordingly. It organised tours to China, meetings and conferences on things Chinese, and dispensed information, films, materials and speakers to schools and educational institutes. SACU gradually acquired an excellent library on China. Over the years, one recurring criticism was that it focused solely on informing the British public about China, but that there seemed to be little interest flowing the other way. Compare that with 2015, where the Chinese are now looking to invest funds in companies and countries worldwide.

Chapters 11 and 12 are not intended to be a roll-call of all the Old China Hands resident in Peking 1965-66, because that undertaking would be too vast, so I can only mention just a few of them. During the New Year celebrations in February 1965, there was a party organised at the Druzhba, and long-standing China resident and medical doctor George Hatem[5] [Ma Hai.de] attended. He talked to a lot of people there, and was a charming, urbane man who was completely at ease with everyone. On another social occasion over that period, we met up with David[6] and Isabel[7] Crook, who were colleagues of ours at the Foreign Languages Institute, and we both liked their open and direct approach. They were teaching at the Peking Foreign Languages Institute itself, while we were teaching at the Attached School, which came under the control and jurisdiction of the Institute. Some evenings they would cycle round to the Druzhba for a meal and to socialise, and we got to know them in this way. They never seemed to restrict themselves to sitting at certain tables, or associating with any cliques.

Within three weeks of our arrival, we were very surprised to be invited to dinner by an American resident Sidney Rittenberg[8] and his Chinese wife, and were joined by our Italian friend Giorgio Zucchetti, who had instigated it, and another American couple, David and Nancy Milton[9]. Maybe it was because Rittenberg was responsible for checking out English-speaking foreigners when they first arrived. We had never heard of Rittenberg before landing in China, and we had no idea that in recent years he had met Chairman Mao several times, including a year previously in January 1964 with three other foreigners, Frank Coe[10], Solomon Adler[11] and Israel Epstein[12], all members of the elite English-language translation team who had worked on the fourth volume of Chairman Mao's Selected Works. Mao had thrown a dinner party for them in Shanghai, by way of thanks, so Rittenberg was truly in the top circle of trusted foreigners in China. It was just as well that we didn't know any of this before the meal, and I can only wince in retrospect when I think of our apolitical level of conversation, coming from a small provincial English background, with a complete ignorance of Chinese socialism, and political science in general. I did know something of modern Chinese history up to the May the Fourth Movement of 1919, but little about the Communist Party and their policies. We must have been a great embarrassment to our friend Giorgio in this respect, and I'm sure that we were well evaluated, in terms of our undeveloped political awareness and mind-set. I never had another opportunity to talk to Rittenberg again during my two year stay. That says it all!

However, much to my amazement, I did see him in a Chinese newsreel shown in the Druzhba during the early days of the Cultural Revolution activity in autumn 1966. He was in a large jeep with Chairman Mao and several others, slowly cruising through masses of Red Guards. Most foreigners, and I am sure most Chinese people, were surprised to see his closeness to Mao. As a measure of his status in China, an article by him strongly supporting the Cultural Revolution was published in the People's Daily of 7 April 1967. However, he became so embroiled in the internal struggles in his workplace, the Broadcasting Institute, that he was arrested and imprisoned in 1968, put into solitary confinement, and was not released and rehabilitated until 1977, finally returning to the US in 1980.

In 1993 he wrote an autobiographical book, with Amanda Bennett, on his times in China, called *The Man Who Stayed Behind*. In this book he mentioned that he had spent thirty five years of his life in China, sixteen years of which were in solitary confinement. It is as well to recognise that his detention in 1968 was without any trial or legal process, and could only have been authorised by the power holders of the dominant political group at that time. To survive those many years in solitary is a measure of the spirit and willpower of the man. Then, out of the blue, I did bump into him twenty years later, in 1985, at an Educational Conference in Hong Kong. He was a consultant on Chinese business links, and I introduced myself as meeting him in the Druzhba in 1965. We had a brief chat, but he didn't seem to remember me.

Around the same time as meeting the Rittenbergs, one evening after dinner, we were invited for coffee to meet another American, Gerry Tannenbaum[13], and his Chinese film actress wife. His name was completely new to us too, and we did not know that he had acted in Chinese films made since 1949. I learnt later, that in 1964, he had even taken the part of the famous Canadian doctor, Norman Bethune[14]. They told us that they lived in Shanghai and were only up in Peking for the Chinese New Year. This time it was a more relaxed conversation, and politics didn't seem to be on the agenda. I well remember that one of my conversational gems was about the Olympic Games in Tokyo in the previous year 1964. This raised the topic of the People's Republic of China's non-participation in that international gathering, where Taiwan had represented China. Similarly, Taiwan held the China seat in the United Nations, as the representative government of the Chinese people, until realism finally prevailed in 1971, and the Peking government was finally admitted to full membership of that body, and replaced Taiwan. Like the Rittenbergs, we did not see the Tannenbaums again either. Even so, in retrospect, I am grateful to both of them for their hospitality at the beginning of our two year stay.

A fascinating portrayal of life for foreigners in Peking before 1949 has been given by Julia Boyd in her book, *A Dance with the Dragon: The Vanished World of Peking's Foreign Colony* published in 2012. During the chaos and upheavals in China after the Boxer Rebellion in 1900, the Emperor had been removed in 1911, and then competing warlords had given way to Chiang Kai-shek[15] and the Kuomintang (Guo.min.dang) armies, with partial invasion and occupation by Japan, and then the growing muscle of the Communist Party armies in the civil war. Throughout those years, 1911-1949, usually termed the Republic of China period, foreign power was gradually waning in China, but that same old consortium of western countries could still exert some influence over Chinese affairs right up to World War II.

Not after 1949 though! When Chinese independence was declared by Chairman Mao on the 1st of October 1949, the playing field changed radically. The imposing British Embassy buildings just off Tienanmen square were requisitioned, and new yellow brick buildings were built in quiet north-eastern suburbs to house a swathe of national Embassies, including the British Charge D'Affaires Office at No 7 Kuang Hua Lu [Guang Hua Road]. Huge new blocks of flats were built nearby to accommodate all the foreign diplomatic personnel. I remember going to the Charge D'Affaires Office quite a few times in the 1965-66 period, and it was a sleepy backwater, with hardly any traffic, and just a few PLA soldiers on duty at the entrances, and on street corners. We didn't need permission to enter these offices, as we got in on our facial looks. The guards only stopped and questioned Chinese or oriental-looking people. With no American diplomatic presence in those days, and declining relations with the Soviet Union and the socialist satellite countries, excepting Albania and Yugoslavia, the emerging Afro-Asian states were a significant force in the diplomatic circles. Today, as Bei.jing has expanded ever outwards in a series of ring roads, that modern embassy area has been overtaken by dynamic China, and the old Kuang Hua road is now a buzzing eight lane highway.

As a codicil to the diplomatic niceties in Peking, soon after settling in at the Friendship Guesthouse, several British residents there frowned when we said that we were going to register at the British Charge D'Affaires Office. It was as if we were breaking some mysterious covenant on the correct commitment towards our Chinese hosts. We went ahead anyway, and as time passed we gradually realised that we were indeed in a minority of British residents who had registered. It was yet another instance of the sort of amateur vetting of political credentials, vis-a-vis New China and socialism, which occurred amongst the foreign residents of the Druzhba. I don't think for a moment that the Chinese were bothered about our action, and I never felt that it affected their treatment of us, as long as we were doing a good job.

The British diplomats, and the resident nurse, were very kind and helpful to us with our two sons, and we appreciated that very much. We received invitations to their social events, such as film shows, a folk-dancing evening (Scottish, of course), and the Queen's Birthday in June, which was held on their desiccated and barely greenish lawn, but we rarely had time to attend any of them. Amazingly, two of the British Secretaries had been permitted by the Chinese authorities to live in traditional houses hidden away in the Peking alleys [hu.tong], and during our first year we went to two parties at one of these, the home of the First Secretary. We learnt that the Secretaries had to spend three months secondment on diplomatic duties in Ulan Bator, capital of Mongolia, which was a comparative quiet backwater, and they all said that returning to Peking was like going to Paris. At these diplomatic dos we met two English language journalists, working in Peking; one from the *Toronto Globe & Mail,* and Vergil Berger from *Reuters.* His placement in Peking ended in 1966, luckily for him, and he was replaced by Anthony Grey, who unfortunately suffered two years of house detention in 1967-69, during the intense heat of the Cultural Revolution.

This relationship between China and the foreigners that she employed after 1949 was new. Every foreign factory, business and organisation, with few exceptions, had been taken over by the Chinese, and the foreign presence had evaporated, so the new emphasis was on equality between foreigners and their hosts, with the Chinese were very much in charge of their own destiny. It would be appropriate here to mention 'Extraterritoriality', the legal concept which had huge implications for foreigners working in China. In the first 'unequal' Treaty of Nanking in 1842, between China and Britain, resulting from the minor conflict labelled the First Opium War, the British had insisted that any of their citizens accused of illegal acts in China would be tried and judged by the laws of Britain, and would not be subject to the jurisdiction of Chinese law. Following this, other countries had similar provisions included in their 'unequal' treaties with the Chinese Emperor and his officials. The Russians had been the first though, by including the concept of extraterritoriality into the Treaty of Nerchinsk 1689.

A fascinating account of the early days of the East India Company trading with China, by H. B. Morse, was published by the Clarendon Press in Oxford in 1926: *The Chronicles of the East India Company trading to China, 1635-1842.* Portuguese and Spanish traders had preceded the British on the China coast, and initially British merchants used such foreign traders or missionaries to act as interpreters. Some British traders may have acquired spoken Chinese, but what happened over the two hundred years was the emergence of Chinese 'Pidgin' English[16] as a means of communication between the two races. It didn't start to decline until the Chinese began to seriously learn the English language towards the end of the 1800s. When stationed in Hong Kong, 1956-57, during my RAF National Service, it was apparent that the rickshaw men, always present outside the Star Ferry terminals, seemed to be using some form of 'Pidgin' English in order to ply their trade, and 'look-see look-see' figured prominently in communications with them. The 'Pidgin' English on the old China coast was a primitive and abbreviated concoction of direct translation from the Chinese, with a disregard for syntax and other components that make up the linguistic matrix of the English language. As a hybrid mixture of two distinct languages, a 'Pidgin' is not the native language of any specific speech community, so in that sense it is not a living language. The earliest examples of a 'pidgin' language came from the Portuguese, the first European explorers. Differing 'pidgins', sometimes called 'creoles', developed in the countries which they controlled or where they traded.

During those first two hundred years of trading up to 1842, the British had been subject to irritating Chinese supervision and obstruction in Macao and Canton, and were well acquainted with the vagaries and exigencies of Chinese law as practised by the high officials on the China coast. When dealing with the Chinese merchants, they had to negotiate arrangements on the financial transactions of selling their cargo and buying China's goods, in a marketplace where the Chinese held all the advantages on their home soil. It was an 'unequal' trading market for the European traders, and they must have suffered much frustration.

The men appointed by the East India Company to carry out this trading had to be multi-talented and diplomatic, and they were justly called 'supercargoes'. Their records of trading are preserved in the Company's archives and they show the amounts of money that had to be paid for gifts, fees, gratuities and bribes. Very fine lines must lie between the definitions of these four transactions. Nevertheless the western traders persisted for all those years in the China trade, even though the trade imbalance was usually against them, as the Chinese desired to buy little of their products. On the other hand, the cargoes they transported back to Europe must have been profitable enough to make the trade worthwhile. The whole economic scene only changed when the opium trading into China developed in the late eighteenth century, and silver currency started flowing out of China instead of inwards. When the British were victors in the Opium War in 1842, they, as a result of their experiences of two centuries trading in a market where the Chinese held the upper hand, insisted on putting a clause on extraterritoriality into the Treaty of Nanking.

Of course, after 1949 all traces of this practice ceased, and foreigners were subject to Chinese law. The Old China Hands who were put into jail during the upheavals of the Cultural Revolution were not given a trial of any kind, and there was no evidence of a legal process being followed. The foreigners were the losers in the power struggles between the conflicting political groups, and they had backed the wrong horses. The old traders of the East India Company on the China coast would have well understood the plight of these Old China Hands, in the absence of a judicial system that was in any way comparable to those of their western world. Apologists might say that China was in a semi-anarchic state during those early, intense years of the Cultural Revolution, and this accounted for the lack of a trial. On the other hand, critics could say it was another example of the 'hollow tree' fragility of the Chinese social infrastructure, when under threat. However, at the outbreak of World War II, both America and Britain interned, without trial, thousands of their population who were ranked as enemy aliens.

60

In 1949, after a hundred and seven years of foreign presence in their country, the Chinese people had finally stood up! The 1950s saw a large influx of experts from Russia and socialist satellite countries to help China re-build and reconstruct. Non-socialist countries, such as Japan, were involved too. Russian became the main foreign language taught in the schools and universities. Then, after the wholesale withdrawal of Soviet technicians in 1960, China had to look elsewhere for the transfer of industrial technology that they needed, and they turned, in particular, towards western European countries. This was because the Americans had long imposed a significant embargo[17] on trading with New China from 1949, which had been loosely followed by the British government too. In 1953 a number of British companies broke this embargo, and went to China to trade, and this group called itself 'The 48 Group of British Traders with China'[18].

Chapter Notes

1. 'Political Pilgrims: Travels of Western Intellectuals to the Soviet Union, China and Cuba, 1928-78' by Paul Hollander, Oxford University Press, 1981.
2. 'The East Wind: China and the British Left, 1925-1976' by Tom Buchanan, Oxford University Press, 2012.
3. Dr Joseph Needham- Wikipedia online
4. Professor Joan Robinson- Wikipedia online
5. George Hatem- Wikipedia online
6. David Crook- Wikipedia and Autobiography online
7. Isabel Crook- Information online
8. Sidney Rittenberg- Wikipedia online
9. David and Nancy Milton: see their book 'The Wind Will Not Subside: Years in Revolutionary China, 1964-69' Random House, New York, 1976.
10. Frank Coe- Wikipedia online
11. Solomon Adler- Wikipedia online
12. Isreal Epstein- Wikipedia online
13. Gerry Tannenbaum- Wikipedia online
14. Norman Bethune- Wikipedia online
15. Chiang Kai-shek- Wikipedia online
16. Chinese Pidgin English- Wikipedia online
17. US Trade Embargo on China, 1949-1969- Information online
18. 'The 48 Group' by Percy Timberlake, The 48 Group Club, 1994.

12

OLD CHINA HANDS, Part II

One China Hand who made an impact on me was Anna Louise Strong[1], a venerable American lady with attitude, who had travelled the world supporting the downtrodden, married a Russian and had written reportage books on Russia and China. After arrest in Moscow in 1949, and for fear of losing her freedom of movement if she returned to America, she eventually settled in Peking for the rest of her life issuing periodic 'Letters from China' focused on the latest developments in China. She was very critical of any negative reactions coming from international quarters. We never met her, and to my knowledge she rarely visited the Friendship Guesthouse, and only had social contact with a limited group of friends visiting her apartment in the old Italian Embassy building, quite close to the Peking Hotel and Wangfuching[2] street. In another flat of that same building was the New Zealander, Rewi Alley[3], who had been in China since 1927, and he was just as remote, although we did spot him at one of the banquets at the Great Hall of the People. Amongst other things, he had been active in the growth of the Chinese Industrial Co-operatives in the 1930s and 1940s, sometimes referred to as the Gung Ho movement.

Robert 'Bob' Winter[4], an American professor at Peking University had arrived in China in the mid-1920s and had stayed. Apparently he had attended a talk in his native Chicago, by a visiting Chinese intellectual Wen Yi.duo, and had been moved to take a look at China. He was now retired and had a very small bungalow on the university campus, with a beautiful garden and small pond, where he was looked after by his Chinese man-servant. He had taught English language and linguistics, and had been a colleague of I. A. Richards and William Empson, Cambridge academics, who had both been Professors of English at Tsing Hua University for periods in the 1930s and 1940s, and he sometimes referred to them in conversation. I was able to meet William Empson briefly, in the summer of 1975 in his Hampstead home, during a two week visit from Peking back to the UK, when I carried a personal letter from Bob Winter to give him. He was quite charming, and took me to his local pub for a beer and a game of shove ha'penny.

Bob Winter was not a 'Sunshiner', and although he weighed his words carefully, we could usually detect his feelings on any matters Chinese that was being discussed. Regretfully, I never asked him about his work with Richards in attempting to introduce the Basic English learning system, devised by C .K. Ogden, into Chinese schools. In principle, it seems a good method for beginners to learn English, but after 1949 the Chinese communist educators would have been critical of Ogden's basic 850 wordlist, which omitted many essential words from the socialist lexicon, such as socialism, class, struggle, dictatorship, proletariat, bourgeois, capitalism, hegemony and so on. Bob was the only one of the Old Hands who mentioned the Bad Famine Years, 1959-61; one of his powerful anecdotes being about when having noodle soup in a little restaurant in nearby Haidian village, a Chinese man suddenly grabbed the bowl from him and wolfed the contents down in next to no time. He also commented on all the trees in the vicinity being stripped bare of leaves, presumably to go into the people's diet.

An old English lady, Rose Smith[5], whom we soon got to know, was adopted by our son Tim as 'Nana Smith' , to compensate for his two missing grandmothers away at home, and in the dining room he always ran over to her table to say hello, which judging by her responsive smile she obviously enjoyed. Although we got on well with her at a superficial level, Rose never joined us at our table, and equally we never imposed ourselves on her table, and this gives some measure of the socio-political undercurrents at play in the world of the Druzhba. As distinct to the middle-class backgrounds of many Old Hands, she was quintessentially working-class, and she had had an amazing and active life history in Britain, involving the communist party, trades unions movement, including as leader of women strikers, and being a journalist for the Daily Worker. Sadly, she has not yet been publicly acknowledged in book form or in the media, except for a doctoral thesis, *The Times and Life of Rose Smith in Britain and China* by Fong Gisela Chan Man at Concordia University, Montreal, Canada in 1998. In China, at the end of her career, Rose was basically a 'polisher' in the English language section of New China News Agency, with no chance to write the news.

One of the Old Hands we got to know well was an English lady, Gladys Yang[6], and her Chinese husband Yang Xian.yi[7], who had met while both were undergraduates at Oxford University. They worked together at the Foreign Languages Press, mainly as Chinese-English translators.   We were introduced to them early on by Bill and Delia Jenner, and we spent many evenings at their apartment, with lively conversation, plenty of alcohol, and cigarette smoking. They always seemed to have an endless supply of genuine whiskey, brandy and vodka on tap, with a back-up of Chinese white spirit, gin and beer when required. Other colleagues of theirs would often be there, including Jack Chen, son of Eugene Chen, one time Finance Minister in the National Government of the mid-1920s, and Clarence Adams, an American PoW from the Korean War who had settled in China. He returned to America with his family in 1966. Other young newly-arrived British residents from the Druzhba, Endymion, Diana and William, also came along and they were regular participants, along with the Jenners and the Hunts. Bill Jenner had been translator of the politically-sensitive autobiography of Pu Yi, the last Emperor of China. This was published in two volumes by the Foreign Languages Press as *From Emperor to Citizen*. Delia Jenner wrote a book entitled *Letters from Peking*, which was published by Oxford University Press in 1967.

My memory is of Xian.yi sitting back in his armchair, with a cigarette in one hand and a glass of Scotch in the other, and enjoying the talking and badinage.   Neither he, nor Gladys, were personalities who needed to dominate the circle, and everyone was able to contribute. The Yangs usually entertained fairly regularly, not only we Friendship Hotel inmates, but also any famous foreign writers, artists and academics visiting Peking, who would all wend their way to see them.   For example, on one of my impromptu visits they were entertaining the Cambridge academic Martin Bernal, who was on a short trip to China.

Our social evenings there were quite strange, and I can only liken the atmosphere to a group of people letting off suppressed steam, away from the gaze of the Chinese dragon. The Yangs were dedicated to their work for New China, and nothing incorrect against the current regime was ever said or implied. Often Gladys would say that she had been isolated for over twenty years from the living English language in Britain, and wanted to keep up to date with it, so she would throw in a linguistic challenge arising from her translation work; one example was the Chinese expression 'Mei you yi.si' (have no interest), and a combined contribution from the assembled guests provided her with a list of alternative English paraphrases and slang expressions.

Evenings with the Yangs meant that after our dinner in the Druzhba, and our reliable Chinese Auntie had arrived to babysit, we would then get a hotel taxi around seven p.m. for the fifteen minute drive through the dimly-lit streets. We were required to sign in at the reception desk in the Foreign Languages Press building every time we visited. As we arrived in their apartment we might hear or catch a glimpse of the Yang's 'bao.mu' (child nurse) clearing up in the kitchen, but she rarely appeared. The children had long grown up, and she was now chief cook and household organiser. When it came time for us to leave, Gladys was usually in bed by then, and we had to drag ourselves away from the irrepressible Xian.yi to the waiting taxi, which was always booked for 9.30 p.m., but unfailingly we were delayed, and the long suffering drivers had to wait in their cars. As different to taxis in Britain, they never complained, and never charged extra for the waiting time. Anyway, ten o'clock in the evening was quite late for everyone, because the Chinese population always seemed to be up very early in the mornings, and we ourselves had to get up around six-ish.

Sometimes Gladys would suggest going out for a meal to the nearby Moscow [Mo.si.ke] restaurant, where we could enjoy caviar and genuine Russian vodka, by-products of Sino-Soviet trading exchanges in the 1950s; a fortunate bounty for many foreign residents. It was a very spacious restaurant, and never very busy because ordinary Chinese people were not allowed in, and the foreign community itself was hardly large enough to maintain a full house every evening. We learnt there that caviar should be eaten with thin pieces of toast and sliced onion, and glasses of neat vodka. On another occasion we went to the sleepy Peace Hotel, which to me captured some of my imagined ambiance of old semi-colonial Peking. Regretfully we saw no other foreign faces there, but my drinking credentials were enhanced by my first gin martini.

For foreign experts, going in to town to eat was a major lift from daily life, and apart from a good selection of Chinese restaurants, there were three central hotels, all within country-walking distance of Tienanmen Square, which catered especially for foreign visitors, namely the Peace [He.ping], New Bridge [Xin.qiao] and National Minorities [Min.zu]. The only downside was the off-putting taxi ride of around 25 minutes to get there, and then the long drive home after the meal. The famous old Peking Hotel had a new towering wing, situated on the corner of Wangfuching Street, and it seemed to host a stream of foreign delegations, but for some reason we never went there to eat. Going north up Wangfuching street, on the left hand side you would reach the Overseas Chinese Hotel, and that was another possible eating place.

A popular venue for foreign experts was the Sinkiang [Xin.jiang Uyghur Autonomous Region] restaurant, where we could get delicious skewers of mutton, and gaze at Uyghur minority peoples dining there. It was strange for us to see groups of bronzed Caucasian faces, and a good deal of mutual staring took place. Their ladyfolk always wore brilliantly coloured dresses, with Uyghur designs, that would have been completely out of place in UK fashions in the 1960s. Someone floated the idea in the Druzhba dining room that the Hungarian and Uyghur languages had some basic linguistic roots, and a message was passed to the only Hungarian couple in residence to ask if they could visit the restaurant sometime and try to communicate with the Uyghurs. They reported back in due course that a few fundamental words in the two languages seemed similar, but they were not able to converse with them using the Hungarian language.

By the end of 1965 native English-speaking teachers had been recruited to work in cities across China, in Harbin, Chinhwangtao, Tientsin, Peking, Sian, Tsinan, Wuhan, Nanking, Chungking, Shanghai and Canton. They were Australian, British and Canadian. As part of their contracts they would be transported to Peking for special events, and in the summer vacation they could relax by the sea at the Pei Tai Ho [Bei.dai.he] foreigners' guesthouse. So for May Day, National Day and the Chinese New Year they would be transported by air or by rail to Peking to take part in the celebrations, and the English-speaking contingent in the Druzhba was suddenly enlarged; it was an enjoyable period of long mealtimes, much talking, and hearing about life in the provinces. For example, Frank Davis was based in Wuhan, and during Chinese New Year 1966 he, along with his partner Rosalyn, was taken by his Institute on a holiday tour around some large cities, ending up in the Druzhba in Peking. They told us that during those travels they had picked up fragments of information about a new political movement in the offing, something big, but had nothing detailed that they could add. We could only listen intently and nod politely, but Frank and Rosalyn were correct, as the first overt shoots of the Great Proletarian Cultural Revolution were soon appearing, even though we didn't understand their implications. We had no prior knowledge of the coming storm.

In the summer of 1966 the Cultural Revolution was just taking off, and schools, colleges and universities were all closed for political meetings, with much activity taking place against any bourgeois admin staff and teachers. P'eng Chen [Peng Zhen], the Mayor of Peking, had been removed from office at the beginning of June, and all this was prior to the irruption of the Red Guards in mid-August. One Sunday morning, mid-June, I decided to cycle round to see the Yangs on a spontaneous visit. Gladys was out, but Xian.yi was there with another scholarly-looking Chinese gentleman, who was a contemporary of his, and who had studied at Cambridge University. My timing was not so convenient, and I only stayed for a short time, but it was long enough for them to tell me that the Cultural Revolution movement would gradually die down, and be over in a few months. This could have been wishful thinking on their part, or just words to satisfy a foreigners questions.

So even Chinese intellectuals could not foresee the enormity of this storm, and the battering of Chinese society to come in the years ahead. Xian.yi and Gladys were arrested in 1968 on charges of being foreign agents, and imprisoned for four years; Gladys in solitary confinement, while Xian.yi was put in a cell with common criminals, which, as he said later, was another education for him, and much better than solitary. Prior to their arrest their bao.mu had left, and during those four years, their flat remained empty and their three children were packed off to various units to do manual work. When the Yangs were eventually released from prison, they were rehabilitated, which meant something like an official pardon, and paid a large lump sum for accrued salaries while in jail. All foreigners imprisoned during the Cultural Revolution were Old China Hands, with the exception of the Gordons. On two year contracts they were detained in 1967 just before returning home. Eric and Marie Gordon[8], and their son Kim, were confined to a single room at the New Bridge [Xin.qiao] hotel in central Peking for two years, and again there was no process of law involved in their detention.

I have often wondered how the ideology of the Old China Hands in the 1950s and 1960s, was affected by the dramatic changes to the economic and political policies in China since the death of Chairman Mao in 1976. Sidney Rittenberg has written at the age of almost 80, some quite compelling words acknowledging his wrong-thinking at times in China, and disclosing some of his regrets, as well as admitting some of the extreme errors of Chairman Mao's policies, and the Chinese leadership. As he puts it "... my life's vision was flawed" during those times:

"When I think back on my nearly eighty years…I can't believe what an interesting, fulfilling and happy life I have had. I am brim-full of thankfulness. Of course, looking back there is much that I regret or find painful. It took me thirty years before I, like most of my Chinese friends, came to realise just how disastrous the Great Leap Forward was, and how many millions died. The Cultural Revolution, too, caused untold suffering -suffering I only fully learned of after my release from prison. In retrospect, I wish mightily that I had been more detached and insightful during the political movements of the late 1950s. I was so repelled by the injustice of the 'old world', and wanted so hard to believe, that I saw what I wanted to see, bent reality to fit my own notions." [9]

I wonder how many of the foreign friends and three hundred percenters of Mao's China in the 1950s and 1960s, felt the same as Rittenberg in their old age, and would admit and acknowledge any failings to themselves, in following Chairman Mao's line wholeheartedly from 1949 to 1976. It could have been very dispiriting for them to concede any weakening of Mao's road to socialism, especially after they had invested so much energy and so many years of their lives to the cause.

Three long-time resident Brits, who suffered prison detention of around five years in length, were Michael Shapiro[10], Elsie Fairfax-Cholmeley[11] (wife of Israel Epstein) and David Crook. At Pei Tai Ho in the summer of 1966 I had briefly met Michael for the first time. He was there with his Chinese wife, and two teenage sons, and we managed some energetic ping-pong games after the evening meals, without any substantial talk about the developing Cultural Revolution. He exactly fitted my image of a typical London East-ender. I gleaned from the grapevine that he had been sent to China in 1950 by the British Communist party, and was now unable to return home. Apparently in 1967 he and Israel Epstein became active in the foreigners Bethune-Yan'an Rebel Group[12] formed in the Friendship Guesthouse.

I have read a thirty page typed accusatory condemnation of Michael Shapiro's book *Changing China* by two young British activists, who were residents in the Druzhba at that time. The nub of their criticism was that the wording of Michael Shapiro's book, on page after page, reflected and peddled the Liu Shao-chi line of bourgeois thinking, as opposed to Mao's correct line on socialism. And that he supported the wrong leadership group in the New China News Agency offices. I cannot say how far their denunciation of Shapiro represented the whole raft of critical judgements built up against him, but in 1968 he was imprisoned in Peking for five years until 1973. I have not been able to find any accounts of his life inside. When I met up with him again in Peking in 1974, he had obviously suffered from this experience, because he was in poor health, a shadow of his self, and his reduced mobility meant that he was quite unable to play ping -pong like he had in 1966.

David Crook[13] suffered five years of solitary confinement from 1968 to 1973, in the same prison in Peking, and he has written a fascinating autobiography that is freely available on the Internet. Soon after arriving in Peking in April 1974 on our second two year contract, I had a chat with him in the Friendship Guesthouse, and I asked him if he felt any bitterness towards China because of his imprisonment. He quickly smiled, and said without rancour "But you don't understand", and then explained that he taken sides in the political struggles of the Cultural Revolution at the institute, and as a foreigner he had thereby interfered in the internal affairs of China, so some form of summary punishment was to be expected. These are some extracts on his reflections on China, after living there for almost fifty years:

"But towards the end of the decade [1980s], with a consciousness sharpened by Chinese and Western friends, including our three sons, I gradually grew critical and disillusioned... Money ruled the roost...now, for the first time in forty years, while my love for the Chinese people remains as strong as ever, I feel at odds with the powers-that-be...The climax of this discord came with the democratic movement of the spring of 1989. I went along with the demand for democracy, as well as the denunciation of corruption, nepotism and bureaucracy. And when the movement was suppressed in blood, when the massacre was denied and followed by a witch-hunt in which the victims were blamed-that was the end of my decades of adulation. I had thought that People's China was humanity's guide to a better world. I still acknowledge her past achievements, but her record has been tragically tarnished."

David is being selective in distinguishing between the Chinese people and 'the Chinese powers-that-be', who had caused this tarnishing. Chinese propaganda always made a conspicuous distinction between the government and the people of China's adversaries. The assumption being that the people were not responsible for the actions of their government, and that they might even rise up and create a socialist state like China. This thinking could also be applied to China, in reverse.

Nevertheless, as well as his publications, overseas talks and lectures, David's main work, along with his wife Isabel, was as a teacher of English, and in this way they were giving a valuable service to Chinese society. David had the satisfaction of seeing many of his students carve out successful, top diplomatic careers and help to re-build their country, and this might partially offset and compensate for his gradual loss of faith in the evolution of China's socialism. Whatever the changes in Chinese political policies over the years, those long-serving foreigners like David Crook and Sidney Rittenberg still had the achievements of their working life in China, with which to assuage any blows to their political belief systems, which may have occurred after Mao had gone.

Postscript One

On International Women's Day, 8th March 1973, Premier Chou En-lai addressed a meeting of Foreign Experts in Peking, and apologised for their mistreatment since the beginning of the Cultural Revolution. In particular, he mentioned David Crook, Israel Epstein, Michael Shapiro and Rose Smith by name. All foreigners had been released from prison by then, except for Rittenberg, who Chou still castigated as being a bad element, and he was not released from prison until 1977, after the Gang of Four had been arrested.

Postscript Two

In 1985, Beijing Review published a small booklet of forty four pages entitled 'Old China Hands Look Back', with contributions from Rewi Alley, George Hatem and Sidney Shapiro[14]. These three were from the elite ranks of long-serving Old China Hands; Rewi Alley had come to China in 1927, George Hatem in 1933 and Sidney Shapiro in 1947. None of them had become politically implicated during the Cultural Revolution, and had not been imprisoned. The worst thing for them would have been suffering pressure and criticisms from Red Guards, and some subsequent isolation from their Chinese friends and contacts. Rewi, in later years though, did remark on his valuable library of books being destroyed by the Red Guards. In retrospect, this booklet seems to represent a valedictory tribute to all the old foreign residents, who had given so many years of their lives in dedicated work for China, and the Chinese people, over the previous fifty years. Now in 2015, China does not have any need for such services from foreigners anymore.

Chapter Notes
1. Anna Louise Strong- Wikipedia online
2. Wangfujing Street- Wikipedia online
3. Rewi Alley- Wikipedia online
4. Robert Winter- Information online
5. Rose Smith- Information online
6. Gladys Yang- Wikipedia online
7. Yang Xian.yi- Wikipedia online
8. Eric and Marie Gordon- Wikipedia online
9. 'The Man Who Stayed Behind', page 448, paperback edition, 2001.
10. Michael Shapiro- Information online
11. Elsie Fairfax-Cholmeley- Information online
12. Bethune Yan'an Rebel Group- Information online
13. David Crook- Autobiography online
14. Sydney Shapiro- Wikipedia online

13

FEAR OF THE EMPEROR

After some time living in Peking in 1965 I gradually realised that there was a high level of conformity among the Chinese people that I could see and experience around me, and as far as I could gather they obeyed the authorities without question in this disciplined society. Perhaps it was more a display of built-in social control, with disciplined mass behaviour of toeing the line, in fear of clear sanctions of some kind against the offenders. Or possibly it was the traditional response of dreading public shame and humiliation through loss of face, in tandem with the historical conditioning of their submission to authority. Whatever the roots, this 'Fear of the Emperor' syndrome must have some origins in the natural consequence of Chinese people living under almost two millennia of autocratic Imperial dynasties and Confucian social hierarchies. This was a much higher level of civil compliance than I had experienced in my UK life, except for the greater controls imposed on the 'home front' during World War II.

Of course there must have been conflicting thoughts against the policies of the Chinese Communist Party, such as had been evidenced in the 'One Hundred Flowers Movement'[1] in 1956, and the subsequent Anti-Rightist[2] movement of 1957. On a visit by foreign experts to Peking prison[3] in early 1965 we were told that out of 1800 prisoners in confinement, forty percent were counter- revolutionaries or political malcontents of some kind. They represented just a superficial layer of people who were dissatisfied with the government of New China. No one knew the size of the submerged iceberg of discontented masses under that tip.

There was no possibility of public questioning of extreme policies which people could foresee were not going to benefit the general population. This phenomenon could occur in any country. In 1958 Chairman Mao pronounced that "People's Communes are Good", and this mass collectivisation movement coincided with the momentum of the Great Leap Forward[4] 1958-59, which was actually the beginning of the second Five Year Plan[5], 1958-1962. We heard from long-time foreign residents in Peking that during this movement a significant slogan had been "Overtake Britain in Industrial Production in Fifteen Years"[6]. The booklet 'China Will Overtake Britain' by Niu Chung Huang, was published in Peking in 1958.

The Great Leap was intended to involve and harness the spirit and energy of the Chinese people in building their country, and it affected all industrial production units, which were usually situated in the urban areas. However one component of this movement also applied to the masses in the countryside. As a result, the Chinese peasantry was coerced into making crude iron and steel in small homemade backyard furnaces in their villages, at the expense of farming and the harvesting of crops. Whatever the progressive planning and worthy aims of the leadership underpinning this movement, the euphoric atmosphere of the times glossed over potential problems in carrying it out. There were serious fault lines in putting the Great Leap into practice in the villages so speedily, and this led to the terrible famines and starvation in the countryside during 1959-61. Mao had already written a lot of sensible instructions on the correct approach that should be followed by cadres in their dealings with the people. A modern set of rules for communist party members, but after only ten years of New China's existence, some cadres were probably still influenced by traditional thinking and values, rather than by Mao's words. That was one possible fault line.

Frank Dikkoter, in his book, *Mao's Great Famine*, which he dates as 1958-62, covers this period in depth, with numerous detailed examples of outrageously inflated declarations for agricultural production, made by local officials all over China. Yet, how could they dare reveal to Peking the gross social and food production disasters occurring in the countryside, caused by the very policies flowing down from the top level, without themselves being blamed for these problems? Some of these extravagant claims, publicised at the time, were so excessive that anyone from a countryside background would have known immediately that that they were an absolute impossibility. School colleagues later told me that a satirical comment made the rounds among the people, to the effect that even Chairman Mao was worried about the challenge of storing this huge amount of grain in the future.

Whatever the many reasons that could have influenced the behaviour of provincial officials, an absence of any feelings of compassion seems to have been a significant factor in the process. There was a medieval Chinese flavour to the events of the famine Bad Years. This disastrous situation in China occurred because of non-negotiable orders from the top leaders down to the people, implemented by a body of officials concerned mainly with protecting themselves and their positions. Thus the impetus of the Great Leap movement could not be modified or reshaped until the order came from the powers above, and only when this happened were the Chinese peasantry released from their nightmare.

An even more relentless critic than Frank Dikkoter, is Yang Ji.sheng a Chinese journalist who lived through those horrific times, and whose father died of starvation. His book *Tombstone* records in great depth all his research work and stories of the famine. Pro-Mao supporters may question the factual integrity of the contents, but they present a similar picture to the findings of Dikkoter. The book is a terrible indictment of the Chinese leadership, Chinese officialdom and the apparent lack of humanity in their society, when 'humanity' is one of the key Confucian virtues. Yang did manage to find a few officials who tried to help the starving masses, often at the expense of their careers. He condemns the authoritarian system in place in China, which produces officials who he aptly describes as "a slave facing upwards, and a dictator facing downwards". The relationship between the masses and officials does not appear to be deferential, but rather more of a fatalistic and stoical submissiveness to those above them in the power hierarchy.

Officials in old China had an ambivalent motivation, where their interests were geared towards family and self, rather than towards the community. That very traditional attitude of the ruling official class was incompatible with the tenets of socialism. Bertrand Russell, writing in 1922, put it like this:

"It is useless to deny that the Chinese have brought these troubles down upon themselves, by their inability to produce capable and honest officials. This inability has its roots in Chinese ethics, which lay stress upon a man's duty to his family rather than to the public. An official is expected to keep all his relations sup-

plied with funds, and therefore can only be honest at the expense of filial piety[7]. The decay of the family system is a vital condition of progress in China."

When we arrived in Peking in 1965, barely three years after the Bad Years, no-one talked about those times, and we had no idea of what had happened. The current movement, then in full flow, was 'Serve the People', led by the posthumous figure of Lei Feng. This movement was purely a morality campaign, and did not cause any suffering to the Chinese people, as did the Great Leap. Marshal Lin Piao is credited to some extent for the 'Serve the People' movement, and for politicising the PLA with Chairman Mao's Little Red Book, which later emerged into public consciousness in the Cultural Revolution.

Provincial officials during those starvation years could have changed the outcome, but they did not help the peasantry sufficiently. Yet serving the masses was a common theme preached by Mao to party members. In retrospect, one is bound to ask how the countryside suffering of the Great Leap Forward period, which was initiated by Mao, could be said to serve the Chinese peasants. Even so, overt criticism of the Party was not present, and was not permitted, and in the narrow circles that we moved in, was not available to foreign ears. It must have been in Chinese minds though, but there was no channel, public or otherwise, through which to express dissent, as even talking with trusted friends or family could be a risk.

Marshal P'eng Te-huai[8] is reported to have criticised Mao and the Great Leap Forward, during a communist party central committee conference at Lu Shan in July 1959. At that time P'eng was ranked second to Marshal Chu Teh in military terms, with Lin Piao third. To give some idea of his high political standing, he had signed the Armistice in 1953 to end the Korean War, and had then become Minister of Defence. Nevertheless, although having support from other top leaders, after those struggles with Mao he was demoted, purged from all influential positions and put under house detention. He disappeared from the scene until the Cultural Revolution, when he was very harshly treated by the Red Guards.

In 1965 China seemed to be a low-energy society, where people were concentrating on surviving, and correctly following all the required political movements, with virtually no options for improving their living standards on the horizon. The basic urban food intake of those days, as I saw at our school, revealed the nutritional limitations of the daily stodgy diet. On the other hand, our students were active and energetic, and some of the older ones were growing taller than the generation of my teaching colleagues. I was average height and none of my colleagues were taller than me, but a few of the senior boys were. Even some of the senior girls were as tall as me.

I had a rough idea of the Confucian[9] concepts of family, human relations and qualities, all interlocking within a hierarchy of unequal social relationships. These virtues could be applied according to the social status of the individual, and everyone knew their place in an ordered society, and followed the rules and conventions. At the heart of Confucianism was a matrix of human attributes. The Classical Chinese characters expressed these values in beautiful calligraphy, with meanings of Benevolence, Conduct, Duty, Filial Piety, Harmony, Humanity, Integrity, Loyalty, Morality, Kindness, Rituals and so on, all emerging from the context of Confucian society in the spring and autumn period of small kingdoms, two thousand five hundred years ago. Bertrand Russell was not inspired by Confucianism:

> *"I must confess that I am unable to appreciate the merits of Confucius. His writings are largely occupied with trivial points of etiquette, and his main concern is to teach people how to behave correctly on various occasions. His system, as developed by his followers, is one of pure ethics, without religious dogma; it has not given rise to a powerful priesthood, and it has not led to persecution."*

Analysts of Russell's views might say that instead of a 'priesthood', China had created a powerful 'scholar-gentry' class.

To my mind, Confucianism was not appropriate to the needs of twentieth century China, when the advent of socialism, and all the resultant changes, initiated a dynamic surge in the building of a new manufacturing, scientific and technological society. It is quite ironic that as part of their 'soft power' strategy, the Chinese are currently establishing a chain of Confucian Institutes worldwide to head up their cultural image globally, and to compete with the British Council, Alliance Francaise and Goethe Institutes, and the successors to the US Information Service.. So old Confucius has survived the severe buffeting of the twentieth century, and is now reviving. Perhaps China needs him back today, to maintain some stability and order in their rapidly evolving market economy and consumer society.

I can't assess how much the Chinese felt that they could rely on foreign experts. If they couldn't trust other Chinese how could they trust foreigners? Personally, at our school, I never felt that my 'bourgeois' outlook and mindset had the slightest influence on my colleagues or theirs on mine. After 1949, outside of Russia and the Soviet bloc countries, a new breed of foreigners had appeared who were willing to give both their ideological co-operation and support to China. They could be representatives from other emerging socialist countries, from revolutionary groups trying to overthrow their governments or just plain believers from the left-wings of the capitalist western societies. None of these groups owned any wealth or means of production in China, and were merely guests in the country, and their thinking was usually based around the core of Mao's distillation of Marxism-Leninism, and his road to socialism. The Hungarian revolution in 1956, and then China's rupture with Russia from 1960, created a schism in the thinking of the western communist parties, and it became inconceivable for a supporter of the Soviet model to be able to work in China.

However, the Chinese authorities at lower levels did not take any chances, and I felt that they essentially treated all foreigners as unreliable 'comrades' in the class war, and kept them at arm's length. For us in the peaceful months of 1965, within such an atmosphere as the prevailing socio-political environment, we detected that it was difficult to build friendships with Chinese people, measured in western European terms, even if both sides were keen to do so. We did have a good relationship when working with our colleagues at school, but it was limited in scope. It is possible that some colleagues may have been quite content with the restraints placed on them, for any 'friendship' with foreigners. In cross-cultural hindsight, I just can't see how real friendships with Chinese people could have flourished then, let alone any forms of 'love' or sexual entanglements. The different facial expressions, body language, politeness, social values, mind-set and life experience were an enormous hurdle to overcome on both sides. Such an eco-system could only produce failed blooms and withered flowers of friendship.

To visit us in our superior quality accommodation in the Friendship Guesthouse Chinese colleagues had to get permission from their work unit or in rare cases they could be instructed to visit us for one reason or another. If they did come it was always in pairs or more, and usually one of them was required to report back to the leadership on the visit. In return we foreign teachers could not visit the homes of Chinese co-workers, often a very minimal, basic apartment of one tiny room for married couples, or unmarried colleagues would living together in larger dormitories. Such fraternising by foreigners could only be done if orchestrated by the work unit, and our school leaders were not willing to allow us to see the poor housing conditions of our colleagues. In later years some of our colleagues told me that they were too ashamed of their accommodation to invite us in.

In our school staffroom, the individual space bubbles between our Chinese colleagues, when standing chatting, were very similar to Britain so we fitted in quite easily. Within our limited purview China seemed to be a non-tactile society for adults. No touching of any kind occurred between the Chinese teachers in front of us, and certainly not male-female, so Waddi and I had to restrain ourselves from natural gestures, and withhold spontaneous pats on the arm or back when with our Chinese colleagues. I had no idea of the tactile interactions between couples, and their child-rearing behaviour towards their children, within the Chinese family home. Any overt shows of affection between Chinese people never happened before my eyes. On the other side, such warm behaviour in public, in my experience, was not very common in Britain in the 1950s, and certainly not between males. As for handshaking in China it was rare, and didn't seem to be a natural part of their social customs. On campus our students seemed more relaxed, and some of the girls would go around arm in arm with other girl classmates, and a few of the boys did the same with other boys; it was never boy-girl.

One pivotal factor in any Sino-Western friendship relationship was the perplexing obstacle of how each side could assess the degree of sincerity and trust of the other, without getting to know each other well. Bertrand Russell's view was:

"Chinese life, even among the most modernised is far more polite than anything to which we are accustomed. This, of course, interferes with efficiency, and also, what is more serious, with sincerity and truth in personal relations."

Russell was writing about his lecture tour in 1921, when he must have mixed only in the intellectual circles at the top universities. Nevertheless, from my two years in 1965-66, to some extent I can relate to what he was saying.

Chapter Notes
1. Hundred Flowers Campaign- Wikipedia online
2. Anti-Rightist Movement- Wikipedia online
3. Qincheng prison- Wikipedia online
4. Great Leap Forward- Wikipedia online
5. Five-year plans of China- Wikipedia online
6. China Will Overtake Britain- www.library.uoregon.edu
7. Filial piety- Wikipedia online
8. Peng Dehuai- Wikipedia online
9. Confucianism- Wikipedia online

14

SOME EMULATORY PROPAGANDA HEROES 1965-1966

Lei Feng[1] was the dominant model hero of the 'Serve the People' propaganda campaign in the early 1960s, and he was endlessly extolled throughout all the media outlets in China available to mass consumers then; these did not include television. Radio, newspapers, film and public notices were the ready communications conduit in the cities, but in the countryside the radio, and maybe a simple broadcast relay system, were often the only instrument for passing on news, apart from having meetings. Even in Peking there was an extensive system of relay loudspeakers along the streets of the central areas of the city. And we had a similar system in all the classrooms of our school.

Many emulatory, revolutionary and production heroes were around in this period, and they could be roughly divided between military and civilian personnel, often Party members, usually posthumous, and sometimes female. Now they have all been consigned to a fragmentary backwater of Chinese history, waiting to be investigated and researched by future generations of doctoral students. Other groups, such as scientists, could be praised as national heroes, for their achievements on the scientific and technological fronts, but they were more in a 'Serve the Country' mode than in the 'Serve the People' mould. Prominent scientific breakthroughs around this period were exploding an atomic bomb on 16 October 1964, and a hydrogen bomb on 17 June 1967.

One powerful production hero, who was definitely not posthumous, was Wang Chin-hsi, known as 'Iron Man' Wang[2]. He came from poor peasant stock, and worked his way up to become leader of the famous No 1205 Drilling Team, which led the battle to open up a new oilfield at Taching [Da.qing] in Heilungkiang [Hei.long.jiang] province; they finally achieved this, striking oil in 1960. Perhaps the Chinese had identified him as their answer to the Russian coalminer, Aleksei Stakhanov[3], who in 1935 had inspired the Stakhanovite movement to reward Soviet workers for outstanding production in their field of work. As a matter of interest, during the Stalinist period, the Soviets created forty two 'Foreign Heroes of the Soviet Union', and not one was Chinese, or British, for that matter. On the Chinese side, in December 1939, Mao had written a moving tribute, 'In Memory of Norman Bethune', to the Canadian doctor, Norman Bethune[4], who had travelled to Yenan and the communist controlled areas in 1938, and had worked as a medical doctor with the Eighth Route Army there, until his death from septicaemia in 1939.

We attended the National Day Banquet on 30 September 1965, in the Great Hall of the People. Wang was present, and he was introduced by Premier Chou En Lai to much applause. Three years later in 1968 in the midst of the tribulations of the Cultural Revolution he was elected to the Central Committee of the Chinese Communist Party, a not inconsiderable leap upwards for a 'poor peasant boy'; but he died from cancer in 1970. One British expert from the Druzhba actually met him on the occasion of this banquet, and they shook hands. He told us later, that Iron Man Wang's hand did not feel like that of a manual worker, a fact which caused us much confusion and questioning of his official biography. Handshaking itself did not appear to be a common form of greeting between Chinese adults, but it did have a beneficial function for foreigners though. When going on visits to factories and communes, we could get some idea of whether the Chinese we shook hands with were manual or mental workers from the feel of their hands. The senior cadres who received us on these trips were always soft-handed, but we might meet some real workers or peasants with rough and hard hands, during the scheduled walkabouts around the factory or village

All foreign experts, but not necessarily their wives, were invited to the banquets on these significant occasions, as were the top echelons of the Diplomatic Corps and any visiting foreign delegations. On our first May Day Eve banquet at the Great Hall of the People on 30 April 1965, I was invited to attend, but not Waddi, so I did not go. At the May Day celebrations next day, our interpreter, Teacher Hu asked me what had happened, and I just explained that I did not wish to attend, because my wife had been excluded. It was possible that unmarried foreign women could become experts in their own right, but the wives of foreign experts, even well-qualified ones, would have to satisfy stringent rules to reach the status of their husbands, and only then were they invited to these events. To rub in more salt, they were still labelled officially as 'Wife of foreign expert X', and did not appear in their own name. Even in those early embryonic days of western Women's Liberation, some of the young foreign women resented this treatment and constantly made their feelings clearly known to their Chinese colleagues. Nothing changed however during our stay.

We were both invited to the National Day Eve Banquet on 30 September 1965. The banqueting hall was enormous and I was informed it had the largest unsupported ceiling in China. A countless number of sizeable round tables stretched away into the distance, and one could only see a fraction of all those present; certainly not Chou En-lai and other top leaders on the opposite side of the hall to us. As the host of this event Premier Chou made the key speech, which was rather long, with regular breaks for clapping, particularly for the extensive list of 'Toasts' to Prince Sihanouk of Cambodia and other important foreign dignitaries present. An English language translation of his speech was available on our table, and the list of toasts covered one page. The only time I could ever see him, was in the far distance circulating around the privileged top tables, in his urbane and sophisticated manner, and paying his respects by toasting guests, probably with a small glass of the powerful Moutai white spirit. I assume that Premier Chou, being the top diplomat that he was, never touched a drop of this potent drink whilst on official duties. Our two school colleagues, who were with us as interpreters, said that Mao no longer attended any of these semi-public functions, but that he had been present during the early 1950s.

Second to Lei Feng, one female revolutionary figure embedded in our school teaching materials was Liu Hu-lan[5] (1932-47). Obviously mature beyond her years, this young teenager was extremely active in her local countryside affairs, and in leading the peasantry to stand up to the landlords. When encroaching Chiang Kai-shek troops descended on the villages in her area to steal their grain and livestock, Liu organised the peasant resistance. This opposition was bound to fail against the soldiers' superior weaponry, and they executed her. Her story rarely failed to produce tears when being read aloud in my classes.

Another PLA hero was Ouyang Hai[6], a 23 year old who had lost his life while moving a horse, which was paralysed with fear and laden with artillery parts, off a railway track just before a train roared through, thereby saving the train and passengers, as well as his squad of soldiers. Even my senior students seemed emotionally affected by his story, often with tears accompanying their reading aloud extracts of his life and death. A popular book in 1965 was 'The Song of Ouyang Hai', and many of the seniors had English language copies of this biography, but it always seemed out of stock in the Guo.zi shu.dian (government bookstore) in town, whenever I tried to buy one. Ouyang Hai's final self-sacrifice, and the many lives he had saved, was way above Lei Feng's league, and set high standards for any subsequent PLA heroes to live up to. Wang Chieh[7], who was canonised six months later, managed to meet this test by throwing himself on a faulty live mine during an exercise, thereby saving the lives of nearby comrades.

One PLA hero who managed to survive his heroic exploits was Liu Hsueh-pao[8], hailed for his courage 'in fighting a vicious counter-revolutionary single-handedly and risking his life to save a bridge from this saboteur's charge of explosive'. During my limited rail trips in China I had been puzzled by seeing sentries on duty guarding any rail bridges that we passed over, and my interpreter would always say that some counter revolutionary Chinese were always looking out for opportunities to damage the socialist cause. I couldn't assess the validity of this standard reply, but to my mind I felt that the anti-Mao villains didn't stand a chance in this New China, although any of their successes would not have seen the light of day, and would never have been acknowledged in the Chinese media.

As it happened, Liu Hsueh-pao lived to fight another day, unlike most of his predecessors, and perhaps this indicated that the government propaganda writers were willing to select living heroes, and were positing the idea that heroic lives be valued at a premium, and should no longer be wasted unnecessarily. On the other hand, posthumous heroes were a safer bet, because they could not upset their heroic image once it was set in propaganda plaster, whereas living heroes, with their human frailties, might cause embarrassment for the Government when paraded in public to celebrate their fame.

An example of a loyal 'production hero' was Chiao Yu-lu[9], the Party Secretary of Lao Kan County (province unknown), which readers were told was a notoriously barren area for farming. He led the local villagers selflessly in their work on the agricultural front and died at the comparatively young age of 42, from a liver disease. Having a less dramatic end to life than the Army heroes, my students seemed to over-compensate in their praise of Chiao, even though I could see that they found it easier to identify with the self-sacrifices of the young PLA men. There were never any tears shed for him in my classes. Older, and married with children, his unselfish image was aimed more at middle-level Party members in positions of responsibility in the countryside.

A contrasting sort of 'national' hero of 1965 was the sailor Mai Hsien-te[10], a 21 year old engine-room artificer, who received a serious head wound during a naval engagement with US-built Chiang Kai-shek ships from Taiwan. Several weeks after the incident he was accepted into the Chinese Communist Party, although not completely recovered and unable to speak. A year later, in the Cultural Revolution, he was quoted in *Peking Review* of August 12, 1966, as saying with great elation:

"We will always study Chairman Mao's works, follow his teachings and be his good soldiers. We will always follow Chairman Mao in making revolution, resolutely carry the great proletarian cultural revolution through to the end, crush the sinister gangs, sweep away all ghosts and monsters and defend the Party's Central Committee and Chairman Mao."

Even heroes such as Mai had to follow the correct political line, and paraphrase their thoughts carefully. By that point in the Cultural Revolution however, after reading so many similar speeches, I could have easily composed a standard statement myself, to go in the *Peking Review*.

The Mai Hsien-te campaign differed from the usual pattern, perhaps because the increasing American involvement in Vietnam posed a greater threat to China's security, and so it became necessary to emphasise the 'Defence of the Motherland' line; and this path was still being pushed in the early days of the Cultural Revolution. A positive struggle against an external enemy could engender a national zeal, which could easily be transferred to the domestic context, and be more encouragement to the Red Guards in their struggles against all the 'demons and monsters', who were following the capitalist road. In 1965 the need to defend the country was mainly sustained by a growing Anti-US Vietnam war campaign. On one occasion our Institute took all their foreign teachers to Tienanmen Square, where in one corner a very small US pilotless drone plane was on public display. These planes, which we were told overflew China regularly, were always at a higher altitude than Chinese MiGs could reach, so this one, which was quite damaged, must have malfunctioned and lost height.

The last PLA hero of 1966 was Men Ho[11], whose campaign bridged the period from the eclipse of Lei Feng into the Cultural Revolution era. He was a mature man, married with children, and more overtly political, as deputy political commissar of an army unit stationed in a troubled Tibetan minority area of Ch'inghai [Qing.hai] province. He died by throwing himself on a home-made hail dispersal rocket, and saved several soldiers' lives; interestingly those whom he had saved were now described as 'class brothers', rather than just comrades of his unit.

His biography shows him to have been a perfect paragon of the 'Loyal to Mao' soldier, and his greatest achievements consisted of making correct decisions to 'Support the Left' during the initial stages of the Cultural Revolution. He was also praised for his efforts to separate the revolutionary wheat from counter-revolutionary chaff, as he tried to resolve the disputes between the rival Red Guard factions in that area. The heroic example of Men Ho was clearly aimed at bolstering middle-level Army cadres who were not fully embracing the correct Maoist line, and who also needed to be reminded of the complete allegiance of the military to the 'Party Centre' headed by Chairman Mao.

The Lei Feng hero era is now a thing of the past, although the Chinese media sometimes refer back to his exploits, but in the market-driven China of today, with its blanket materialism, I don't feel that he would be granted any respect by the individualistic Chinese. It would be impossible for me to imagine his presence in the Chinese media of 2015. From my visits to China in recent years I get the feeling that he would, more likely, be regarded as an irrelevant absurdity of a past age that the older generation wanted to forget, and he would be condemned as a simple man. His life could possibly go down in history as a naïve Chinese fable to rival 'The Foolish Old Man who Moved Mountains'.

Mary Sheridan[12] in her article 'The Emulation of Heroes' points out that heroic figures have been present in folk stories and literature throughout China's history, and even occurred in the pre-1949 days of the Communist Party, during the Yenan period. The ones that I encountered in 1965-66 were all ordinary people who were lifted into the political limelight by their actions, real or alleged, and by the propaganda machine of those times. Today, all those forgotten Chinese socialist heroes, dating from fifty years and more ago, are transfixed in a time-warp of those short years of Chinese history from 1949 to 1966. The Chinese media may occasionally harp back to Lei Feng, and say how valuable his virtues would be in today's society, but the Chinese people wouldn't hear this message at all, as they are devoting all their time and energies to surviving, making money and bettering themselves!

Chinese Romanisation Concordance Table

Old Romanisation	New Romanisation [Han.yu Pin.yin]
Lei Feng	Lei Feng
Wang Chin-his	Wang Jin.xi
Liu Hu-lan	Liu Hu.lan
Ouyang Hai	Ouyang Hai
Wang Chieh	Wang Jie
Liu Hsueh-pao	Liu Xue.bao
Chiao Yu-lu	Jiao Yu.lu
Mai Hsien-te	Mai Xian.de
Men Ho	Men He

Chapter Notes

1. Lei Feng- Wikipedia online
2. Daqing Oil Field (Wang Jinxi)- Wikipedia online
3. Aleksei Stakhanov- Wikipedia online
4. Norman Bethune- Wikipedia online
5. Liu Hulan- Wikipedia online
6. Ouyang Hai- Information online- Chinese compound surname- Wikipedia online
7. Wang Jie- Information online
8. Heroic Soldier Liu Hsueh-pao- Information online
9. County Party Secretary Chiao Yu-lu- Information online
10. Battle Hero Mai Hsien-te- Information online
11. Men Ho- No information online
12. Mary Sheridan, 'The Emulation of Heroes', *The China Quarterly*, No 33, Jan-March, 1968., and more information can be found online

15

ON CHINESE FACE[1]

I well remember a small incident that happened in the autumn of 1965, well before the onset of the Cultural Revolution and rampaging Red Guards. There were various restaurants in different parts of Peking that were familiar to the resident foreigners, and four of us went out for an evening meal in the Hsitan [Xi.dan] district. This was a new restaurant for me. We travelled in one of the Warszawa taxis, built in Poland, from the fleet operated by the guesthouse, and would be picked up by another one at the time we specified. When I say 'evening' I mean between 6pm and 8pm because in those days all stores, shops and restaurants were closed by 8 or 9pm, rather like a curfew, and the Peking side-streets that we drove through, all very poorly lit, were silent and empty. Such a staggering contrast with the bustling high-rise dynamic Bei.jing that I found in October 2015, fifty years later.

We sat at a table, hidden in a corner, and we were all wearing standard Chinese blue padded winter jackets, so we didn't stand out too much as 'foreigners'. It was a fairly large restaurant and everything was quite quiet, until we heard voices raised in altercation from a table in the distance. I was amazed to see three old Chinese men, who looked past retirement age, standing there arguing loudly over who would pay the bill; they were in serious dispute, indeed one of them was quite white-faced. Restaurant staff quickly dealt with the situation, probably even faster because four foreigners were present, but that fleeting experience gave me a flavour of 'Chinese face'. Of course, such incidents might occur anywhere in the world, and I didn't know the social context of that particular situation, but the intensity on display surprised me.

So I got the impression that Chinese face is a powerful force which can create social conflict, or even more serious underlying problems, if not dealt with on the spot. Sometimes it can be resolved on the surface by the intervention and conciliation of third parties. However, in that scenario I couldn't comprehend the full extent of the feelings of the white-faced old man, the frustration of not maintaining his face, and any possible fall-out in his relationships with his fellow diners.

The other time I had seen it in action was when cycling into town in daytime, and remember, there were thousands of cyclists everywhere, on the streets of Peking. Suddenly I reached a huge crowd of dismounted cyclists watching a confrontation between two ordinary-looking Chinese men, somewhere in middle age. They were facing each other with straitened faces, unmoving and unspeaking, but as soon as I arrived they saw me, and that seemed to reduce the tension. Chinese people could not risk a scene in front of a foreigner, as that might rebound on them, so as nothing was happening I decided to cycle on. Maybe my arrival gave them an excuse to end the impasse, and avoid losing face [diu mian]. It was often in such situations that street policemen on patrol could step in and defuse the atmosphere by listening to the grievances of the confronters, and then apportioning blame to each one on the ten units system, before sending them on their way. No doubt the policeman would also include consideration for the 'face' of the parties involved, when making his final judgement. But it is difficult to know if the parties would accept the decision of any third-party conciliator, and when no neutral arbitration was available, their responses and the outcome might be unpredictable.

Many commentators, both Chinese and foreign, have entered the discussion on Chinese face, looking at it from various viewpoints. The different human traits involved in public face can be expressed by a variety of English nouns, such as authority, dignity, honour, integrity, prestige, pride, reputation, status. Should any of these personal attributes and qualities be threatened or questioned in public, then the individual, whatever their nationality, might possibly feel a mixture of humiliation, shame, resentment or anger, at this loss of face.

Lu Hsun (1881-1936), famous Chinese writer[2], reported in one of his stories that foreigners living in China in the nineteenth century were often fascinated by 'Chinese Face', because they felt an understanding of it might give them a key to the Chinese mentality. In his book *Chinese Characteristics* published in 1894, Arthur Henderson Smith[3], devotes a chapter to 'Chinese Face'. Smith had spent twenty two years as a missionary of the American Board in China, quite a considerable length of time. His writings reflect the attitudes of a superior 'White Anglo-Saxon Protestant'[4] (WASP) living in old China.

He didn't think that honour, presumably as defined in his own culture, was involved in the subject of face, and he focused on the giving and receiving of gifts, and the lengths that Chinese people would go to in order to avoid losing face:

"The question of 'face' is never of facts, but always of form. If a fine speech has been delivered at the proper time and in the proper way, according to the traditional rites of Confucian propriety, the requirements of the play is met. Properly to execute acts like these in all the complex relations of life, is to have 'face'. To fail of them, to ignore them, to be thwarted in the performance of them, this is to 'lose face'. Once rightly apprehended, 'face' will be found to be in itself a key to the combination lock of many of the important characteristics of the Chinese."

He constantly mentioned that foreign barbarians were unable to fully comprehend the workings of Chinese face:

"It should be added that the principles which regulate 'face' and its attainment are often wholly beyond the intellectual apprehension of the Occidental, who is constantly forgetting the theatrical element, and wandering off into the irrelevant regions of fact."

Face still seems to be significant in China today. The sublimity of the Olympic opening and closing ceremonies in 2008, and the superb organisation of the Bei.jing Games in every small detail, seemed to indicate the extremely high value placed by the Chinese on their international public image. Every host country would surely try to achieve such a positive impression, yet this did produce a mild backlash from some foreign reporters. Little comments to the effect, that it was a mechanical display of perfection, with a lack of the joy factor.

Some commentators have loosely categorised East Asian countries, such as China, as 'shame'[5] societies, while Christian countries, with a religious component, could be labelled as 'guilt'[6] societies, although both human syndromes are present in all societies. Much debate and analysis has gone into differentiating between the two, and a broad consensus seems to place feelings of shame as usually occurring within a public scenario, while guilt is a more personal and internalised emotion. On the other hand, shame and guilt may sometimes be difficult to tell apart, especially when being present in the same emotional response. Western people did not like public embarrassment or humiliation either, and during the Middle Ages the shame of the village stocks was often used as a punishment for minor wrongdoings.

Much research has been carried out by Chinese and foreign academics over the past fifty years, and 'Oriental face' is a very complex issue. Michael Harris Bond[7] an academic based in Hong Kong has been quite active in this field, and he edited the *Oxford Handbook of Chinese Psychology* published in 2011, by Oxford University Press. Some writers today ascribe both shame and guilt to Chinese face; *Mian.zi* stands for the prestige obtained through getting on in life, and being successful for all to see, and any decline in this status would be a psychological blow to that person. *Lian* represents the moral character and integrity of the individual, the loss of which would internally undermine the normal functioning of that person in the community.

In today's world, potential loss of face for westerners doesn't seem to have such quiescent power as that contained in oriental face, and may lead to different reactions and outcomes. Maybe westerners are more attuned to the concept of compromise, and the rule of law, as a means of settling disputes. During the Cultural Revolution news slowly filtered out that some Chinese academics, intellectuals, writers and artists committed suicide after being humiliated and ill-treated by Red Guards. Here, it is hard to know to what extent 'face' was a contributory factor. Suicide seemed to be the only course of action left, perhaps a final gesture of defiance to the attackers. In China it is not necessarily regarded as a blot on the character of the individual.

When 'oriental face' is involved in larger political decision-making then it becomes a significant factor in East Asian and international affairs. The impending crisis over the contentious disputation of the sovereignty of the Diao.yu-Senkaku[8] islands is slowly building up. These eight uninhabited islands are situated in the East China sea, north east of Taiwan, and the claimants are China and Taiwan lined up against Japan; that is, Chinese nationalism versus Japanese nationalism. The two nations have history, and patriotic face looms large on both sides of this equation. It might need the wisdom of Solomon, and possibly UN arbitration, to resolve this potential conflict peacefully. With regard to the need for a process of compromise in settling a dispute, it is not clear to what degree oriental face will accept this form of crisis conciliation, or whether compromise itself is deemed to be a sign of weakness, and thus a loss of face. In the same way the dispute over the Spratly islands in the South China Sea looks to be another crucial issue for the world community. In this case the countries staking claims are Brunei, China, Malaysia, the Philippines, Taiwan and Vietnam. Hopefully, having more numbers involved may temporarily defuse this simmering discord, and leave it on the back-burner.

During the SARS[9] (Severe acute respiratory syndrome) international epidemic crisis of 2002-2003, which originated in Guang.dong province in China and then moved to Hong Kong, the Chinese government were slow to release any information on their internal situation to the WHO (World Health Organisation), or make active attempts to co-operate with other nations affected worldwide.   Traditionally China has always been secretive, and with the blame for SARS being placed on their backs, the People's Re-public may have viewed this novel and unfamiliar predicament as a potentially face-losing endgame, so it initially prevaricated before finally being forced to open up. Of course, information about the epidemic from mainland Chinese people was humming around the Internet, and this showed that any internal Chinese matters, especially of great import, could no longer be hidden from foreign eyes.   Taiwan, on the other hand, was much more open and informative on their SARS situation, and gained some status from the international community. It seems that 'oriental face' might need to be reck-oned a meaningful factor in future international affairs.

Chapter Notes
1. Face (sociological concept)- Wikipedia online
2. Lu Xun- Wikipedia online
3. Arthur Henderson Smith- Wikipedia online
4. White Anglo-Saxon Protestant (WASP)- Wikipedia online
5. Shame- Wikipedia online
6. Guilt (emotion)- Wikipedia online
7. Michael Harris Bond- Information online
8. Senkaku Islands dispute- Wikipedia online
9. Severe acute respiratory syndrome- Wikipedia online

16

TEACHING PRIMARY THREE AND JUNIOR ONE- 1965-66

After our 'apprenticeship' term from February to July of 1965, the School leadership gave us a special project for the start of the upcoming academic year in September 1965. It would be teaching a class of new entrants to the school for one session every day, a sort of semi-intensive experimental course. Waddi would teach Primary Three (ages 9-10), and I would teach Junior One (ages 12-13), and it was hoped that after one year of our daily classes, they would be more advanced in oral/aural English than previous years. Two ladies were assigned to work with us. Teacher Wu would team up with Waddi for Primary Three, and Teacher Yu, who was quite tall and nicknamed Da Yu (Big Yu), was to work with me on Junior One. Of course we still had other classes to teach in our weekly timetable, but none of those were on a regular daily basis.

We both saw this as quite a challenge, and prepared in detail our teaching plans, outlines and materials, and had long meetings with our support teachers. Those two lady colleagues were invaluable in the process, as they provided materials for the core vocabulary and grammatical structures to be covered in the first term, and they also gave us copies of the two cyclostyled booklets handed out to the pupils, one for reading passages and one for grammar notes. By the time all this preliminary work had been effectively integrated within the fruits of our last term's experience, we felt well-prepared and ready for the challenge. We concentrated on using as many direct method activities as possible in class, a very demanding schedule in practice, especially for a double period of one hour and forty minutes, with only a ten minute break in the middle. In reality, through the judicious use of reading and phonology exercises, and teacher talk, we were able to provide some breathing space in class for the pupils, and for ourselves.

An immediate issue was that these classes had over forty pupils. So the full class had to be split into two halves of around twenty pupils each, and we were given one of these groups to focus on, while for the other half we only managed a couple of classes per week. I learnt that the other half of Junior One were very disappointed at seeing me less frequently, but Da Yu assiduously made extensive notes during my classes, and faithfully replicated everything I covered, in an identical class that she gave for them later in the day. I once sat in on that class and was astounded at her reproduction of the idiomatic classroom expressions, correct stress, and the body language that I used, as was her handling of all the differing oral activities and exercises, including simple phonology and pronunciation. Her spoken British English was excellent, and it was great to see this carbon copy of me in action, doing a brilliant job for the other half of Junior One. As well as that, she taught grammatical usage to the whole class in the afternoons, and faithfully covered all vocabulary needs, reading exercises, listening to tapes, chanting rhymes and singing songs in her daily duties. Da Yu was the veritable lynchpin of the course. Likewise, Teacher Wu had the same crucial role in supporting Waddi's success in teaching English to the two classes of Primary Three.

As Junior One progressed during the first term I became over-enthusiastic, and thought that they could be taught other subjects through the medium of English. As I had some experience of teaching Maths to 'O' level at my old grammar school, I suggested to the leadership that I taught some Maths to Junior One in English. They seemed appreciative of my keenness, and thanked me for my suggestion, but nothing came of it. However, as a sop, they allowed me to sit in on a senior maths class, and when I arrived mid-lesson it was algebra and differential calculus. The large blackboard was completely full of quite complex equations involving roman letters, x and y, dx/dy, a^2 and b^2. There were hardly any Chinese characters on the board.

For my Junior One class, most of the pupils did quite well, and three girls reached an outstanding level of spoken English for their age-group: Lu Chiang, Chang Chieh-p'ing and Huang Mei. Their English accent, language understanding, and ability to answer the most demanding questions on the spot, gave me great satisfaction. They were closely followed by Hu Hsiao-mien and Sung Hai-wei. There were four girls and one boy in that top group. On my recent Bei.jing trips Lu Chiang has always acted as my interpreter and minder.

Waddi and I both became very attached to our classes, and we would exchange ideas on the activities and materials that worked well or not, and on everyday problems that arose in class. As proof that we were doing something right, our classes would sometimes be attended by visitors from other schools and educational groups. This was the only sign of our success, because towards the end of the second term, from June 1966, the Cultural Revolution cranked up a gear, as a result of the May 16 Circular[1] issued by the Central Committee of the Chinese Communist Party. A key directive then came down from above: "Ting ke nao ge.ming" (Suspend Classes and Make Revolution!), and classes were stopped. The movement took over the lives of everyone at school. We had no further meetings with the school leadership after that, and we never did hear their views and evaluation of this experimental year with Primary Three and Junior One. But in later years, we did get positive reactions from some of those pupils that we had taught in 1965-66. As time has passed, we have come to realise that we are the beneficiaries of the old Chinese respect for the teacher.

Just before the 'Suspend Classes' directive, during a Junior One class in early June 1966, a short, loud message, unintelligible to me, came over the broadcast relay system, the class erupted in joyous cheering and pandemonium, and no more teaching took place. I was informed that P'eng Chen [Peng Zhen[2]], the Mayor of Peking, had been deposed. That evening Old Chang [Zhang] phoned me and said that I wouldn't have any classes tomorrow, because all the pupils were having meetings. He would phone me when my classes re-started. They never re-started, and for the last seven months of my contract I had no classes. However Waddi was able to go into school to teach her primary classes for another two weeks, before they were finally suspended too. Neither of us had any further teaching responsibilities at school for the rest of our contracts, right up to our departure in December 1966.

From then on, I went into school once a month to collect our joint salaries, which they faithfully paid for the rest of our stay, and it was a strange atmosphere on the campus. I would be met at the entrance by Old Chang, and he would take me to the accountant's office, where I would be given a thick envelope of banknotes, usually five or ten yuan. These were the maximum value notes that we were given in 1965-66; smaller ones in circulation were two and one yuan, and then fifty fen (cent) and twenty fen (cent). The accountant always asked me to count the notes, and sign a receipt.

108

Sometimes, I would see some of my pupils in the school grounds, but they would all be looking in other directions, and I couldn't make any eye contact. On one visit, Deputy-Head Han was doing some labouring work in the playground, and he looked away too. This was after having a series of meetings on our contracts with him, during 1965. I didn't like this behaviour at all, and became very critical. It took me some time to register that in this developing Cultural Revolution movement it was not politic for any Chinese to show any attention, let alone a friendly manner, to a foreigner, who by definition was 'bourgeois'; the very malaise that they were meant to be stamping out in their own society. Over time, I came to see their avoidance of eye contact as being the risk of standing out in the crowd, and becoming the butt of political criticism, or suffering even more serious sanctions. It was purely for their self-survival. For me, however, this was a new side of Chinese society, and of the Chinese people too, and I found it very hard to reconcile myself to that reality.

On a working trip to Bei.jing in January 2005, I unexpectedly got a phone call from Lu Chiang, my old pupil from the Junior One class, as a result of our old colleague Teacher Hu having given her my hotel details. I was delighted that four of them could come to my hotel for a meal the next day, and it was my first time to see them since summer 1966. Apparently they had not kept in touch as a class until the year 2000, when computer emails enabled them to hold their first reunion. Now they have their own website and hold annual reunions. In October 2007 I went to Bei.jing, and they organised a large gathering and banquet attended by thirty one of my old pupils from Junior One and Junior Two. Teacher Yu, still fit and active, was there too. It was an enjoyable day for me, ending with some of them singing snatches of English songs that Teacher Yu had taught them.

I could only respond with one Chinese song that came to mind; a revolutionary Sin-kiang [Xin.jiang Uyghur Autonomous Region] song, in praise of Mao, which I had learnt by heart in 1966 because I liked the catchy tune. Not an apt choice on my part, for a generation trying to forget the bad old days of the Cultural Revolution, in which their formal education was cut short, and their lives disrupted. Nevertheless, some of them joined in with my singing; all these songs were an indelible part of their school memories. I did note that most of my old junior pupils, now in their fifties in 2007, seemed quite confident and successful in life. Presumably, pupils with negative memories of their school experience did not come to the reunions. The ones who still used their English, all had British accents, and that was very pleasing.

Then, in October 2015, I went to Bei.jing for ten days to see again my old colleagues and pupils on the fiftieth anniversary of our arrival in Peking. I was able to meet up with seven old colleagues, and many old pupils from the junior years, and also some of the seniors, at a series of lunches, dinners and banquets. Because we were able to meet in smaller groups, I was able to ask them about our classes all those years ago. Most of them had positive memories, with a few exceptions, and I got some honest answers. The first thing that Junior One told me was quite a surprise. In August 1965, before they had even entered our school, they had done two weeks farm work in the Western Hills[3] quite close to Peking. A few of them now referred to this work as 'brain-washing'. They had been housed in the Long.quan (Dragon Spring) Temple[4], and had walked to work in the fields every day. Another story from a Junior One boy was that when I entered the classroom I put my wristwatch on the desk, and checked it regularly, and always finished the class on time. He said words to the effect that I was a time-watcher because I was paid by my teaching hours.　I had to laugh at this explanation, and then moved on.

The next Junior One pupil said that sometimes I was late arriving for the 8 a.m. class, and once I tried to cover up my lateness by running into the room and teaching them the verb 'to run', on the spot.　One man claimed that I didn't ask him questions in class.　I was upset by this probable blind spot in my early teaching techniques, to which I had no answer decades later.　However I asked the other classmates about this, and they all said I went round the class asking questions in turn. Little recompense for him, because he had been carrying this disregard for all those years.　They also told me that one time I got annoyed with the class, and walked out midway, leaving Teacher Yu to sort things out.　I have absolutely no recollection of that incident at all.

On another occasion, when doing some pronunciation drills on new words, which included the word 'pillow', I asked one of the boys to read out the list of words, and he had had problems saying 'pillow'.　Indeed, on his first attempt, all the class laughed, and I didn't know why. After class, Teacher Yu was not able, or was unwilling, to enlighten me.　So, fifty years later, the old classmates explained that his English version of 'pillow' sounded the same as a crude expression in the Peking dialect.　That's why they had laughed.　And what is more, they had then given the poor boy the Anglo-Peking nickname of 'pillow'.　They said that he didn't come to any reunions of their class.

Quite a few of them said how important that first year of English had been, and how it had helped their future careers, after the Cultural Revolution had died down in 1976, and life returned to some normality.　Several of them spontaneously affirmed how glad they were to have a British English accent.　Two of them explained that they had travelled extensively around continental Europe in their work, and their hosts had always praised their spoken English.　They also told me that in the early days of the Cultural Revolution in 1966, the School Head had broadcast over the school relay system, and warned everyone to be on their guard with the foreign teachers, and not to trust them.

One of the Junior One girls, now aged 62, and Professorial Head of a Research Unit at the Peking Union Medical College, said that some time previous to our arrival in 1965, the Foreign Minister, Marshal Chen Yi had issued a call to all the top echelons of cadres, administrators and the military, to support the Attached Foreign Languages School, and send their children there.　Her parents put her name forward, but she objected because she wanted to go to the Girls Attached School of Peking Normal University, which had had a high reputation at the time.　Needless to say, she was pressurised into going to our school.　She also said that when the Cultural Revolution started, she, and her older brother in a French class, publicly opposed the movement and said it was wrong.　They would not take part in Red Guard activities either. To stand out against the tide at that young age, was very brave, and neither of them changed their mind, so they were both sent to the countryside quite early on, as a punishment, and as a way of removing their negative presence at school; and possibly for their protection.　She didn't expand on those lost years, but at the end she casually added that her Father was working alongside Premier Chou En-lai at the time.　Her classmates now admitted she had been right to oppose the Cultural Revolution.

Senior Three students informed me that one day, I had told them the story of polishing my new boots when I started national service in the Royal Air Force.　They all grasped the polishing part easily enough, but I hadn't explained the context clearly, so on the campus I became known as the 'Shoe-polisher'. I never got to know about this until 2015.

The senior classmates, now in their late sixties, were not well-organised like the junior classes in holding reunions, but one of the ladies came to my hotel for afternoon tea. She said she came from a wealthy Manchu[5] family, owning several properties in Bei.jing, and her father had been a medical doctor, later followed into this profession by six others in the family. By 1966 they had acquired a significant collection of treasured antiques, furniture, scrolls and paintings, and when the Red Guards arrived at their home, and saw all these beautiful works of art, the family were immediately classified as 'bourgeois'. She did not enlarge on her family's subsequent fate at the hands of the Red Guards, but she said that a large lorry had been sent to collect all their valuable possessions, and it had been packed full when driven off. Since then, they had never been able to recover any of these stolen items.

At one lunchtime banquet with the junior classes, small glasses of white spirit [er.guo.tou][6] were flowing freely amongst the men, and as a result of this alcoholic in-take, I received some criticism. Towards the end of the meal, one of them approached me, and told me a little story, in English. He said that one day on the school campus, he had asked me if I loved Chairman Mao, and I had replied that I was not Chinese, so I couldn't answer him. I could see from his manner that he had taken this as a 'no', which it was, and it still rankled with him, decades later. I was only rescued from this edgy situation by several female classmates sitting nearby, who engaged him in conversation, and fortunately he didn't re-appear at our table again. We closed the banquet with everyone standing around in a circle at every table, and singing 'Auld Lang Syne'[7], using wordsheets that I had managed to bring with me.

Chapter Notes
1. May 16 Circular- Information online
2. Peng Zhen- Wikipedia online
3. Western Hills- Wikipedia online
4. Long Quan Temple- Information online
5. Manchu people- Wikipedia online
6. Erguotou- Wikipedia online
7. Auld Lang Syne- Wikipedia online

17

CHINESE ESSENCE AND WESTERN APPLICATION

By 1860, during the turbulent times of mid-nineteenth century China, she had suffered humiliation in the two Opium Wars[1], first at the hands of the British, and secondly from Anglo-French forces. This led to a situation, where non-Asian foreign residents were permitted in five eastern seaboard towns and cities, as laid down in 1842 by the Treaty of Nanking[2]. Additionally, the small enclave of Macao[3] had been occupied by the Portuguese since 1557, and then there was the tiny closed area permitted for foreigners and warehouses in Hong Kong and Canton[4]. Other non-Asian penetration into China had taken place previously, in the form of Russian incursions into the Amur basin from the seventeenth century onwards, as evidenced by the Treaty of Nerchinsk in1689.

Another huge event in those times, was the internal Taiping Rebellion (1856-67)[5], a massive civil insurrection that was finally put down by Tseng Kuo-fan [Zeng Guo.fan][6] and his armies, supported by foreign military forces, with an estimated twenty million dead. He, along with other powerful figures like Li Hung-chang [Li Hong.zhang][7], realised that, amongst her list of many immediate practical needs, China had to modernise her thinking, and learn from western science and military weaponry. They were strong supporters of the Self-Strengthening Movement[8] from the 1860s onwards, which promoted the approach of grafting western science onto traditional Chinese structures.

This policy was encapsulated in the eight character slogan "Chinese learning as the Essence, Western learning for the Application" [Zhong xue wei ti, Xi xue wei yong]. It was based on the long-established Chinese concept of Ti-Yong, meaning 'Essence-Function'[9]. According to this view, 'Essence' represented the very roots, and Chineseness of their culture and thinking, which had to be preserved from the creeping depredations of the 'foreign devils', while 'Function' corresponded to the practical applications. The slogan can also be seen as an example of the old traditional division between mental and manual work, with the Chinese emphasis being very much on their superior moral philosophy and Confucian traditions, while the foreign barbarians merely provided the military weaponry coming from their practical science and manufacture. Whatever the effectiveness of such thinking, it was a stepping stone towards 1949, when China finally overcame the inertia of tradition, freed itself from foreign straitjackets, and became an independent nation.

After some months of living in Peking in 1965, the rest of the world gradually receded from our immediate life. London, Paris and Europe all seemed very remote; even Hong Kong was around two thousand kilometres away by air. Over mealtimes in the Friendship Guesthouse, we foreigners were always talking about things Chinese and trying to understand what was happening, and this became the focus of our attention. Our main source of news from outside China came through the large, shiny radio we had bought in town on arrival, and it was a reliable prop throughout our stay. This radio would give us the BBC World service, other English-medium radio stations, and the English language broadcasts of Radio Peking. Also freely available every day were the typed New China News Agency news sheets in English, and other languages, covering selected international happenings. From family and friends at home, we would sometimes receive news and cuttings, and of course we had a regular exchange of letters and mini tape-spools, with the two grandmothers.

The third most frequent of our mailing correspondents was my bank manager in Hucclecote, near Gloucester, to whom we were transferring small sterling deposits almost every month. Against our clear instructions, he once addressed a letter to us in the 'Republic of China' (postal title for Taiwan), instead of the 'People's Republic of China'. It was returned to the bank unopened several months later. As for censoring mail, many of the inmates of the Friendship Guesthouse were uncertain about whether the Chinese authorities opened our outgoing and incoming letters, and we ourselves never noticed any signs of tampering of letters received. When posting letters, we had to stick the stamps and envelopes down with the messy glue and brush available in every post office. We couldn't see how they could ever be opened without trace, especially the aerogrammes that we used quite a lot. We felt that incoming parcels might be opened, and this seemed quite reasonable to me. I never believed that 'short-term' foreign experts were deemed of sufficient consequence to constitute a security threat to the Chinese, and thereby warrant a high level of scrutiny.

The topic of 'Form' and 'Content' sometimes came up over mealtimes in the Friendship Guesthouse restaurant, and it was a fascinating issue. Such discussions usually arose from the many events and manifestations of Chinese life. It seemed that no matter how impoverished the quality of the Chinese reality around us, 'Form' always had to be expressed positively, and be well-wrapped verbally. Public statements and political pronouncements were always a virtual enhancement based on the projected goal of the sunny climes of 'Socialism' for all the people. I was constantly bemused by the many public speeches or articles by top leaders and Party cadres that started with the positive statement that 'the situation in China is excellent…' and carried on in this vein, as this was completely out of kilter with my reading of the Chinese actuality that I saw every day, and their position and status in the world. On the other hand, from the viewpoint of the Chinese leaders, the situation in the mid-1960s could well have been regarded as excellent, when compared to the harsh realities of life prior to 1949.

So the Chinese seemed to place a lot of importance on 'Form', rather than on 'Content', and in propaganda terms of keeping the country informed of the progress under socialism, it was absolutely essential for maintaining public morale and work output. This emphasis on appearance, could possibly be related to Chinese face and traditions, and should not be claimed as an original characteristic of New China. One notable leader with a more balanced approach was P'eng Chen [Peng Zhen[10]], Mayor of Peking up to June 1966, who listed a litany of shortcomings in his speech at the National Day Parade on 1st October, 1965. Bearing in mind that most political leaders tend to shy away from speaking of harsh realities, one can find faint echoes of this approach in other countries too, though it is not so common in Britain, because of the freedom of information, and an active press and media. China then only had government-controlled press, radio and film.

This Chinese pattern of overstatement was a different ballgame to the classic British 'understatement' trait of my first years 1943-45, during World War II, at the Crypt Grammar School, in the City of Gloucester, where boasting and exaggerating your achievements, with a few notable sporting exceptions, were not exactly the accepted norm. British society in the 1940s was more deferential than now, with clearly defined class divisions, and where everyone should know their place. To suddenly meet with this apparently overblown Chinese rhetoric, where a spade might be more than a spade, was quite unsettling to me. Another source for absorbing British social values came from living with my grandparents during the war, with grandma's homilies littering my brain. One of them related to giving presents to family members, and her mantra was that however modest the present, it is the sincerity of the thought that counts! Since living in China, and with the exception of genuine Chinese friends and my old Chinese pupils and colleagues, I have rarely been able to assess the 'sincerity' of a Chinese present, because of the complex web of polite and social obligations within which they are culturally enmeshed.

Over time in Peking I gradually adjusted to this new format of Chinese hyperbole, and I focused attention on trying to extract the underlying truth from the official texts. It was a challenge for foreigners to try and penetrate the politico-cultural code, which shrouded the articles and official translations, in the Peking Review. Easier-to-read articles were in the English language magazines of *China Reconstructs* and *China Pictorial*, which were more factual in content.

On the Chinese side, my school colleagues were scanning the pages of the *People's Daily*, and seemed to be able to interpret what was going on at a superficial level, if not behind the scenes. They knew that relevant political information would be conveyed to them through the meetings held at school. This leads on to the re-writing of modern Chinese history for educational and propaganda purposes. Right from the beginning, the New China government has revised modern Chinese history, especially the Republic of China period from 1911 to 1949, and the history of the Communist Party from 1921. Of course, Chiang Kai-shek[11] and his Kuomintang party[12] and army, came out of it very poorly. Yet western commentators have noted that the Kuomintang armies did engage in battles with Japanese armies at various times, while the Communist armies were mainly limited to guerrilla actions.

When comparing the nineteenth century message of 'Chinese Essence-Western Application' with the 1960s, the appropriate slogan during our stay could well have been 'Western Essence-Chinese Application'; the direct opposite of the original slogan. In effect, China was now attempting to practice a form of socialist government based on the European philosophy and writings of Marx and Engels. Admittedly these ideas had been tested and shaped by Lenin, in the furnace of the Soviet Union's revolutionary struggles, before being taken up by Mao, who had then combined this thinking, plus his own original ideas, into a socialist mould appropriate to the Chinese reality. This may have made socialism more understandable to the Chinese people, if not necessarily more acceptable. It was a sublime effort by Mao to attempt to change the thinking and culture of his country, after more than two thousand years of unbroken history, by imposing a socialist system of governance, structured on foreign theories, onto China. Perhaps this was asking too much of the Chinese people.

By the time of the Cultural Revolution the underlying philosophy had metamorphosed into 'Marxism-Leninism-Mao Tse-tung Thought', a troika of Marx, Lenin and Mao, with Maoism as the leading ideology. Although absorbed into the 'democratic centralism'[13] structure of the communist party, a concept that was practised in the Russian revolution, the Chinese leadership, not unexpectedly after two thousand years of tradition, still exhibited some imperial similarities with the old dynastic styles of governing.

Mao and Teng, the last two veteran leaders of twentieth century China, who had survived from the early days of the communist party, showed Emperor-like tendencies at times.

When first meeting the idea of 'democratic centralism' out of the blue, I felt quite puzzled as it seemed to be a contradiction in meaning, but on investigation it proved to be much more complex. I see it, in one way, as an attempt to limit and control any growth of individual power in a party structure. That is, by requiring shared decision-making at all levels of the hierarchy, it was to be a check and restraint on any one man, such as Mao Tse-tung, acquiring total autocratic authority, just like the Emperors of old. James Bertram[14], a New Zealander who was working in China for the *London Times* newspaper, interviewed Mao on this very topic of 'democratic centralism' in October 1937, and the talks are recorded in Volume II of the *Selected Works of Mao Tse-tung*. When viewing Mao's supreme personality cult during the Cultural Revolution 1966-76, one can only wonder at how effectively 'democratic centralism' worked in China during those days. It is difficult to assess exactly how much Chinese officialdom, in a self-protective mode, helped to boost and elevate the cult during the social maelstrom of the Cultural Revolution, and how much Mao himself encouraged it. Mao, in one way, could be seen as a privileged prisoner in the hands of the top layers of the communist party leadership.

Nevertheless, it should be said that socialism itself was, in essence, a foreign and invasive ideology, even when embodying a solid rump of Chinese reality, and when resting on the four pillars of Volumes I-IV of the *Selected Works of Mao Tse-tung*. To implant it into Chinese culture, was a daunting task and it would surely need continual distillations until it became a purer form of 'Chinese' socialism. This was not to be, because when Teng Hsiao-ping finally replaced Chairman Mao as the paramount power -holder in the late 1970s, he changed the priorities on policies, and China took a new direction, although still adhering to a modified socialist framework. In 1979 Teng Hsiao-ping declared the 'Four Cardinal Principles' underpinning China's future:

1. *We must keep to the socialist road*
2. *We must uphold the dictatorship of the proletariat*
3. *We must uphold the leadership of the Communist Party*
4. *We must uphold Marxism-Leninism-MaoTse-tung Thought*

Chapter Notes
1. First Opium War- Wikipedia online
2. Treaty of Nanking- Wikipedia online
3. Macau- Wikipedia online
4. Canton System- Wikipedia online
5. Taiping Rebellion- Wikipedia online
6. Zeng Guo.Fan- Wikipedia online
7. Li Hong.zhang- Wikipedia online
8. Self-Strengthening Movement- Wikipedia online
9. Essence-Function- Wikipedia online
10. Peng Zhen- Wikipedia online
11. Chiang Kai-shek- Wikipedia online

12. Kuomintang (Guo.min.dang)- Wikipedia online
13. Democratic Centralism- Wikipedia online
14. James Munro Bertram- Wikipedia online

18

LOOKING AT MY DIARY-AUGUST 1966

Saturday 6th August 1966

We arrived back from a delightful seaside holiday at Pei Tai Ho [Bei.dai.he] [1] by train, into Peking and its 'tiger heat'. The stifling humidity and stickiness was such that we drank many bottles of lemonade between four of us in the dining-car during the journey. Back home in the Druzhba, friends told us that during the preceding week many flat-back lorries, crammed full of standing people, had been passing the Guesthouse to go to Peking University [Bei.da] to see the struggles going on there, where the Principal, Lu P'ing, and other leaders, were under heavy criticism and attack. This is the same Lu P'ing who, eight years previously during the Great Leap Forward, had complained "So many factory workshops have been established on the campus. Shall I be the director of a university or a factory?"

Not much heavy traffic had passed by the Druzhba in the previous eighteen months of our stay, and now we were able to see for ourselves this extraordinary movement of lorries and people over the next few days. The main traffic was in the mornings and returning in the evenings. The people, judging by their age and clothing, seemed to be mainly students and teachers, office staff and factory workers, and we estimated their numbers in the thousands; but as far as we could see no peasants were involved. It was the busy season in the countryside.

Monday 8th August

Went in to school in a Guesthouse taxi to see our Head of English, and to request a Letter of Permission from the school for me to travel to Sian [Xi.an] and Loyang [Luo.yang] on my own, for a five day visit. Old Chang [Zhang] said that he would get this done, and so I went to the central Railway Station, and flushed with the guileless belief that I would get the coveted stamp of bureaucratic approval, I advance booked a soft sleeper berth to Sian for the following Friday afternoon. From a political angle, and quite unbeknown to us, this date of 8 August 1966 was highly significant for China, because the Central Committee of the Chinese Communist Party issued their Sixteen Points[2] decision on the future implementation of the Great Proletarian Cultural Revolution. After months of infighting at the top over the way forward, it signified that Chairman Mao was finally in control.

Wednesday 10th August

I collected the letter from school and went straight to the central Kung An [Gong.an] public security office to complete an application form for permission to travel to Sian, giving 12th August as my leaving date. A friendly Chinese man in the waiting room helped me to fill it in. The official said I should collect it on Friday.

Waddi and I went to the Kung An office by taxi and collected my travel permit which I discovered was for Loyang only, and not Sian. So I had got a yes and a no; half success, half failure. I can see now that the constant struggles that foreigners had with Chinese bureaucracy created an adverse environment, and we knew we could not win. I should have been satisfied to get this travel permit and gone solely to Loyang, but I did not. I had to act quickly about my already booked soft-sleeper to Sian for that afternoon. Our taxi was waiting outside, so we got in and headed off straight to school.

We found Old Chang and he said that they had been told by phone that foreigners were only permitted in Sian when accompanied by an official interpreter. I said that I would prefer to wait until that could be arranged, and in fact I did make a three day excursion with a Chinese colleague to Sian in November 1966. At my request, Old Chang then phoned the railway station and cancelled my soft sleeper. Although he had helped me quite a lot, he still looked rather embarrassed, and he gave us our salaries on the spot, three days in advance. No doubt it was a sop to foreign feelings, but it was good psychology too.

Bolstered by eight hundred yuan in our pockets, in five and ten yuan notes, we went to Liu Li Ch'ang³ and collected an old scroll that had been sitting there for many months being restored, and then we indulgently went straight to the Peace Café in Tung An market for a western meal. The Peace Café was empty, except for the part-owner, one of the few fat Chinese men I ever saw over my two year stay, sitting in his usual chair by the bar, and we exchanged a few words. Just to be clear, he was plump and fat around the waist by Chinese standards, but he was nowhere near the obesity of today's western world. Although he acted as though he was overseeing a major fiefdom, the cafe had nothing special in its atmosphere, except that there was a nondescript inner door at the back, which led into a Japanese restaurant. His cafe was just a little western-style restaurant in joint ownership between the state and private enterprise, and that's where he came in. It was a cosy environment for foreigners though, and we treated ourselves to iced coffees and mixed grills. We had no inkling, that with only six days to go before the first Red Guard Mass Rally in Tienanmen on 18 August, and the subsequent release of those shock troops on urban society, the fat proprietor's world was about to be shattered and his privileged days finished. I never saw him again.

As a further indulgence, we then went to No 19, the Friendship Shop, still open to foreigners, which was just round the corner from the Peace café, and spent some time gazing hypnotically at the gold, silver and jade, as well as the mass of gemstones and jewellery. Most of the valuable gemstones on display had never impinged on my life before China. In my previous existence, I had been quite content to buy tiger-eye and coral jewellery, within the budget of a teacher's salary. Now I was elevated into a world of new favourites of turquoise and lapis lazuli, not to mention jade. In the end we bought a cheaper rubystone ring.

Sunday & Monday 14th & 15th August

The last week had seen a gradual decline in the passage of lorries taking people to Peking University, but this was offset by an increasing number of marchers in town with red flags, drums, cymbals, other noisy instruments, and posters of Chairman Mao. As a sign of the growing instability, more and more shops and stores might be closed at any time, with notices on the doors saying 'Kai hui' (Meeting). The large parades reached a peak on Sunday and Monday, August 14 & 15. We heard reports that on the Monday a huge 'Exhibition' meeting of 60,000 people had been held in the Workers Stadium, where Lu P'ing and other leading capitalist roaders from Peking University were criticised and humiliated.

Tuesday & Wednesday 16th & 17th August

On Tuesday the tempo in town was much quieter with minimal parading. Wednesday saw a gathering of parades near to the Hsin Hua [Xin Hua] Gate, the entrance to the Zhongnanhai[4] compound, where Mao and the top leadership lived.

Thursday 18th August

No transport left the Friendship Guesthouse, and foreigners were kept away from Tienanmen and central areas, where the first Mass Red Guard Rally took place. According to reports, at 5 a.m. that morning, way before the rally speeches started, Chairman Mao was in the Square meeting groups of Red Guards. He was wearing an olive green military uniform with a very visible Red Guard armband. The opening address was by Ch'en Po-ta[5], leader of the Cultural Revolution Group, which, for a time, became almost as powerful as the Standing Committee. Other speakers were Nieh Yuantzu, a student leader from Peking University, and college and middle school students from Peking, Harbin, Changsha and Nanking. The first key person to speak was Marshal Lin Piao, Minister of Defence, who gave a rousing speech of incitement aimed at unleashing the Red Guards on to the streets. Premier Chou spoke next, using a heavily watered-down and paraphrased version of Lin's sentiments. Seeing the weekly newsreel of the event a few days later, Chou looked so pale and pressurised that I felt his heart was not in it. I noted that (President) Liu Shao-chi's name had dropped down to eighth place in the list of the leadership hierarchy, as recorded in Peking Review.

Friday 19th August

Went into town on the 10 a.m. coach and returned on the 11.30 a.m. one. It gave us barely an hour in town, but we could see events in Wangfuching, and also the nearby section of Chang An boulevard. It was quieter today, although there were large numbers of students with red arm bands, both plain and printed, on the streets.

Saturday 20th August

Purposeful groups of Red Guards, definitely in organised groups, were going into shops, stores, hairdressers, cafes and all establishments along Wangfuching, and checking them out. There were little groups of animated activity everywhere. Red Guards were starting to remove, cover or break up any existing shop names that could be regarded as feudal, non-socialist or non-revolutionary.

That evening we had dinner in the Moscow Restaurant with Professor Bob Winter, who taught at Peking University, and he gave us an outline of the situation there, and confirmed that the huge rally criticising the leadership had taken place on Monday 15 August. One change in the restaurant that we immediately noticed was the number of

Chinese dining there, so the previous rule of 'foreigners only' must have been modified. The Moscow was an extremely large, cavernous restaurant with very high ceilings, and one of the restaurant walls had a huge mural of Moscow on it, which was now completely covered over by white sheeting. It made me wonder if anything had happened to the carved-in-stone inscription from the 1950s, at the nearby Exhibition Hall, that stated "Sino-Soviet Friendship is Indestructible". Suddenly, in the middle of our meal, six male Red Guards walked in and surveyed the place. I assessed them as higher education or research students. Several displayed distinctive Chinese traits of power, with the aplomb and swagger of generals that reminded me vaguely of the stylised body language of old Peking Opera. Their presence severely disconcerted all the diners, Chinese and foreign, who eyed them discreetly and nervously, until they withdrew. I was sure that they would be back in force the next day, to 'struggle' against the management.

Sunday 21ˢᵗ August

We all went into town on the 10 a.m. coach, and returned on the 11.30 a.m. one. On reaching Wangfuching the coach was reduced to barely a walk, because the street and pavements were jam-packed with people. An air of intense expectancy was around. All the old stores and shop names had been covered over and replaced by sheets of paper with new, handwritten names boldly inscribed on, such as Revolutionary, East Wind, Advance, Long March, East is Red, Red Flag, Victory, Cultural Revolution, and 'Peasants-Workers-Soldiers'. For some reason the Big Store [Bai.huo da.lou] still retained its name, and had been spared this onslaught. Tung An (East peace) market was now Tung Feng (East wind) market, Wangfuching was Great Revolutionary road, and Chang An avenue was Communism avenue. Shop frontages and glass windows were being covered with small hsiao tzu-pao and large ta tzu-pao [6] handwritten and cyclo-styled posters, reciting all the key points from Lin Piao's speech, and these were being issued by various Middle Schools, most prominent of which were Nos 13, 21, 29 and Coal Hill.

No-one paid much attention to us as we soaked it all in, and we slowly made our way to the dear old Peace café, now also temporarily renamed the Tung Feng (East wind) café. It was chaos there, as the headwaiter and two staff members were vainly defending the entrance, and saying it was only for wai.bin (foreign guests). They happily welcomed us in, as two real-life examples, and we found the interior fully lit and bare, and for the first time, a few Chinese customers sitting in place. The electric fans, coloured neon lighting, cut-outs of peace doves, extraneous decorations and the menus had all disappeared. The old, fat joint-owner was not present either.

Monday 22ⁿᵈ August

We got the 10 a.m. coach into town. Wangfuching was again very crowded, with a tense atmosphere. A lot of people filled the Advancing Barbers shop, with Red Guards controlling the doors, and a huge crowd standing outside. The staff there were undergoing criticism and being denounced for their bourgeois tendencies of offering western-style haircuts. Similar scenarios were occurring up and down Wangfuching. The road seemed packed with thousands of people and I felt that the mood was unfriendly. I also felt quite vulnerable as I was carrying a camera slung around my neck.

We gradually realised that we were being trailed by two Red Guard girls, aged, we guessed at around 15-16, so we made our way to the sanctuary of the Friendship Store, which was closed to Chinese people. After a suitable cooling down period, we ventured out and made another visit to the Tung Feng café, while noticing that this time two young Red Guard boys were trailing us, but they didn't enter the café. Even more changes had taken place since yesterday. This time all the bottles behind the counter had gone, and the wall mirror there was covered by an exhortation of Lin Piao's: "Read Chairman Mao's works and Listen to Chairman Mao's words", with a big picture of Mao above it. A saying of Mao's covered another wall, but we could see that the original Peace Café neon name sign was still in place.

Tuesday 23rd August

Atmosphere much the same as yesterday, with a continuation of little struggle meetings taking place in shops, and along the pavements of Wangfuching. According to the new names, all the shops and stores in joint ownership had been changed to public control. There seemed to be thousands milling about on the street, and small groups of Red Guards would randomly accost any bourgeois looking passers-by. If their answers were not to the Red Guards' satisfaction, then within seconds the recipients suffered a criticism and denunciation scene on the spot. Narrow trousers had one leg cut off, western-style clothes were ridiculed, permed hair criticised and the traditional long plaits cut off. In effect the trousers, clothes and permed hair manifested a bourgeois mentality, while the long plaits were examples of decadent, old Chinese habits. I was told that the female Red Guards wielding large scissors on the streets were called the 'steamrollers'. Hong Kong styles were in the firing line too, and this was seen as an oblique attack on Shanghai and Canton as spheres of real or potential bourgeois tendencies. The wall posters, big and small, and of various colours, now covered every inch of space on shop frontages, and the layers were getting thicker. Content wise, the posters had four main threads: Criticising, Denouncing, Warning, Suggesting.

Wednesday 24th August

A brief foray along Wangfuching, which was not so crowded today, and I saw the 'steamrollers' in action. They accosted one young woman of around thirty with two long plaits, walking by with an older man who I took to be her husband, and he was holding a young child. The young female Red Guard brandishing the scissors looked about 16, and in less than ten seconds she had cut off one plait, while both the victim, and her husband, seemed dazed and unable to speak. There was no discussion. The victim was guilty because her hairstyle represented one of the Four Olds[7] (Old Customs, Old Habits, Old Culture, Old Thinking) of the exploiting class, the main targets for the Red Guards, as instructed by Chairman Mao. I just had time to get my camera out and focus it, before I was pushed back by a swarming crowd of onlookers, and then the second plait was neatly chopped off. As I walked away I realised that I was very lucky that as a foreigner, openly using a camera on a crowded street in central Peking, no-one had apparently noticed me, or at least had done anything about it. This freedom, which I tried not to abuse, continued for the next four months in Peking, until our two year contracts expired.

Walking further up the street I saw a crowd ahead, which slowly broke up and from it emerged two young women who looked to be in their twenties. They were arm in arm, with one crying her eyes out, and the other, who happened to have short bobbed hair, was smiling and holding her friend's two long plaits, that had just been cut off.

Thursday 25th August

I went into town on the 10 a.m. Friendship coach, and even as we drove into town, things looked more serious today. As we slowly sailed through the Hsitan [Xi.dan[8]] intersection, everyone could see that there was a cowed man and voluble Red Guard standing together on a table, surrounded by a large crowd. After some initial comments from other foreigners, we all went rather quiet, and then just after that a three wheeled truck passed by, with a man tied up and three Red Guards guarding him. As we watched from the safety of the coach, one Red Guard roughly forced his head down as he was trying to look up. It was my first glimpse of the violent side of the Cultural Revolution. And definitely not a day for taking photos.

Wangfuching was packed with people again, and there were still small groups present in most of the shops and stores. The loudspeaker relay system was broadcasting non-stop to the crowds, while many lorries driving by were full of Red Guards in khaki type uniforms, probably off on assignments to storm some bureaucratic enclave. Not many PLA soldiers were out and about on the streets, but several were on duty guarding the Friendship Store, and the only policemen I saw were those on traffic duties at the main junctions along Chang An boulevard.

Friday 26th August

We went into town on the afternoon coach and decided to visit the Catholic Convent of the Sacred Heart, situated just off Wangfuching, and close to the Hsieh Ho Hospital. I had never questioned the anomaly of this foreign presence in the very political heart of socialist China, but had just accepted it as being one of the few perks of life for foreign families. The nuns were Belgian and French, and they ran a tiny English-medium school for foreign children, with a small contingent of pupils from Druzhba families travelling there every morning in a mini-bus, and coming back at lunchtime.

Digression

Our oldest son Tim, after reaching his fifth birthday, had become a pupil there for the spring term of 1966, and he seemed to like it. It was definitely old-style teaching of the Three 'R's, combined with strict discipline, and very reminiscent of my own primary school days, twenty five years before. We always went to meet Tim off the school bus every lunchtime, and one day we had a great shock because he was not on the bus. None of the other pupils or the driver knew anything of his whereabouts or could help in any way. Completely bewildered and desperate, we thought of phoning the convent so we rushed to the Foreign Experts Bureau office to get them to phone, but it was closed for lunch. Then we decided to get a taxi downtown straightaway, calling in to our school to pick up an interpreter, when suddenly in the middle of this frantic melee, the daily coach back from the Friendship Store arrived, with Tim safely on board. Somehow he had missed the departure of the school bus, and couldn't get back into the school because the doors were closed. Crying his eyes out, he had had the wits about him to run to the nearby Friendship Store, about three hundred metres away, where he was able to explain himself to the Chinese staff, and they looked after him until the

Guesthouse coach left soon afterwards. In later years he told us that while running to the Store, several old Chinese ladies had asked him what the matter was, but he didn't stop to talk to them.

Friday 26th August Continued

As we walked towards that convent on that Friday afternoon, I felt the atmosphere, judging by the sea of Chinese faces, to be very unfriendly. All the convent windows were full of Red Guards, red flags were flying everywhere, with a lot of activity going on, but there were no signs of the nuns. Wall posters stuck on convent walls said things such as "Yang gui.zi gun.dan" (Foreign devils be off[8]), "Foreign Imperialist women be off" and "Foreign Imperialist women get out of China". Over the entrance doors it said "Your time is near!" We didn't stay, and I didn't risk taking any photos. On the coach journey back we witnessed two separate incidents on the streets of a man, and then two youths, being led off by Red Guards, presumably for further investigation. I was beginning to be glad that I was not Chinese.

That evening we got a taxi to the National Minorities Hotel in central Peking to meet our friends Neale and Deirdre Hunter, who had just finished a holiday tour around China, organised by their host Foreign Languages Institute in Shanghai, and they had only arrived in Peking the previous night. They had spent the day trying to visit religious establishments in Peking, and one of their first calls had been to the Convent of the Sacred Heart, but the road was closed to them. It turned out that that very morning the nuns had been paraded outside the Convent, publicly denounced, and forced to bow and kneel before the Red Guards. Rather reminiscent of kowtowing[9] to the Emperor in the old days. We soon heard on the BBC World service that eight nuns had been expelled from China, and were now in Hong Kong.

Neale and Deirdre had also been barred from visiting the mosque, but they heard that a pig's head had been placed inside, and the imam had been manhandled. All the churches and two cathedrals that they could get close to were closed, with wall posters of criticism on display, and one church had most of its windows broken, plus a large red flag flying from its steeple. They were both visibly shaken by their day in Peking, and after our meal, we had coffees up on the roof garden, before a violent downpour sent us indoors. Another disturbing event for them was the news of the suicide of a Chinese businessman, married to an English woman they knew, in Shanghai. The next day they went to get their train back to Shanghai, and found that the railway station was packed with Red Guards. As they made their way to their comfortable soft sleeper compartment, they realised that the train was transporting a huge contingent of Peking Red Guards, the first of many, going down to Shanghai to carry out Chairman Mao's orders, and to wreak havoc in the process. Their train arrived in Shanghai on Sunday 28th August 1966.

Postscript

Right at the beginning of September 1966, we received a letter by post from the British Charge D'Affaires Office in Peking, saying that they were ready to help any British subjects who needed it. It was much appreciated by us, but the Institute and our school were looking after all the foreign teachers, and anti-foreign Han chauvinism[10] had not fully reared its head. It grew through 1967 though, culminating in August with the attacking, and partial burning of the British Charge D'Affaires Office, and the manhandling of diplomatic staff. Other Embassies in Peking, and their staff, were hounded by Red Guards too.

Chapter Notes
1. Beidaihe District- Wikipedia online
2. Sixteen Points: see Cultural Revolution- Wikipedia online
3. Liulichang- Wikipedia online
4. Zhongnanhai- Wikipedia online
5. Chen Boda- Wikipedia online
6. Big Character poster- Wikipedia online
7. Four Olds- Wikipedia online
8. Xidan- Wikipedia online
9. Kowtow- Wikipedia online
10. Han chauvinism- Wikipedia online

19

RED GUARD RALLIES IN PEKING IN 1966

18 AUGUST   31 AUGUST   15 SEPTEMBER   1 OCTOBER (National Day)

18 OCTOBER   3 NOVEMBER   18/19 NOVEMBER   25/26 NOVEMBER

During the four months from August to November 1966 Chairman Mao reviewed eight huge Mass Red Guard Rallies[1] in Peking, the first six of which took place in Tienanmen Square, with Chairman Mao and top leaders on the rostrum of the main gate. At the penultimate rally, Chairman Mao and top leaders were in a convoy of cars that slowly traversed along the length of Chang An boulevard. The final rally, over November 25/26, was held at Tienanmen Square, and on the second day at Hsiyuan military airfield in the western outskirts. This meant hundreds and thousands of Red Guards[2] had to walk there in around sub-zero temperatures. The vast numbers involved and logistics for organising these eight rallies must have been an enormous problem for those responsible in the Cultural Revolution Group. These rallies were never to be repeated in the years following. To relieve pressure on the inhabitants of Peking, on the feeding and housing of these extra millions of mouths and on the transport systems, after the last rally it became necessary to start to return the Red Guards back to their home provinces.

Selected foreigners and visiting foreign dignitaries, were invited to attend some rallies, but for foreign experts there was no official movement of coaches or taxis leaving the Friendship Guesthouse on those days. The one exception was National Day, 1st October 1966.

In the early years of the People's Republic of China, every October the First was celebrated as National Day, and it was a public holiday, during which an imposing and lengthy parade, replicating the Soviet model in Red Square in Moscow, and lasting for several hours, took place through Tienanmen Square in Peking. Later that evening there would be a marvellous fireworks display over the square. On the eve of National Day, a magnificent Celebratory Banquet hosted by Premier Chou En-lai would be held in the Great Hall of the People, and all the foreign experts would be invited. Chairman Mao did not attend such public events, and the keynote speech would be given by Premier Chou.

We were lucky enough to see the last of these parades in 1965 before the onset of the Cultural Revolution. It consisted of many huge, colourful mechanised floats showing the achievements of 'workers and peasants' since liberation in 1949, interspersed with huge numbers of them dancing, singing or performing. The militaristic side included highly disciplined groups of marching soldiers and a small display of military hardware that we had to assume came mainly from Russia, while the basic transport equipment on show, included lorries and jeeps that were home-produced. China had imported a few UK Land Rovers, which we sometimes saw on the streets, but on that day they didn't appear. Presumably the Chinese were already working on the production of their own manufactured version of it.

According to the traditional agricultural calendar the weather in Peking in early October was completely predictable and always good. No weather forecast was needed because we knew in advance that it would be dry with blue sky and sunshine; quite a difference to the vagaries of the British weather. And that year one group of male soldiers paraded in swimming costumes, while another small detachment was doing the 'goose step'. Pollution was not an everyday issue in those days, and there was no sign of any noxious layers hanging over Peking. However, during our second contract in 1974-76, we often went to the Western Hills, and everyone could see the thin veil of pollution lying over the city then. Unfortunately, the level of pollution there today is dreadful, and on some days a yellowish blanket hides the sunshine and blue sky.

The first Red Guards rally, on Thursday 18 August 1966, was the crucial day on which the educated youth were given Mao's instructions by Lin Piao, to take to the streets, and destroy the Four Olds (customs, culture, habits, ideas) of the exploiting class, and build the Four News. *Peking Review* of 26 August 1966 headlined it as "Chairman Mao Joins a Million People to Celebrate the Great Cultural Revolution". Here is a brief extract from Lin Piao's speech:

"The Great Proletarian Cultural Revolution is a great new creation in the Communist movement and in socialist revolution. It must eliminate bourgeois thinking and build proletarian thinking. We must destroy the old thinking, culture, customs and habits of the exploiting class. We must remove those in power who follow the capitalist road, bourgeois reactionary authority, bourgeois royalists and all monsters and devils. The masses are the creators of history. If they use Mao Tse-tung's thinking they will become an irresistible force with unlimited power."

The weekly film show in the Friendship Guesthouse always included documentary newsreels of things happening in China and these were excellent historical records of those times. None more so than the newsreels of the early months of the Cultural Revolution. After the third rally on 15th September we saw film of Premier Chou looking ashen-faced, obviously in a turmoil about what was happening, but he seemed to be hanging on to his battered political status and prestige. And he gave the secondary speech after Lin Piao, at the first four Mass Rallies. Then in October, coming into the top tranche of leadership faces was a new effeminate man in army uniform, who foreigners didn't recognise, until told by their Chinese colleagues that it was Chiang Ching [Jiang Qing- Mrs.Mao].

October 1st, National Day, in 1966, was quite different because of the Great Proletarian Cultural Revolution which had officially taken off in May that year. This National Day Parade was in actual reality a Cultural Revolution Rally, where Chairman Mao received the masses of revolutionary Red Guards and teachers. Tienanmen Square itself, said to cover 400,000 square metres, was packed tight with Red Guards, many tens of thousands, even before the parade started. Ch'en Po-ta [Chen Bo.da][3], as head of the Cultural Revolution Group officially opened the proceedings. Marshal Lin Piao, who was closely working with Mao Tse-tung at that time, and was his mouthpiece at such events, again made the key speech, which was relayed over the extensive loudspeaker system covering a wide area around the city centre. His words were completely direct, welcoming the Red Guards, praising them and supporting them in their actions since 18 August of carrying out this great Cultural Revolution according to the instructions of the Great Leader, Chairman Mao. As with the previous three rallies, the supporting speaker was Premier Chou En-lai, but his words were calmer, and did not have the ardour and zeal of Lin Piao's speeches.

Later on, as the Cultural Revolution developed, Mao was accorded the accolade of the Four Greats: Great Teacher, Great Leader, Great Commander and Great Helmsman. Mao is reported to have criticised the growth of his personality cult, but for any sycophants and cynical acolytes at all levels, it was in their self-interests, and for their self-protection, to raise his national prestige to sublime heights. As for the believers in Mao and his Way, even though they might not like these machinations, how could they oppose his elevation to exalted status?

Then the march past began, led by an advance guard of twenty thousand PLA and militia men, followed by a huge, wide river of Red Guards waving their Little Red Books, who slowly walked and eddied from east to west along Chang An (now renamed 'The East is Red') boulevard, and past the rostrum on the Tienanmen Gate where Mao stood. Peking Review of 7 October 1966 reported that one and half million Red Guards took part, walking 140 abreast, including worker and peasant groups, revolutionary intellectuals, cadres, teachers and students; and the parade stretched for dozens of kilometres! They were carrying banners, placards and slogans exhorting their support for Chairman Mao and the Cultural Revolution, and chanting continuously 'Mao Chu-hsi wan sui' [Mao Zhu.xi wan sui[. "Long Live Chairman Mao" was the key slogan of the Red Guards. Movement was very slow and disorganised, because every one of them wanted to see Chairman Mao on the rostrum, and so the whole process took more than six hours.

On either side of the great Tienanmen Gate and below it, there were a series of sixteen smaller reviewing side stands which housed an amazing assortment of 'Special Categories' of guests and visitors from all over the world: Invitees were from a range of fraternal socialist countries, including little Albania, their leading supporter in Europe. Various African states just liberated from colonial control e.g. Ghana and Algeria. Independence leaders, freedom fighters and revolutionary groups from Latin America, Arab and African states such as Colombia, Mozambique, Palestine and South Africa. North Vietnam was fighting her war of unification in 1966, so they were represented. As were any 'friendly' countries well-disposed towards China.

On the diplomatic side, the Ambassadorial corps in Peking were all present. The major absentee from this line-up was the US[4], who didn't establish full diplomatic relations with Peking until 1979. From the capitalist west, any Marxists or progressives, accorded the status of 'foreign friend', and who supported the Chinese line rather than the Moscow line, might be invited, as well as the small body of 'foreign experts' resident in China. As Peking Review described it "Reviewing the parade on the rostrum were noted revolutionary fighters against imperialism from the Five Continents. Friends from more than seventy countries and regions attended the National Day celebrations". On the rostrum itself, with Mao, there were twenty six of the top Chinese leadership, including President Liu Shao-chi and General Secretary Teng Hsiao-ping, with the last name on that list being Chiang Ching. This was public affirmation of her increasing political involvement, which culminated in her becoming de facto leader of the Gang of Four, until her arrest in 1976, after Chairman Mao's demise. Also present on the rostrum in the background were a vast array of Central Committee members.

I remember that day as very noisy and frenetic. During the course of the parade, Chairman Mao came to each end of the rostrum to wave to the masses, so all we side-standers could see this recognisable head and shoulders above us on the main gate. Foreign experts, being of lowly status in this Chinese hierarchy of importance, compared to this array of foreign dignitaries and guests, occupied the furthest stand from the main gate so we only saw a very small silhouette of Chairman Mao.

But our humble vantage point had unexpected advantages for us. We were right next to smaller, temporary stands, which were packed with chanting Red Guards. We could watch them freely, and what's more photograph them without fear of causing an incident. Something that could be distinctly unwise and unpredictable if done at any time on the streets of Peking. And the constant background noise level came from hundreds of thousands of Red Guards continually waving the Little Red Book and repeating the rallying-cry of "Long Live Chairman Mao".

From the beginning of the Cultural Revolution, the bulk of Mao's 'Little Generals' were aged around 15-30, coming from junior and senior middle schools, colleges, universities and higher education institutions. On this day the ones I was close to on the adjacent stand looked like tertiary students in the 18-25 age group. Many of them seemed to be in a state of trance-like intensity, exhausted by endlessly repeating their mantra, with some of the girls in tears. The mass fervour was out of the norm to my eyes, and certainly I had not seen such a public display of emotion anywhere for the previous twenty one months of my stay in Peking. Up to then, I had felt, in my limited experience, that the Chinese generally kept their inner feelings under wraps in public, especially if foreigners were present.

On 5 September 1966 an edict had been issued that Red Guards could travel anywhere within China to exchange experiences [Chuan.lian]. Rail and bus travel was free for Red Guards, so many of them were able to come to the capital city of their country, the great majority for the first time in their lives. Legions of small bands of Red Guards, walked hundreds of kilometres to Peking, re-creating the daring spirit of the epic Long March of the mid-1930s, while many Peking students walked to Yenan [Yan.an], the revolutionary home of the Long March survivors from 1935. Some took on the much longer march to Mao's birthplace in Shaoshan [Shao.shan]. From September to November 1966, Tienanmen Square was awash with countless groups of provincial Red Guards having meetings, relaxing, sightseeing or setting off somewhere on a Long March. Numbers started thinning out in December 1966.

The educated youth tramping through the vast Chinese countryside were somehow fed and housed by the peasantry in their villages and communes. It's not clear how much the central or provincial governments helped the peasants financially in this task. According to Liang Heng[5], a Red Guard from Changsha in Hunan province, who went on a mini 'Long March', the peasants were not unfriendly and provided roadside stands supplying boiled water. In larger villages, hospitality stations, with rest shelters and primitive bedding, had been set up. Hot boiled rice in huge wooden barrels was available, but very little in the way of meat and vegetables. Similar scenarios must have been endlessly replicated across China.

In return for this support in the countryside, the Red Guards were expected to act as cultural propaganda teams, by spreading the political messages, and performing the revolutionary operas and songs of the day. Some of Mao's sayings had been put to music, in a dramatic style, so they were necessarily in vogue, and the safest pieces to sing. In effect they were coded passwords to show the correct revolutionary feelings of the singers. Red Guards were not permitted to disrupt the countryside and the peasantry, but had to concentrate all their efforts in the urban areas. In those early days, when I asked my colleague Old Chang about the Cultural Revolution, he explained that in the 1950s they had carried out Land Reform in the countryside, and now a similar type of rectification campaign was taking place in the towns and cities.

The emotional reactions of the Red Guards at this National Day rally were possibly stimulated by having had the unbelievable freedom and power to act as a destructive and hostile militia on the urban dwellers of Peking. Another ingredient could well have been some form of adulation for the charismatic figure of Chairman Mao, who was more important to them than their parents. Perhaps it was youthful belief in a powerful 'Emperor' Father figure, and the moral righteousness of being selected to carry out his instructions. To balance this idealised interpretation of Red Guards' outlook and motivation, it's as well to read Ken Ling's book[6] of his days as a young Red Guard in his hometown of Amoy [Xia.men] in Fukien [Fu.jian] province, in which he quotes the feelings and attitudes of many of these teenagers, who were anything but supportive or respectful of Chairman Mao and his policies. But they knew it was an opportunity for them to travel, and have more freedom. It was a traumatic release from their traditional shackles, and expected norms of behaviour.

For the young generation, one way of escaping the traditional family bonds of subordination to their elders, was through higher education. As educational opportunities expanded in the 1950s, more children from peasant-worker families were able to enter higher education, usually in a college a long way from home. One of our colleagues, Old Yang, was a classic example. A bright peasant boy from a village in the Nanking area of Kiangsu [Jiang.su] province, he had eventually graduated from the Peking Foreign Languages Institute, and was now a resident in the capital. He told us the saying about peasant children who left home to further their studies: "First year native, second year other, third year don't know Father-Mother".

Mao's orders to attack officials and power-holders was one area of stress for the students whose parents were very high in the political hierarchy, as it could mean Red Guards having to criticise their own parents and other family members at their places of work. In reality the Red Guards virtually had power over anybody, whether they were party members or not, by simply accusing them of being bourgeois, and against Chairman Mao's line. Red Guards were able to pick on anyone in the streets, and through the neighbourhood committees they could identify potentially bourgeois families in the urban population. They would ransack the homes of these unfortunates, and confiscate whatever they wanted. Once they had focused on a victim, a merciless onslaught of verbal denunciation, public humiliation, deprivation, physical isolation, and possibly beatings could take place. This could sometimes be so severe that the victims died or committed suicide. It is impossible to know how many such deaths took place all over Peking, and other major cities, in the first months of the Cultural Revolution in 1966.

Often the Red Guards would punish victims by exiling them from Peking, and sending residents back to their village and provincial ancestral homes. For us travelling by taxi or coach around Peking in late 1966, we could often see the consequences of this policy, when piles of old traditional furniture would be standing along the pavements await-ing disposal at the hands of the Red Guards. The second-hand shops catering for for-eigners were bursting at the seams with beautiful old furniture at very reasonable knockdown prices, but for us the expense of packing it and transporting to the UK by sea was too much.

With regard to the Red Guards behaviour on National Day 1966 it seems that the term 'hysteria' could not be applied to them. Mass hysteria usually implies some physical symptoms of discomfort arising from a period of stress, but to my eyes those young Chinese may have been under emotional stress, but they were definitely not in a state of discomfort or fear. Rather the opposite, it seemed to be a frenetic outpouring of blind idolisation of their charismatic leader, who they would give their lives for. It was may-be closer to an assemblage of religious devotees seeing their spiritual head for the first time.

These 'shock troops' seemed to carry an extreme intensity of feelings, and it is well-recorded that some of them carried out their political struggles with a fanatical holy zeal, which always led to humiliation and physical suffering for the victims, with some-times fatal consequences. Those young Chinese had little fear of arrest or reprimand because the police force and most instruments of law were submerged by the civil chaos of Chinese life. Their initial onslaught after 18 August 1966 must have impacted on the leadership though, because at the second rally on 31 August, Lin Piao warned the Red Guards specifically against using force and coercion, and instructed them not to hit peo-ple. Whatever effect these words had, it was difficult to stop their momentum.

It is not easy to assess Chairman Mao's charisma based on western criteria. He never gave public speeches, so it was not based on his oratory. As an Emperor-type figure he still had a tenuous hold on the Mandate of Heaven, even after the three years of starva-tion and deaths of 1959-61 following the Great Leap Forward. His influence and pow-erbase had been weakened and he had lost some control in the interim, but he had led the Chinese people to stand up and regain their self-respect, independence and sover-eignty in 1949, and he was the figurehead of New China. Those Red Guards at the mass rallies were effectively in sway to him, whether they were believers or not, and they obeyed him implicitly. I felt that if they had been told to save Chairman Mao from drowning in the Yangtze river, most of them would have jumped into the water regard-less of whether they could swim or not.

During the beginning of the Great Leap Forward movement in 1958, Ke Qing.shi, a close comrade of Chairman Mao, had allegedly issued this command to the educated youth: "Believe in Chairman Mao to the degree of blind worship, Obey Chairman Mao to the degree of blind faith." These precepts were being revived in the Cultural Revolu-tion, as the Red Guards were being asked to use all their efforts to destroy the adminis-trative structure of their country. No wonder the Chinese people describe that period from 1966 to 1976 as the Ten Lost Years. The social disorder, civil upheavals and in-ternal struggles were at their worst over the three years 1966-68, and those years are the historical timeframe of the last great movement of Mao's tenure in power.

Even though there was semi-anarchy in parts of China during those years, the military remained in place to control the excesses of the Red Guards. The top government ad-ministration just about functioned and lumbered along, with industry and the communes working on. Premier Chou En-lai, and other like-minded cadres, worked ceaselessly to preserve some semblance of social order in their country. An example of this business as usual was China's shop window to the world, the bi-annual Canton Trade Fair (Chinese Export Commodities Fair), which continued without a break during the Cultural Revolution. Twice a year for two weeks, in the spring and autumn, Canton [Guang.zhou] was host to hundreds of foreign business personnel eager to buy Chinese products. In autumn 1966, the foreign visitors were subject to the Red Guards enthusiasm for spreading the gospel of Mao's Thought. One apocryphal story concerns a foreign businessman whose evenings in his hotel room had to include reading Chairman Mao's sayings with a small group of male and female Red Guards. After two sessions he had had enough, so the next evening when they knocked on his door he opened it naked, and the shrieking Red Guards retreated down the corridor.

Bertrand Russell, in his book *The Problem of China*, proposed a Chinese characteristic, which may be relevant when contemplating the anarchic conditions of the Great Proletarian Cultural Revolution. He visited China on a lecture tour in 1921, the very year of the foundation of the Chinese Communist Party. That was only ten years after the seismic collapse of the Imperial dynastic system of government, and the subsequent social instability of those times may have influenced him:

> *"I have been speaking of the Chinese as they are in ordinary life, when they appear as men of active and sceptical intelligence, but of somewhat sluggish passions. There is, however, another side to them; they are capable of wild excitement, often of a collective kind. I saw little of this myself, but there can be no doubt of the fact. The Boxer Rebellion* [7] *was a case in point, and one which particularly affected Europeans. But their history is full of more or less analogous disturbances. It is this element in their character that makes them incalculable, and makes it impossible even to guess at their future."*

Ninety five years after Russell's visit, China is now one of the most powerful economies in the world.

Chapter Notes

1. Red Guards (China)- Wikipedia online, or see Peking Reviews 1966, at www.massline.org/PekingReview
2. Ken Ling, *Red Guard in Mao's China*, Macdonald, London, 1972.
3. Chen Boda- Wikipedia online
4. US-China Relations- Wikipedia online
5. Liang Heng, *Son of the Revolution*, Hogarth Press, London, 1983.
6. Ken Ling, *Red Guard in Mao's China*, Macdonald, London, 1972.
7. Boxer Rebellion- Wikipedia online

20

CHINA AND DEMOCRACY: SOME THOUGHTS

One 'Western' definition of a democratic state: *"A country with a government that allows freedom of speech, religion and political opinion, that upholds the rule of law and majority rule, and that respects the rights of minorities"*

In 1911, after a history of virtually two thousand years, the imperial dynastic system of government was overthrown by the Chinese people. The Chinese claim that their civilisation has been unbroken for three thousand years, with the implication that it is an advanced and superior culture. Yet after that prolonged period of time China was still a feudalistic, agricultural society, and it had produced only an autocratic form of governance, by Emperors with absolute power. The long distillation of this form of self-governance could have only come from the Chinese people themselves. That is, excluding the times that China was governed by 'barbarians': the Mongols in the Yuan dynasty, 1271-1368, and the Manchus in the Ch'ing dynasty, 1644-1911.

In the nineteenth century, apart from textiles and porcelain, the small industrial base came mainly from western sources. Whatever ideas had emerged from Chinese political thinking during the previous three millennia, no forms of remotely democratic structures could be seen at work in the governing of the country in the final centuries. The sole institution to have some apparent independence from the Emperor's grasp was the Imperial Examinations system that selected capable officials to administer the nation's affairs. That was abolished in 1905.

Compare this with Britain since the Magna Carta of 1215, where during the seven hundred years up to 1915, the power of the ruling monarchs had been slowly whittled away until state power lay in the hands of a representative parliamentary government. Granted that there was still no full democracy in the British electoral system after those seven centuries, because not all men got the vote until 1918, and women had to wait until 1928. At the same time, in other parts of Europe, states with forms of autocratic systems of governance were still in existence.

As a rule, Confucianism[1] is held to be the main bulwark of traditional Chinese social values. It was a practical construct, without any overt religious beliefs, based on a complex framework of rites and rules, and a hierarchy of relationships, containing clear inequalities. A cultivated morality for daily life was advocated for the top educated men in society (jun.zi[2]), as something to aspire to, and everyone else was subordinate to the power-holders. This Confucian social value system, which became permeated, over time, with elements of Daoism and Buddhism, had sustained the Emperor's power base over an agricultural and feudalistic China, for unchanging centuries. There had been Chinese thinkers who had acquired the requisite theoretical science base and knowledge, but they did not translate this learning into any forms of empirical practice and manufacture, such as Europeans had done in their industrial revolution. The full extent of Chinese scientific knowledge is comprehensively covered by Joseph Needham[3] in his monumental series of twenty seven volumes, entitled *Science and Civilisation in China*[4].

In 1949 the Chinese people, and Confucianism, had to come to terms with the new philosophy of socialism, which was the prevailing ideology of the incoming leadership. Socialism looked to be a powerfully dynamic force, which could bring about change and modernisation by means of mass co-operation. In contrast, the old established philosophy of the sages appeared to be a static, conservative form of thinking, concerned with establishing a standard of morality for the male individual, through social rites, virtues and behaviour. Old China's history had seen huge numbers of forced labourers, ordered by the Emperor's edicts, to work on large public projects. Mao's socialism attempted to galvanise people to take part in such work by using political movements to inspire and persuade the people, especially the young educated urbanites, towards ambitious goals. In the compulsive pressure of such movements, it was difficult to separate the degree of willingness of an individual from the degree of coercion imposed on an individual. Movements like these were commendable in theory, but often had disastrous outcomes in practice, such as in the Great Leap Forward in the countryside, and the Cultural Revolution. Socialism appeared to have a group dynamic at its core, whereas the Confucian way only preached a code of ethics for the educated man.

A different, and more positive, assessment of Confucianism has been taking place, especially since the economy took off in the 1980s and 1990s. Some Western, Chinese and other academics have written on the key virtues of old Confucian China that seem to have been of distinct value in contributing to the recent success of some Asian economies. In recent decades, countries such as China, Japan, South Korea, and the smaller 'Tiger' economies of Hong Kong, Singapore and Taiwan, have all prospered. Professor Geert Hofstedt[5], Emeritus Professor of Organisational Anthropology at Maastricht University in The Netherlands, has focused on cross-cultural analysis, and has researched a wide range of national cultural differences. He analysed each culture according to six dimensions, in order to identify culture-specific characteristics. His research shows that particular Confucian virtues have appeared to be cornerstone values that underpin the economic success of China, and the other oriental nations. One of his most popular books *Culture & Organizations: Software of the Mind* was published by Harper Collins in 1994, and he also has an extensive collection of published work to his name in this field.

For socialism, the weighty problem was that it did not come from Chinese roots, but from European barbarians, via the harsh realities of the Russian revolution. One of Mao's achievements was to adapt and paraphrase Marxist-Leninist ideology into Chinese terms, and so integrate it into the Chinese reality, thereby, making this foreign import more understandable to the Chinese people. In the 1950s, Chinese books tended to talk about Marxism-Leninism as the basic source of socialist theory, but by the time of the Cultural Revolution in 1966 this had been expanded to Marxism-Leninism-Mao Tse-tung Thought.

When Western powers in the nineteenth century, armed with superior weapons and scientific technology, became more bellicose, China had no united front, either nationally, politically, militarily or in applied science, with which to combat them. So Britain was able to overcome any Chinese resistance in the first Opium War, leading to the unequal Treaty of Nanking[6], 1842, and the establishment of Treaty ports[7]. The British, as victors, entitled the Nanking document as 'A Treaty of Peace, Friendship and Commerce between Her Majesty the Queen of Great Britain and Ireland, and the Emperor of China.' From then on it was all downhill for the dynasty, even though some Chinese intellectuals and leading activists advocated minimal reforms and modernisations. Any such changes were swamped and neutralised by the conservatism and inflexibility of old China, and the dynasty slowly declined and collapsed in 1911. By that time China was reduced to semi-colonial status, with the eastern seaboard controlled by a cohort of western European countries, plus Russia, America and Japan. In 1949, Chinese historians assessed China's position then as being a semi-feudal and semi-colonial country, which had suffered a century of humiliation at the hands of foreigners.

In the political and social upheavals that followed the downfall of the dynastic system in 1911, China had to find a way out of the morass. The intellectual ferment produced waves of new thinking, such as the 'New Thought Movement' of 1915-1919, which looked outside China for solutions to her instability and woes, and favoured various forms of constitutional government. It looked inwards too, and Confucian thinking came under criticism. At the same time, democracy was praised, even though China had had no traditional experience of this form of governance. Chen Tu-hsiu [Chen Du.xiu[8]], a famous intellectual of the time constantly talked of Mr. Sai (science) and Mr. De (democracy), both of which he saw as crucial to China's survival and development. In 1921 he became a founding member of the Chinese Communist Party. It seemed that 'Science' and 'Democracy' were regarded as the two magical keys that could unlock China from her feudal past and set her on a road of modernisation.

Democracy has many layers and forms, and it is hard to know what the Chinese meant by democracy in those times. A new freedom for them was not to have the Emperor's yoke on their backs, and any slight relaxation of the social restraints on the Chinese people was regarded as 'democracy'. Yet in those days the huge majority of the Chinese masses in the countryside were uneducated and illiterate, which was hardly a favourable environment for the introduction of any real 'democratic' structures. The Chinese people had had a deep-rooted exposure to one man leadership, and this was possibly another inhibitor of rapid change. To change from an autocratic Emperor system in 1911, to the rule of a Standing Committee of the Chinese Communist Party in 1949, was a leap in primitive democracy. For the past hundred years since 1911, China has been toying with the concept and forms of democracy.

In 1912 Dr Sun Yat-sen[9] (1866-1925), one of the leading reformers, who became a revolutionary activist, was made provisional President of the newly-created Republic of China, with the novel political structure of a constitutional parliament. He only lasted for three months in office before being replaced by a local warlord; it was too much to expect a country of such traditions, to go from autocratic to parliamentary governance in one year. Dr Sun, a convert to Christianity, had been developing his ideas on saving China for a long time, and he promoted them in a series of lectures in 1924. These were collected into a book, *San Min Chu I* [San Min Ju Yi], translated as the 'Three Principles of the People', which were People's Nationalism, People's Sovereignty and People's Livelihood.

They were the proposed means to lead China towards salvation. In the English translation it is hard to follow some of his reasoning, because in his idea of People's Sovereignty, he intermingles the words of equality, liberty and democracy, without giving definitions of them. As I see it, by People's Sovereignty he means the freedom and independence of the masses, and he equates that to democracy. This short extract illustrates his thinking:

"So our revolutionary party in its inception took liberty and equality as aims in its struggle, but made Democracy-the Sovereignty of the People-its principle and watchword. Only if we achieve democracy can our people have the reality, and enjoy the blessings of freedom and liberty. They are embraced in our principle of the People's Sovereignty."

In this section, he had explained the political histories of the US and western European countries, and how they had had to fight for liberty and equality, before achieving the embryo of democracy. Yet here he seems to be using the reverse argument, that by achieving a degree of democracy, the Chinese people would then have some freedom and liberty. Democracy, Equality, Liberty and Sovereignty…all western concepts that were not present in theory or practice in the old dynastic China, and they might take many decades to introduce into Chinese society. They represented Sun's dream for China's future.

Yet the biggest underlying question in his lectures, still to be resolved, is how far China will go in following the foreign notion of democracy, always assuming that the Chinese feel it is the right path for China to adopt. Chairman Mao wrote a seventy nine page booklet 'On New Democracy' in 1940, which was a realistic analysis of China's current history, and was an update of Sun Yat Sen's three principles, which he replaced by the 'Three People's Principles of New Democracy'. These were the cardinal principles of alliance with Russia, co-operation with the Communists, and assistance to the peasants and workers.

In 1965 I found that Dr Sun Yat-sen still commanded a major position in the pantheon of Chinese patriots, and he was regarded as the 'Father of the Revolution'. On May Days and National Days a huge portrait of him would be erected towards the southern end of Tienanmen Square, facing Chairman Mao's portrait, which occupied the chief position on the main gate leading into the Imperial City. Portraits of Marx, Engels, Lenin and Stalin were positioned on the edge of the square where it merged with Chang An boulevard. Large portraits of two Chinese and four Foreigners! I can't imagine that happening in the China of 2015.

The western notion of the 'State' was completely foreign to the old Chinese mindset of cultural superiority over the surrounding tribes. This European idea was that a country consisted of an accepted territory and physical borders, and contained an organised political community, controlled by one government. In addition it required diplomatic equality and respect between nations. Mao is quoted in the Constitution of the People's Republic of China (1975): 'An organisation must have rules, and a State also must have rules; the Constitution is a set of general rules and is a fundamental charter.'

For the first time in its history, after 1949, an independent and unified China attempted to set up diplomatic relations and designated borders with all the countries adjoining it, on the basis of mutual respect and equality. On the question of physical boundaries with bordering countries, the 'mutual respect and equality' was marred by minor border disputes; with India in 1962,the Soviet Union in the late 1960s and Vietnam in 1979. Offshore, China has made massive territorial claims over sets of uninhabited islands within the adjacent seas. These borders have been disputed by neighbouring countries, and have not yet been resolved.

A crucial component of representative democracy is the willingness of the citizens of a state to accept the rules and laws of their courts and government, even for a majority decision of 51-49. And in return they are given some limited input into the selection of the political power-holders governing them. It would seem that majority decision-making at all levels is a difficult concept for people to accept, especially in countries where an old authoritarian system has been the traditional norm. Even in Britain, majorities are sometimes required by law, or by agreed rules, to be 'two thirds', or some other percentage larger than 51-49. The concept of majority rule may become a more significant issue in the future development of democratic practice.

The old system of governance in China was based on the framework of a specially selected educated class ruling over the rest of the people. Mencius[10] [Meng.zi, 372-289 BC] had proposed the notion of the scholar class governing the manual workers, and this idea has long been nourished in China. The elite corps of scholar-officials never soiled their hands in manual labour, as a sign of their superiority over the masses of the common people. When looking at the industrial and scientific success of China today, it appears that brain and hand are working together in the manufacture of goods and wealth. Though whether the mental outlook of Chinese intellectuals is changing at all is not clear. I still feel that the inherent attitude of the educated classes towards the masses of their fellow citizens is one of superiority.

Mao himself came from a reasonably well-off peasant family, and he was constantly fighting against this entrenched mentality of old China, which could be viewed as a serious obstacle to scientific and technological progress. One of his educational policies was that all the young people in urban schools should spend a period of time working in factories or in the countryside, so that they could experience manual work at first hand. The Cultural Revolution emphasised manual work in the curriculum, and our school set up links with urban communes, army units and local factories. Two factory workshops were set up on the campus, one of which produced small wooden fold-up stools. Senior pupils would spend several weeks living in a village, while junior classes would have shorter periods helping in local communes, such as with pea-harvesting, and gleaning the fields after harvesting.

Citizens of a democratic state have both rights and responsibilities. China has not yet produced an organic society in which the conditions allow minimal citizens' rights to be practised. Chinese people up to now, when voicing their appeals for democracy, tend to focus their claims on having more freedom and rights, while failing to acknowledge their responsibilities. It is as though they equate democracy to freedom. And perhaps they feel that they already bear an overload of duties from their inherited traditions. The new socialist approach had a progressive form, and the rights and duties of citizens were clearly laid down in the printed book of *The Constitution of the People's Republic of China* which first appeared in 1954[11], and was then revised in 1975, a year before the demise of Mao and the end of the Cultural Revolution in 1976. It was re-written in the Teng Hsiao-ping era in 1982.

The 1954 Constitution was overflowing with democratic principles. It was a significant blueprint for the Chinese people to ponder over, laying out their status and involvement in developing China's future, and it came from the Communist Party leadership, the new rulers of China. In effect, it was a modern 'Mandate of Heaven' accord, in writing, between the Chinese rulers and the Chinese people. And it was a mixture of realism and long term hypothetical aims.

Article 27 set out the right to vote or stand for election, the right to work and to education, and the right to complain about transgression of the law or neglect by any organ of state. In all of these, women enjoyed equal rights with men. Various freedoms were listed in Article 28: speech, correspondence, the press, assembly, association, procession, demonstration and the freedom to strike. On religion, the freedom to believe or not, and the freedom to propagate atheism. Of course, all these freedoms and rights could be reduced, controlled or removed at any time, according to the internal situation of China, and the responses of the country's leadership. On foreigners, Article 29 is strikingly brief: "The People's Republic of China grants the right of residence to any foreign national persecuted for supporting a just cause, for taking part in revolutionary movements or for engaging in scientific activities."

All these considerations of citizens' rights did not come out of the blue. Similar ideas had emerged in China in the previous hundred years, from the manifesto of the Kingdom of Heavenly Peace [Tai.ping Tian.guo, 1856-67] [12], the provisional constitutions of the Republic of China, right up to the Common Programme[13], which was adopted on 29 September 1949 at the Chinese People's Political Consultative Conference. But these rights were only written on paper, and sufficient independent institutions to uphold them were not in place. They had to be absorbed into the thinking of the people too. Nevertheless the written word carries weight in China, and it was a revolutionary step forward.

A crucial Chinese inheritance from tradition that inhibited the growth of any form of western-style democracy, was that the power of the executive and of the judiciary lay in the hands of one man, the Emperor himself. When these autocrats were on the Dragon Throne, their appointed scholar-officials throughout the country combined these two functions in their designated role as magistrates, and they had absolute power over the masses under them. Socialist China started along the path of separating the powers of the Judiciary and the Executive, and by 1975, Article 25 of the Constitution, consisting of sixteen lines, set out the Chinese position on 'The Judicial Organs and the Procuratorial Organs'. It stated that "The Supreme People's Court, local people's courts at various levels and special people's courts exercise judicial authority." It then specified that these courts were responsible and accountable to the corresponding organs of the People's Congresses. All very vague to my mind, and it did not address the question of independence of the judiciary. In practice, the crucial person in any court decision was the highest-ranking political cadre present, who would be working in tandem with legal officials.

Rudimentary democracy could be summarised as elementary rights, rule of law, and some contributory participation for citizens in the political process. The last two points have yet to be achieved in China. It can hardly be said that China has satisfied her people's democratic rights, let alone their human rights, even if they had wanted to. It remains to be seen how long it takes for such notions to become acceptable to the mass of Chinese people, as has happened, within limits, to the people of some neighbouring East Asian countries, since World War II. Maybe the increasing prosperity of the comparatively small, Chinese middle classes will bring about faster social changes if they become involved in the politics of their country.

But by any reckoning, hundreds of millions of Chinese must still be on the fringes of this gathering of real wealth, and no-one knows how they will react. Taking only one small sentence of the 1975 Constitution that "Citizens have the right to work and the right to education", this represents one of the many enormous tasks for the Chinese leadership to fulfil, throughout the largest population in the world. Today, China's rapid economic growth has outstripped their modernisation of the old social infrastructures, and there is a pressing need to create necessary new structures and institutions. It seems that western-style democracy is still quite irrelevant to this current stage of China's progress, now under the leadership of President Xi Jin.ping[14].

Chapter Notes
1. Confucianism- Wikipedia online
2. Junzi- Wikipedia online
3. Joseph Needham- Wikipedia online
4. Science & Civilisation in China- Wikipedia online
5. Professor Geert Hofstedt- Wikipedia online
6. Treaty of Nanking- Wikipedia online
7. Treaty Ports- Wikipedia online
8. Chen Duxiu- Wikipedia online
9. Sun Yat-sen- Wikipedia online
10. Mengzi- Wikipedia online
11. Constitution of the People's Republic of China- Wikipedia online
12. Taiping Tianguo- Wikipedia online
13. Common Program (China)- Wikipedia online
14. Xi Jinping- Wikipedia online

21

FARM WORK AT MARCO POLO BRIDGE COMMUNE, AUTUMN 1966, Part I

The Cultural Revolution ratcheted up considerably following the first Red Guard Rally in Tienanmen Square on Thursday August 18, 1966, when one and a half million youthful Red Guards and revolutionary teachers were reviewed by Chairman Mao. They were directed by Marshal Lin Piao to carry out the Chairman's express instructions for their great revolutionary work of destroying the 'Four Olds'[1](customs, culture, habits, ideas) of Chinese society, and building the 'Four New'. The first public stages of their deeds took place on the streets of Peking during the next few days, which we were able to observe when we went into the city centre on the morning coach run from the Friendship Guesthouse. Any foreigners travelling around the city's main shopping street of Wangfuching[2] could immediately see public manifestations of the Red Guards' activities; changing the names of shops, stores and roads, and thickening layers of wall posters, large and small (tatzupao and hsiaotzupao), covering all the shop windows and buildings. An eye-opener for foreigners, who were used to the Chinese always hiding their internal struggles from outside eyes. This was different.

From then on, some of the more committed foreigners based in China, whether from the ranks of 'foreign friends' or 'foreign experts', wanted to be involved in this movement, instead of being permanently excluded, as was the usual fate of foreigners. Soon rumours circulated around the Friendship Guesthouse in the September of 1966 that some American foreign experts, of top status in Chinese eyes, had written a powerful wall poster criticising the discriminatory, and implied 'racist' treatment of foreigners by the Chinese authorities. They strongly protested their right to take part in manual work in the countryside, and productive labour in factories. Cyclostyled copies of their unsigned wall poster appeared on the walls of the dining-room in the Druzhba, and I managed to acquire a copy. It is only in later years that I have learnt the names of the four people[3] involved; Joan Hinton[4], her husband Erwin Engst, Bertha Sneck and Ann Tomkins. Needless to say, at that time in Peking, I had never met any of those foreign experts, and had only heard the name Hinton in passing.

As we could see law and order gradually disintegrating in Peking we had no real idea of who was in control or what might happen next. In fact, we all listened to daily BBC World service news on the radio, as they were able to include in their coverage various reports from international sources such as Agence France-Presse, Reuters, Tanjug, Toronto Globe & Mail, Japanese agencies and others. Thus we were able to glean a little more general information on what was happening in Peking and China. During those uncertain times all foreign experts were well protected inside the walls of the Friendship Guesthouse, with PLA guards on duty at the gates, and I never had any worries about the safety of myself and family.

Whatever the coincidence of reasons, and Mao himself had apparently said a few words in favour, mentioning specifically "revolutionary foreign experts and their children", suddenly, in October 1966, foreign experts in the Druzhba, regardless of their 'revolutionary' hue, were invited to live in the countryside for a week, in order to do manual work with the peasantry. I don't know how Chinese officialdom coped with

Mao's words on the 'revolutionary' status of foreign experts, and how they assessed them, but I never heard of any foreigners being excluded in the selection process. To be allowed this freedom to work on the land was a minor revolution in itself, but it wasn't to everyone's taste.

There was a very limited take-up from the foreign ranks, and when we set out on our expedition from the Friendship Guesthouse all the foreign participants didn't even fill one bus. We were given a basic minimum list of clothes and living kit to pack, and the authorities informed us that in the village we should expect no concessions towards the standard of living normally enjoyed by pampered foreigners in the Guesthouse. There would be no more comfortable, centrally-heated apartments, with three restaurants on hand, and all the Chinese and foreign dishes to choose from; not to mention the excellent Tsingtao beer. Now that the foreigners had made this breakthrough into real Chinese life, the authorities made sure that this concession would come as a rude shock to the foreigners' privileged life-style, and I am sure they hoped it might act as a deterrent to any future campaigning from foreign residents to live and work with the Chinese masses shoulder to shoulder.

We had no medical check-up in advance but maybe the authorities in charge did actually investigate our medical records before sending us into the fields. I personally don't think so, because everything seemed to be very last-minute. Allowing foreigners to work in the countryside was so unusual that Chinese officialdom had had little time to prepare for it. I can't remember signing any forms of consent, but in those days there was little emphasis on the responsibilities of the authorities towards their foreign employees, except when looking after their health and well-being, and curtailing and constraining their movements and activities. Health and safety was only of the minimal kind in 1966. Awareness levels of hygiene in cooking, eating and preventative precautions looked abysmally low on the Chinese side, and I felt that foreigners were not much better informed on these issues either.

For example, my main concern was contracting roundworms or threadworms, the parasites that thrived due to unhygienic practices in food preparation and cooking. If it had been 2015 I would have had a long list of medical questions at the ready, and I doubt that I would have gone to the countryside. And I'm sure that the Chinese authorities on their side would have been just as cautious. But we did have a medical doctor from the Guesthouse, who accompanied us to the villages, and was on call if needed. Such a medical presence on the ground was essential, because any unfortunate injury sustained by a foreigner would have been a serious blow to the reputation of the Foreign Experts Bureau, the Ministry of Foreign Affairs and the Chinese government. It would have been a setback to China's isolated and beleaguered world standing in those days, even though China had a small circle of friends from the developing countries.

At the beginning of November 1966 a collection of foreigners, mainly males, were bussed to Lukouch'iao [Lu.gou.qiao], Marco Polo Bridge commune, a few miles to the west of Peking, where we were greeted by a large group of peasants, and an efficient-looking Chinese newsreel team, who were filming continuously throughout our arrival. I never did see any of this film about our visit, but I would like to think that it must have been stored away carefully in some dusty Peking film archives. Today, it's quite astounding for me to realise that this visit of ours to the Peking countryside was only seventeen years after Mao had made the historic declaration of the foundation of the

People's Republic of China on October 1st 1949.   I was obviously not too aware of history then.

Two small groups disappeared off to be billeted in nearby villages, while five of us, all males, were allocated to Tat'ui [Da.tui] village.   We consisted of two South-East Asians, and two Europeans, plus our Chinese interpreter-cum-minder Wang. I never did find out his personal names. Comrade Yang, our host, was not there to greet us, being still working in the fields, but his wife, a capable looking woman in her forties, took us to their home which was a single-storey brick house comprising two rooms, each with a concrete floor and a large kang^5, also made from bricks, for sleeping on. Within a short time we realised that Mrs Yang wore the trousers, and got things done. A large portrait of Chairman Mao was on the wall, plus a few selected sayings, but their framed collection of family photos was even bigger than Mao's portrait.   They had got their priorities right, and I was impressed.

Leaning against a wall in a corner were two sacks of grain for the family use, their insurance security against any bad times in the immediate future. One of them I could see was sweetcorn, and in fact the ubiquitous sweetcorn cobs were everywhere, as nothing was wasted. A pile of the shorn cobs was drying out in the courtyard and were used for fuelling the stove. It reminded me of my childhood during World War II when I remember an atmosphere where things were re-cycled to the nth degree, usually by Grandmother, and nothing was thrown away.   No food was left on plates at the end of the meal. It was the same here.

The family consisted of Mr and Mrs Yang, his Mother and their two children, one girl and one boy, not yet teenagers. For sleeping, they occupied the kang in the larger room, while we foreigners and our interpreter, five of us in all, slept on the other kang in the smaller room.   A large table with chairs and stools constituted the dining facilities. Back of the house was a small pigsty with one pig, with a collection of poultry everywhere outside. The toilet facilities were in a small hut in the corner of the courtyard.

We only had a few moments to throw our bags onto the kang, and then we were off to the production team office where we were pronounced members of the Great Proletarian Cultural Revolution Team (West Branch), of the Red Guard Brigade in the Eternally Red Commune; in other words our team consisted of the inhabitants of Tat'ui village in Lukouch'iao commune, just outside Peking.   In the early 1960s the commune had been designated as the Sino-Romanian People's Friendship Commune, but there was no mention of this during our stay. As a nominated commune this meant that they were used to foreign visitors, and that must have been why they were chosen to receive us.

The middle-aged male team leader immediately launched into the facts and figures of the production team.   There were 335 people living in the village, from 65 families, with 121 able bodied workers (56 men and 65 women) and 15 work animals.   The land under cultivation was 322 mu of land (53 acres, where one mu equals 0.165 acres) and production was mainly concentrated on Chinese cabbage, plus a variety of other vegetables, watermelons, castor beans, maize, winter wheat, some other grain, pigs and poultry. Before 1949 their peasant houses had been made of wood and earth, but since then all new houses were built of bricks.   The majority of the villagers were classified as poor or lower-middle peasants. No mention was made of the old landlords before liberation, and I didn't see any men walking around with a black diamond patch sewn on their sleeve to indicate this dreaded status.

The leader proudly pointed out that the commune now had electric pumps for irrigation, compared to the old human treadle system, which could only irrigate two or three mu per day. This meant that before 1949 the low grain yields averaged only 100 jin (1 jin equals 1.102 lbs) per mu. Since electrification all the 322 mu could be watered in four days, and as a result, by 1965, yields had risen to 560 jin per mu.

In terms of real money, the village income over the past four years had risen from 128,000 Yuan[6] to 139,000 Yuan, marred only by one bad year, when hail had destroyed the watermelon crop and damaged the grain, resulting in a lower figure of 108,000 Yuan. By covering the income of only the last four years 1962-65, the team leader was able to avoid mentioning those calamitous days of famine during 1959-61, and how it had affected their village. Whatever had happened in Tat'ui during those years, the next day I was able to see the younger men of the village in action digging and building the clamps; they had stripped to the waist, and they looked quite strong, healthy and muscular.

The team leader finished his report with some current standard of living statistics. Over fifty of the households had a radio set, every family had an alarm clock and at least one bicycle, and between them there were twenty wrist-watches and sixteen sewing machines, with adequate clothing for all. He stressed that such standards were unattainable before 1949. From the vantage point of 2015, such basic levels of living, with not a TV in sight, seem ludicrously low. Finally he got down to business and outlined our work schedule for the week.

The keystone product of the village economy was Chinese cabbage [bai.cai], and they had to build three large underground earthen clamps in which to store all the Chinese cabbages during the freezing months of winter, that is, roughly mid-November to mid-February. In other words, it was man-made refrigerated storage, as the cabbages would survive unspoiled in the clamps, and then be periodically released for sale to the state distributor, and thence onto the Peking streets, as a welcome addition to the winter diet. There was little time left. The traditional agricultural calendar predicted that all the land would be completely frozen over in just three weeks' time, about November 20th.

Our daily work schedule was a harsh reality check: the work day began at sunrise and ended around five o'clock at fading light, but fortunately for we 'soft' pen-pushing westerners, there were four rest periods in the day. Breakfast break was from 08.00 to 09.00, followed by mid-morning 10.30 to 11.00, then lunch 12.00 to 13.30 and mid-afternoon 15.00 to 15.30. Work points were allocated according to individual or small group performance, and the type of work involved. The leader stressed that the production team held regular monthly meetings to discuss any problems over the work and allocation of work points, and the finer distinctions between assessing different tasks. He added that all problems were solved by the application of Chairman Mao's thought, when key quotations were studied by groups of around ten villagers in selected homes at night. Resolving such issues was a serious matter, because the number of work points determined the income of every worker and their families. Thankfully, foreign guests were excluded from the work point allocation process.

As an afterthought, the team leader offered the Mao quote "What is work? Work is struggle" as being very apt in relation to the current situation in the village. To my mind this simplistic statement, even without any political significance, could be applied to all the hundreds and thousands of villages throughout China, but like our fellow villagers, we foreigners would not question the merits of such polemics even if we had wanted to. Going against the political tide was not life-enhancing for a Chinese person, and even for we foreigners such perverse behaviour would surely have made its way into Friendship Guesthouse gossip, and left hefty black blots on our copybooks.

Looking back at the work timetable I don't know if it had been modified for the arrival of the incoming foreigners, because in actual fact those privileged foreign experts could contribute as much or as little as they were able to do, providing they were unaffected by losing face of course. When confronted by physical labour in the fields, the foreign experts reacted in different ways. Sometimes it seemed as if common-sense went out of the window. Some of those with a strong belief in the Marxist-Maoist system would start at their task frantically, which I presumed was motivated by their desire to be fraternal comrades, and work side by side with the Chinese peasants. In this way they could prove their political mettle, both to themselves as much as to the Chinese, and to other foreigners too.

This was a risky business, because in realistic terms they led sedentary lives and had 'soft hands', so they soon acquired allied complaints like cuts, blisters, strains and muscular aches, or more seriously back problems needing medical treatment. Their bodies and muscles just weren't used to this level of physical activity and they over-taxed themselves in their devotion and enthusiasm to show the correct socialist spirit. Most ailments could be settled by our doctor in the village clinic, and by 'rest'. No-one was rushed to hospital in Peking. Other experts phased themselves, and were able to do some reasonable work but not for long periods. They knew they could always take a breather whenever they wanted. As for our diet in Tat'ui many of the experts took time to adjust to the peasant food, but no-one would admit it was a problem, and no one mentioned the low levels of hygiene.

Our first meal that evening was prepared and cooked by Grandma, a little, wiry old woman with bound feet. She was in her sixties, and was the mother of our host Comrade Yang. Thick handmade noodles of varying consistency in a meat gravy, some heavy brownish bread and a shared plate of fried vegetables, all served and eaten in clean-looking enamel bowls , with drinks of hot water available from huge thermos flasks. I must admit that the first evening I was embarrassed to be only able to finish half my bowl. Then I made the huge mistake, to my great shame, of getting up with my half-finished meal and going outside round the back of the house to tip the remains into the pigsty. No comment was made, although later on alone in our room my fellow experts severely criticised me for this, and said the food would have been re-cooked and eaten by the family. All the Yang family finished their bowls of food in good time.

However things were moving fast, and meals were apparently of short duration. After dinner other villagers appeared, and suddenly we were in the middle of a political study group, discussing the theme of 'The Foolish Old Man Who Removed the Mountains'. The Old Man Yu Gong[7], featured in a Chinese folk fable, which was adapted by Chairman Mao in June 1945. It was one of the 'Three Stories' that were part of the political propaganda themes of the time. The other two were 'Serve the People' (September

1944) and 'In Memory of Norman Bethune' (December 1939). The aim of the Yu Gong parable was to educate and encourage the mass of the Chinese peasantry to throw off their old fatalistic attitude of "Mei you ban.fa" (There is no way out!) and to show them that by mutual co-operation and self-reliance they could achieve much more in the long term. It seemed quite a worthwhile objective to me, so I was right behind Chairman Mao on this one.

At first I think the villagers were inhibited by the presence of us two European 'big noses'[8] in the meeting, but then a middle-aged man began to speak. He outlined the story, discussed the issues involved and correlated them with his own work and life in a genuine and subjective manner. At the time I asked myself if he had been placed in the group in order to impress us. It was really a pointless thought in terms of the well-buttressed Chinese bureaucracy, which was not answerable to any of its citizens, and which kept a tight control of information on all news. Whatever my thoughts on this were, that man did a good job. Other villagers slowly joined in and the discussion livened up and was surprisingly mature. Foreign friends present were not invited to participate, and I was glad of this.

This meeting followed the regular practice of having no real debate on issues by participants, but merely producing repetitive stress on the correct political road to follow, according to the tenets of socialism. When we questioned Wang about this, he told us that serious talks might take place amongst groups of peasants on agricultural matters affecting their village lives, but that was all. For the peasants, this new movement was just another phase in the constant socio-political changes that they had been subjected to during the sixteen years since 1949. The political litany of their liberated years, after 1949, was packed with mass movements causing many upheavals in the countryside. Key campaigns in the 1950s were the Land Reform movement, the creation of Mutual aid teams and Co-operatives, the formation of the People's Communes, and steel production in the Great Leap Forward. That was followed by the famine years of 1959-61, and now, from 1966, the turmoil of the unfolding Cultural Revolution, although the countryside was on the periphery of the movement. It must have seemed to the villagers to be a never-ending succession of social disruptions during those years, but whatever the practical outcome in terms of village life, they stoically followed the party line and got on with their work and survival. They didn't have any options in this closely-controlled society, except for rebellion and insurrection!

The political study group ended with a singsong. We all joined in singing several revolutionary quotations of Chairman Mao which had been put to music. These were played ad infinitum on Peking Radio and other radio stations every day, so even the foreigners knew the words by heart and we sang them with gusto. It was the only contribution we made to the evening, and was the least we could do after eavesdropping on their group discussion. Who knows what they made of those foreigners singing the words of Mao:

"Be resolute, fear no sacrifice,
And surmount every difficulty to win victory"

This quotation also comes from the Yu Gong story.

Postscript[9]

In January 1967, Minister of Foreign Affairs Chen Yi addressed a meeting of foreign experts in Peking about the implications of the foreigners' wall poster and Mao's reply. The Minister said that foreigners would be allowed to take part in the Cultural Revolution, by participating in Chinese groups or by forming their own rebel groups. As for the privileged lifestyle led by foreigners, they were free to reduce their salaries and move into humbler accommodation if they so wished. He added that on these questions there might be differences between the choices of long-term and short-term residents. He did stress the harsh realities of living like the Chinese, as follows: "To live like us, foreign comrades, is to live without bathroom, telephone and elevator. Ours is a hard life, which we accept in the certainty of a better future." A year later in 1968, a few of the old China Hands, who had been present and heard Chen Yi's words, were imprisoned without trial for some years.

Chapter Notes
1. Four Olds- Wikipedia online
2. Wangfujing- Wikipedia online
3. For more information see Anne-Marie Brady, *'Making the Foreign Serve China'*, Chapter 6, 2003.
4. Joan Hinton- Wikipedia online
5. Kang- Wikipedia online
6. Yuan (Chinese currency)- Wikipedia online
7. Yu Gong- Wikipedia online
8. Big noses- Traditional Chinese way of describing 'Westerners'
9. See note 3 above.

22

FARM WORK AT MARCO POLO BRIDGE COMMUNE, AUTUMN 1966, Part II

I awoke next day at 6 a.m. to the strains of the 'East is Red' coming over the village relay broadcast system. We washed face and hands in the cold water of the courtyard well, and put on more layers of clothing. Time for a quick drink of hot water, before we tidied the yard and set off to work. We were given the task of carrying long tree-trunks, stripped of bark, from a nearby pile to the partially-constructed second clamp, where they would be used as roofing supports and ceiling beams. Two of us cautiously carried one tree trunk at a time, although a strong male villager would carry one on his own, when it was properly balanced on the shoulder. But as there was no pressure on us, we could relax. We soon realised that the villagers themselves would easily construct the three clamps effectively, without our assistance or hindrance. In fact, the first one had been completed before we arrived, and the second one within three days of our arrival. Thankfully, the powers that be had decreed that we were definitely not permitted to use a shovel or spade to dig up or move earth in any backbreaking way. To my mind, sensible precautions by the Chinese.

The first day's work being a novelty for us, time passed pleasantly, and I noted the steady but relaxed pace of work of the village men and women. They obviously didn't worry about our intrusive presence in their lives and daily existence, or what we thought of them; in fact on that first day there was a degree of horseplay and laughter between the sexes, ending with one of the young men losing his padded jacket. Quite an eye-opener for me, as back in my school, which was only about twenty kilometres away from this clamp-building, none of my Chinese colleagues, all educated to university level, would behave in any way like this. They would laugh and joke with each other in the staffroom, but we never saw any horseplay.

I roughly paced out the length and breadth of the clamps, and estimated the depth according to the height of the men standing in there working. Each clamp was about 100 feet long and 18 feet wide, and the internal height when completed about 8 foot. Bearing in mind that the headroom resulted from the villagers having dug out a large trench, four feet deep, and then built up earth banking around the sides of that trench by another four feet. The tree-trunks were used as both vertical roofing supports and horizontal crossbeams, which were then covered by long rolls of wide padded matting made from agricultural products, covered over by sheaves of dried-out maize stalks or other produce, closely packed together, and topped off with many layers of earth. A sloping earth ramp led down into each entrance. The finished clamp was impressive and compact, and when all the land was frozen over, it must have worked very effectively as a refrigeration unit. It reminded me of nothing else more than larger versions of the air-raid shelters in my primary school playground during World War II, but lacking the sandbags and corrugated sheets of metal.

The clamps required constant peasant management and attention. I was told that once all the cabbages had been safely stored in a clamp, they had to be turned every three days, and later every six days. Manpower for this crucial task came from each family, who were allocated a certain section to look after. Old retired male villagers, on a rotation basis, would spend the whole winter daylight inspecting the clamps, to check that the cabbages received adequate ventilation and to eliminate decomposition. It was a classic example of combined community effort and perseverance to reach their goal, which was to get their key produce in best condition to the state distributor.

All through my days in Tat'ui I found the villagers to be quite direct in conversation, which was a refreshing relief after working with educated cadres and teachers, who were much more concerned about showing us China's best side. And all this, was regardless of the bleak economic reality that we could see around us. To be fair, our Chinese colleagues at school tried to be as open as they could be in explaining things about their society, but unlike the peasantry, they knew something of the backwardness and inadequacy of the Chinese standard of life, when compared with the West. So some of them were touchy and defensive, and problematic topics that we brought up were gently ignored, and shunted into a cul-de-sac. When interpreting for us at official functions we were completely dependent on them to decode Chinese euphemisms, so that their translations retained some of the culture-specific meaning.

The lunch and evening meals in our Tat'ui home were very similar to the previous day, and this pattern followed throughout our stay. Some of us had brought supplies of fruit and biscuit snacks with us which helped to balance our diet. It was a Spartan existence, and there was no let-up in evening activities for the foreigners. We were taken to a meeting of the brigade leadership, where the main theme was appealing to the commune members for greater efforts at such a crucial part of the agricultural year. Especially the gathering of pig manure to use as fertiliser on their land. Most households had at least one pig, so this would be a considerable financial saving for the production teams, when compared to buying chemical fertiliser from the State.

Our daytime work of moving tree trunks barely lasted two days, and then we did all sorts of petty routine work in the interim, in the fields or around the home, until clamp number three was under construction and we could help out on tree trunks again. After clamp number two was virtually completed we were allowed, under supervision, to re-cycle earth over the top and tamp it down. During another of the afternoon breaks there was a lot of laughing when an older villager passed by. They referred to him as 'our foreigner', because he undeniably had a large nose, that was absolutely un-Chinese. He silently went on his way and did not respond to their ribbing, presumably having already suffered a lifetime of it.

At times we only had minor routine jobs just to fill in the time, for example I spent some time scrubbing the corn off maize cobs, so gradually my break periods became longer and longer. One lunchtime in the courtyard I found a bamboo shoulder carrying pole, and I tried my hand at carrying two lightweight loads, one at each end. It was impossible for me to get the right balance with appropriate movements of legs and hips, and with the two baskets ballooning uncontrollably in all directions, my hopeless antics reduced the kids to laughter, and even Grandma was smiling. After that I had the greatest respect for all shoulder-polers carrying heavy weights, as they smoothly covered the ground at considerable pace and poise.

One diversion for me was to wander around the nearby fields looking at everything. I discovered that some of the larger expanses were winter wheat, something that was news to me, as a city dweller. I met an old man in passing and we had a chat, he asking me where I came from, was I Russian, was I married and how many children did I have; the usual direct frontal Chinese practice in the countryside. When I said "Ying.guo", which passes for both England and Britain, he didn't know it, so I said it was further west past Russia. I admitted that I was married and in fact had three sons. He looked at me with a kind of respect, and said something I didn't understand, but I noted the words and asked Wang about their meaning later that evening.   Wang said they were words to the effect of "You are blessed!" I then managed to get in a question of my own asking about his children, and he replied "I have three children, two daughters and a son, and my son is a tractor-driver!" Said with pride. That was the gist of our conversation. One break time I had a similar interrogation from our host Old Yang, and he wanted to know my age.   When I told him he smiled and said "You're younger than me, but you look older!" He didn't ask how much money I was earning, which I would have politely avoided answering. My monthly salary of 460 yuan was probably closer to his annual income,

Mid-week evening was a Bathhouse night in the village and we were all invited. Three of us stayed at home and washed our feet in bowls of hot water, but not so our intrepid companion of rotund girth, who the village children had labelled 'Old Fatty' on our arrival in Tat'ui. He had that special kudos accorded by the Chinese to fatter than normal people, a very rare species in China then, and he was always the centre of interest and attention whenever he appeared. So he ventured into the bathhouse, which we heard later was packed with expectant male villagers, all waiting to run their eyes over his figure. In the bathhouse he was weighed, and to everyone's delight he came out at 180 jin, where the Chinese jin equals half a kilogram, so he was indeed 90 kilograms. From then on in he was known as '180 jin', and we always knew when he was about because we would hear the village children shouting "Yi bai ba.shi jin lai.le!"(180 jin is coming!) He came out of the bathhouse with even greater status than before. At least he gave some light relief to the villagers, after the daily grind of work, the evening millstone of studying Mao's Little Red Book and political meetings.

One evening we foreigners came back earlier than expected, and there we found Grandma washing one foot in a bowl of water. She was very disturbed by our invasive presence, and obviously had got her timing wrong that evening. She happened to be drying one foot with a towel, and in a quick glance we were horrified to see that bound foot[1]. I was quite embarrassed by this unexpected spectacle, and we all shot into our room without any polite niceties, leaving her alone. From day one we had noticed her bound -feet condition, and yet in spite of this deformed mutilation and having to hobble around on her heels, she seemed to cover the ground in the house and courtyard fairly sharply. Talking about bound-feet was one thing, but seeing the reality was a shock.

After dinner one evening we were visited by an old peasant man who recounted the story of his pitiful life before 1949. Owing to the chaos and disorder in China during that previous civil war cum Japanese occupation period, such stories as his were well-documented and authenticated. Everything seemed quite plausible, and almost certainly could be corroborated by millions of other peasant voices. On the other hand, surely all of China's villages couldn't have been as bad as this, even during the chaos of the 1930s and 1940s, and the ravages of the limited Japanese occupation[2]. One answer could be the fact that the Communist Party had developed a powerful propaganda machine, which flourished and expanded after they had achieved political power. This machine expunged all historical input from other unacceptable sources, such as Kuomintang[3] (KMT) government officials and records before 1949. It is difficult to say if and when China might review her modern revisionist history, and to record a more balanced view of it. But this will only happen, when it suits China's interests so to do.

This talk by the old peasant was a warm-up for our next activity, which was to put on thick cotton-padded clothing, and carrying our very small stools, walk to the little village square to see a film. A travelling mobile film unit had set up a large white sheet on a wall, and we all sat on the mini-stools, quite a skill for large-beamed foreigners, and watched the 'Red Lantern', with most of the villagers squeezed in around us. Red Lantern[4] was one of the approved model plays during the Cultural Revolution. The theme, portrayed in very simple black and white terms, represented the terrible life in the 'Bad Old Days' before liberation, and focused on the struggle against the Japanese army occupiers and Chinese landlords. Most foreigners had already seen it at the Guesthouse cinema, but this time there were no subtitles or dubbing, and in this village environment it seemed to me more pertinent and relevant, and I followed the film quite closely.

A memorable incident did occur though, in the middle of the film, when there was a sudden commotion and shouting, and we all had to pick up our stools and quickly disperse, as a very stinking night-soil cart, with the large metal container tank fixed on it, slowly creaked and trundled right through the square,. It was pulled by two oxen under the whip of a cart-man, dressed in the usual long animal hide jackets and filthy-looking clothing of his trade. No-one could have planned that event. Night-soil collectors, although doing a crucial job of transporting night soil from the urban areas to the countryside for use as fertiliser, did not enjoy any social status. Attempts had been made in the past to habilitate them, and praise them, but they were still night-soil collectors. On one occasion some of them had been invited to a state event, and Liu Shao-chi (President 1959-66) had shaken hands with them. The photo portraying this scene in 'China Pictorial' (English language edition) had the caption "President Liu felt a warm glow spread over him as he shook hands with the Comrades".

With Peking City being so close at hand I never felt completely isolated in the countryside at Tat'ui, and from the fields we could see traffic on the nearby road into Peking. There were always plenty of small groups of Red Guard 'Long March' squads going in both directions, as they exchanged revolutionary experiences. While based there we didn't see any of these marching groups intrude or bother the villagers. Perhaps Tat'ui had some special protected status, and anyway it was rather too close to Peking for the incoming Red Guards marchers, who must have been eager to reach a resting place in their capital city.

On 3 November 1966, we were treated to a full-volume relay broadcast of events from Tienanmen square, where yet another huge rally of Red Guards, the sixth one since August 18th, was being reviewed by Chairman Mao. We could hear the familiar high-pitched voice of Marshal Lin Piao addressing and exhorting them on behalf of Mao. More than two million students and teachers took part that day as they walked along Chang An boulevard and through the square where Mao and other leaders were on the rostrum. President Liu Shao-chi and Teng Hsiao-ping were still in attendance on that day, but they were never shown on the newsreel coverage; by then they were sliding down the pecking order fairly rapidly. After being subjected to a critical onslaught from Red Guard wall-posters, and the government media, and being labelled as leading 'Capitalist Roaders', they were losing their power, and by 1967 had disappeared from view. Liu died in house confinement in 1969, but Teng bounced back in the 1970s and returned to the top, where he initiated dynamic politico-economic changes that created the powerhouse of today.

Our minder, Comrade Wang looked to be in his thirties, so was probably in his forties, and even though his English was only passable it was enough for our needs. His main asset was confidence, and he had plenty of it, as he looked after our interests in the fields of Lukouch'iao commune. I automatically assumed that he was a Party member, but in the end I never did find out the truth. One trait of his that was soon revealed to us was his complete disdain and arrogance towards the peasants. I was quite appalled as I had never seen it in action at close-hand. He was quite open in his manner, and did not try to hide it. It was the traditional superiority of the educated urban classes towards the countryside masses, and Chairman Mao himself had well-realised this powerful negative dichotomy in traditional Chinese society.

That is why Mao had always insisted that manual labour be an essential part of the school, college and university curriculum for every educated student to experience, and this approach was manifested in the curriculum at our school, even before the Cultural Revolution began. For example, the senior classes, aged 17-18 had worked for four weeks on building the Miyun Reservoir Dam project near Peking during the second half of 1964. They all wrote me an essay on their experiences as soon as I started teaching them in February 1965, and it proved a valuable trigger for useful oral work in class. Those seniors told me that manual work helped them 'to wash away their bourgeois thinking', and to attempt to become 'working-class intellectuals'. One very popular slogan of the times for the educated youth was 'Be Red and Expert'[5], where Red equated to a socialist political heart, and Expert meant mastering their field of work and study. It was meant to be a harmonious goal, but in practice it had to cope with inimical traditional values, and that often made it difficult and divisive. Waddi made a visit to Peking University on Thursday 25 February 1976 to see all the wallposters on campus. She found one which listed some of Teng Hsiao-ping's alleged comments and statements over the years, showing his wrong political attitudes. One quote from March 1965 related to the 'Be Red and Expert' slogan as follows: "The students of physics learn Lei Feng's diary and Chairman Mao's works off by heart every day. Such people are neither red nor expert."

At the time of our departure from Tat'ui village, clamp three was virtually finished, but as yet no Chinese cabbage had been placed in any of the three clamps for winter storage. On saying farewell, we realised that we had got somewhat attached to our families in only a week, and we promised to come back and see them. I heard later on that some of the foreigners had gone back to see their hosts, and that others had since spent some time in Tat'ui. In 2015 it would be impossible to do that, because the old Lukouch'iao ex-commune has been drastically affected by the outward expansion of Bei.jing, and has been heavily developed with roads and buildings in the past decades. So much for all that arable land and the Chinese cabbages, which could have yielded such valuable produce every year to help feed the capital city.

Chapter Notes
1. Footbinding- Wikipedia online
2. Legend of the Red Lantern- Wikipedia online
3. Kuomintang- Wikipedia online
4. Legend of the Red Lantern- Wikipedia online
5. Red and Expert-www.marxist.org

23

SHANGHAI FAREWELL: DETAINED BY RED GUARDS

Some months before our contracts ended on 7 January 1967, the school leadership, wanting to arrange our transport back to Britain in good time, asked how we would like to travel. Initially we had toyed with the idea of going by sea and getting cabins on a merchant ship from Tientsin, but with three small sons to look after, reality finally prevailed, and we decided to go by air, first of all staying eleven days in Shanghai, and then flying to London via Dacca and Beirut. Most of our possessions and belongings had to travel by sea, so the school had four large wooden crates made for us, and Waddi slowly and methodically filled them up. Our tape-recorder and bicycle we sold to the second-hand shop in the Friendship Store, and we got good prices for them. Then at the beginning of December our four crates were transported by lorry to the customs shed at Andingmen railway station, and we followed behind in a guesthouse taxi.

The customs officials questioned us about any Chinese books we had, and I explained that we had language books, dictionaries and lots of children's books. As a diversion we then showed them the small pieces of Chinese traditional furniture and other bric-a-brac that we had acquired, but they didn't seem very interested, and these were all quickly passed for export, with red wax seals, much to our surprise. They persisted in their quest for books, and systematically searched all the four crates thoroughly, checking every individual book, turning things upside down and reducing Waddi to tears as she tried to re-pack everything. We had gone full circle, because Waddi had been tearful on our first day in Peking two years ago, and now on departing it had happened again; but the customs men were impervious to her tears.

In after years when meeting up with other former British residents, I learnt that customs were searching for proscribed books, especially the small book *How To Be a Good Communist* by President of the People's Republic, Liu Shao-chi[1]. The English edition consisted of ninety five pages, and was first published in China in 1951. It so happened that by December 1966 Liu had been branded as the No 1 Capitalist Roader, under severe attack at that time, and the book was labelled 'poisonous'. On reading it today, in political terms it seems remarkably bland and inoffensive, but it may have been stigmatised because of what was left out of the text. I did actually possess a copy of that book, and kept it safely in my jacket-pocket, when passing through customs on finally leaving China at the end of that month.

So we left Peking, by an internal flight, on 20 December 1966 to spend the last 11 days of the month in Shanghai, staying with friends, Neale and Deirdre Hunter, in their comfortable foreigners' guesthouse that was way up Yenan West road at No 914. We had been given a family exit visa which permitted us to visit Nanking, Hangchow and Soochow, as well as Shanghai, before leaving China. Our Institute was fulfilling their contractual duties, and we had Pakistan International Airline tickets from Shanghai to London. They also sent along Old Yang, one of our Chinese colleagues, to look after us in Shanghai, and we were very glad of that. The foreigners' guesthouse was an old and large western-style house that looked as though it had been probably built around the turn of the century, with five storeys and many rooms. When we checked in, I immediately obtained details of all their accommodation charges, so that we could marshal the limited funds we had budgeted for our stay there. All our other money had been changed into foreign currency, for our short stay in Beirut. The guesthouse had informed the local Kung An Chu [Gong.an.ju-Public Security office] of our imminent arrival, and I went there to complete the formalities, and get our visa stamped.

Most importantly, Deirdre had organised a very mature and competent-looking Chinese 'Auntie' to help look after our three sons, and without her daily services our activities would have been severely curtailed. We had comfortable rooms and the Fuwuyuan [fu.wu.yuan], Chinese service staff, appeared relaxed, even though the Red Guard propaganda struggles were raging outside in the streets of downtown Shanghai. The little basement dining room was a great bonus for us, as at every breakfast, the rolls, toast, butter, jam, milk, bacon, scrambled egg, porridge and so on, had a closer to home taste. And the Chinese meals were delicious too, so we were all really pleased about that. Our mood was that the western food here was much better than in Peking. As befitting the most dynamic of the old Treaty Ports, from 1843 to 1949, and having the largest International Settlement, Shanghai[2] knew all about foreigners, and their tastes.

I had spent two days in Shanghai in July 1965, so I knew about The Bund on the river front, with its huge solid stone buildings, very similar to parts of the City of London. One of those buildings, the famous Seamen's Club[4], was reputed to have the longest bar in the world, and during that brief stay I had managed to get in and see it, before my credentials were questioned, and I was politely asked to leave. My overnight room had been on the sixth floor of the Shanghai Mansions, just across the way from the British Consulate[5], at the Soochow creek end of the Bund, and in their garden was one of the tallest flagpoles I have ever seen, with the Union Jack flying rampant. That evening I had been invited to dinner by the British Consul, and also present was a Secretary from the British Charge D'Affaires Office in Peking. We were joined for the meal by a Dutch writer called Hans Koningsberger[6], resident in America, who was on a short tour collecting notes for a book, and the four of us had a stimulating discussion about China that evening. The excellent dinner was cooked and served by silent, white-jacketed Chinese males, and the whole evening seemed like a replay of my image of Old Shanghai before 1949.

Hans did produce his book, *Love and Hate in China* published by McGraw Hill, a year later in 1966. I often wonder if his book came out after the early struggles of the Cultural Revolution, and whether the title had been changed in order to fit the reality. In 1966 the terrible excesses that the Red Guards inflicted on their fellow Chinese indicated that 'hate' was the order of the day, rather than 'love'! In fact, over our two year stay I had no idea of the 'compassion quotient' present in the Chinese psyche, and I never witnessed any examples of it in practice. Or indeed any demonstration of public affection between Chinese.

I was amazed to hear that the Consulate still organised a western film showing once a month, and at least three elderly Shanghai residents of European origin would turn up on these evenings. Apparently they were long-time residents, who had decided to stay on after 1949, and China had accepted them. The next morning, as I was getting up, I swear that I could see the dear old Union Jack from my bed on the sixth floor of the Shanghai Mansions, a stone's throw away. In terms of presence and prestige along the Bund, that flagpole was a remarkable relic of history. It may have been erected before

1949, all credit to some bright spark in the Foreign Office or the Shanghai community of those times, but it only had one year of life left under British control.

In December 1966 when we ventured down to the Bund we found the famous old Peace Hotel[7] closed and locked up. Its walls were thickly blanketed with handwritten paper posters (tatzupao), and some of the latest ones, written in very large characters, called for "Down with Teng Hsiao-ping", "Down with Liu Shao-chi", and "Down with Ts'ao Ti-chiou" (Mayor of Shanghai). In all my wanderings around central Peking during November and December 1966, I had never seen a poster decrying Teng Hsiao-ping or Liu Shao-chi. The imposing British Consulate had now been taken over by Red Guards, with a mass of posters explaining their actions, and how they had recovered this Chinese territory from the British Imperialists, and driven them out. The impressive flagpole, now flying the Chinese flag, was still standing.

The atmosphere in the downtown streets was very tense, with layers of wall posters stuck on every building and shop window, and propaganda sheets of different bands of Red Guards lying around all over the place. Frissons of activity occurring regularly on the streets kept us all on the alert, so at our request, we often had Old Yang, our Chinese colleague, come along as 'bodyguard' to negotiate unexpected problems, and also to translate any posters that took our fancy. One spectacular event was that sometimes large quantities of paper propaganda leaflets would come floating down from high buildings like a huge snow storm.

We tended to gravitate towards the Bund and the river whenever we went downtown, and one morning in one of the small back streets there, called Cohen Road[8], a pedicart slowly approached us. I noticed the old pedicart man pedalling slowly and staring intently at us. He was clearing his throat, and as he passed by, with great facial contortion he said 'Good Morning' in a perfectly English upper-class voice. I was lost for words, but for some reason, his mimicry cheered us up.

Along the Bund the old Headquarters of the Hong Kong & Shanghai Bank[9] was all boarded up, and the two impressive lion statues guarding the entrance had vanished. Of considerable size and made of metal, their removal indicated the determination of the Shanghai Municipality to protect their heritage, even when it was of foreign origin, from the ravages of the Red Guards. Two days later, when visiting the city museum with Old Yang, we went up to one of the top rooms, and by chance looking down on the streets below, I was pleased to see the two lions lying safely in a yard opposite, protected from the eyes of passers-by by the high walls. The Museum being open was another show of Shanghai's resolve not to allow the Red Guards, who had come from other parts of China, to disrupt daily life in their city.

Neale and Deirdre explained that warring Red Guard groups, from different cities in China, had been fighting for overall control of Shanghai, since the first Peking contingent had arrived by train on 28 August 1966; the Hunters themselves had been on that same train. But Shanghai was putting up fierce resistance against these intruders, and during our stay we saw several huge street demonstrations by masses of the Chihweitui [Chi.wei.dui-Scarlet Army], officially set up on December 5th 1966, and they were a new name to me. They were patently mature workers, well above student age, and obviously assembled by the old Shanghai administration to oppose and defend against the depredations of those rampaging Red Guard 'outsiders', who were intent on destroying the old power structure.   In Peking I had never heard of any such 'Scarlet Army' groups, so we obviously weren't getting reliable accounts of the struggles in Shanghai from the New China News Agency, or from Peking Review either.

Historically the Chihweitui were not a new phenomenon, because according to the Chinese-English Dictionary produced by my institute, and published by the Commercial Press in 1978, this was the name given to paramilitary units of the masses who were operating in the revolutionary base areas during the Second Civil War 1927-37.   In the dictionary they were translated as 'Red Army' units, but in the Cultural Revolution the English term 'Scarlet Army' was used, so as not confuse them with the Red Guards. Interestingly, David Crook, a British lecturer at the institute, was named as the advisor of that Dictionary.   And this was after he had been imprisoned in solitary confinement for almost five years, during the height of the struggles, only being released on 27 January1973.   Other contributing foreigners acknowledged in the dictionary's preface were Frank Wylie, Nancy Hodes, Elsie Fairfax-Cholmeley and Norman Shulman.   I saw a practical manifestation of the effects of solitary confinement on David in 1974, when he lent me his copy of Engels' *The Condition of the Working Class in England,* which had been one of his allowed books in prison.   All the spare space on every page, outside of the printed words, was filled with his handwritten annotations and notes, written in very small script.   It was a second book within a book.

Following the same approach as in Peking I was very cautious when taking photographs in the streets, and I tried to avoid any potential situations which might arouse Red Guard suspicions and reaction.   I always wore the lapel badge of my Peking Institute, as some form of insurance cover, and this proved to be a sensible precaution. Whatever my best intentions though, all the intense activities along the streets proved irresistible to me, and so I had to keep taking photos of what I saw as 'living history'.

One morning Waddi and I decided to take our two small sons for a walk down Nanking road on our own, and we eventually reached a busy cross-roads right by the famous old Wing On[10] Department Store.   But no traffic was now passing through because it was all roped off; a helpless traffic policeman was sitting immobile in the elevated police traffic box on the corner, bereft of any power.   And large numbers of pedestrians were walking past taking it all in, without any obvious reactions.   Inside the ropes many Red Guards were sitting down or talking in groups; it was a sit-down demonstration against the Municipal authorities, and yet another pregnant 'waiting for something to happen' moment.

I had my camera hanging around my neck and I casually lifted it up and started taking photos of the scene.   We walked around to another side of the roped off area, and then suddenly I was surrounded by four young male Red Guards who led me into the enclosed demonstration area to question me about my photos.   They were not wearing their school or institute's lapel badge so I didn't know where they were from, but they spoke standard Mandarin (pu.tong.hua), and they sounded very Peking-ish to me.

I immediately explained in Chinese that I was a 'foreign expert' (never was I so glad to use that title!), teaching English in Peking at the No 1 Foreign Languages Institute for the past two years, as evidenced by my lapel badge, and that I had taken many photos of Red Guard activities in the streets there without any problems.   I said that I was sorry that I hadn't understood the different situation in Shanghai, and I handed them my cam-

154

era, and asked them to take out the black and white film. Fortunately I had my little Identity card, issued to all foreigners, and I showed them that too. They said I should wait on that spot while they rushed off somewhere, clutching my camera, for guidance from above.

So there I was, standing around filling in time in the middle of the Red Guards, none of whom seemed interested in my fate, and imagining the possible outcomes of my predicament, while Waddi and sons, Tim and Matt, were watching anxiously from a discreet distance. It seemed like an age before a middle-aged man, with Red Guards in attendance, came up to me, and said that they had discussed my case. As I was a "foreign friend" (his words) they had decided to release me and he handed back my camera untouched, saying "Zhe shi ni.de zi.you!" (This is your freedom!) I was so relieved by this outcome that I can't remember clearly what happened next, except that I quickly rejoined Waddi and the boys, and we walked straight back to the Guesthouse to have a much-needed cup of tea, and to tell Neale and Deirdre all about it. And those black and white photos were some of the best that I took during the Cultural Revolution. Nevertheless I was much more cautious taking photographs of Red Guards after that.

We were only in Shanghai for eleven days, but lots of things were happening as we lived through those momentous times. The Hunters were spending a lot of their time reading wall posters, collecting leaflets and talking to their institute colleagues, while at the same time writing up daily notes and their analysis of the Shanghai scene. I was impressed by their discipline and dedication, which they apparently maintained until their departure in April 1967, and this painstaking investment was later converted by Neale into his book *Shanghai Journal* published by Praeger in 1969. Even though they were eye-witnesses, and had their colleagues and students in the Shanghai Foreign Languages Institute to talk to, it was a tremendous tour de force for a foreigner to write such an in-depth book on the complex political struggles taking place there.

One day Neale suggested to me that we cycle to the Airport because he had learnt that there was an Albanian Song & Dance Ensemble cultural group arriving that evening. So we set off early amongst the mass of cyclists in the evening rush hour. Waiting at a set of traffic lights we both noticed a young male Chinese cyclist alongside, who was eyeing us up discreetly. Like most young Chinese of those times, he was of thin and slight build, all sinew and muscles. Nothing was said but we both got his message, and as soon as the green light showed we were off pedalling furiously. This was a case of national pride being at stake, or more accurately, Westerners versus Chinese. All three of us were going at a frightening speed which defied common-sense, and as well as that we had to negotiate a way through the masses of cyclists going at a normal lick. It was neck and neck for a considerable distance, the next traffic lights being a long way ahead, and when we eventually reached them we three were still side by side, and I was completely out of breath by this time. I was very thankful when our challenger, with just a sideways glance, took the right hand turn off the main road, and honours were shared. So even with our greater body weight, a healthy, sporting life-style in our younger days, and a childhood diet of meat and milk, we two competitive Caucasians couldn't shake him off. I knew that we were both reasonably fit because that previous summer, Neale and I had spent a lot of hours at the Pei Tai Ho holiday resort locked in a series of very tight Anglo-Australian tennis matches. So that young Chinese man made quite an impression on us.

We ambled on to the airport and made our way to the arrivals hall. Noticing a balcony overlooking the area we slipped up there to get a good view. Looking down, we saw a huge crowd of welcoming Chinese personnel waiting there, some carrying cymbals and erhu fiddles[11], and some, obviously performers, with traditional greasepaint on their faces. The mood was getting more and more excitable, and then to tremendous noise and applause the Albanian troupe appeared and were mobbed immediately by their hosts. Equally animated and overcome by their reception, the Albanians were also on a high, and singing broke out spontaneously from both sides. This closely-packed mass of people filled the arrivals area, gently swirling around as welcome bouquets and presents were exchanged between the groups, while the short speeches were drowned out by the noise and charged atmosphere. I wasn't used to all this raw emotion from the Chinese. To my mind, it wasn't the usual Chinese way of doing things, with all the social control and correct protocol being thrown to the wind.

And it was a European group being warmly welcomed by China. After China's relations with the Soviet Union had soured in 1960, Albania was the only European socialist satellite country to follow China's political line. All very bizarre, and by our reckoning Albania was 'the mouse that roared'. As a result of this special growing relationship, the Chinese had produced a song in celebration of these fraternal links with Albania, presumably churned out for all appropriate politico-cultural events. I had never heard the song in action, but it must have been recorded on one of the many 78 rpm records of 'revolutionary songs' that were readily available in the stores at that time:

"Peking-Tirana, China-Albania,
Heroic cities, Heroic countries,
The great peoples are dauntless,
The heroic peoples hold their guns tightly
Long live Mao Tse-tung, Long live Enver Hoxha[12],
Long live our great Parties,
Long live Peking-Tirana."

Peking Review always gave glowing reports on visiting delegations from the People's Republic of Albania, and referred to them as coming from the 'Land of Eagles'. Apparently, Albania was very active at the United Nations in 1971, in helping the People's Republic of China to gain the Security Council place, previously held by Taiwan. However, this extraordinary relationship was not to last, and the final rupture to their close friendship occurred in 1978.

Deirdre had plans for us all to spend Christmas at the very famous West Lake Hotel[13] in Hangchow, and she had built up supplies of special foodstuffs to take with us, including a large turkey, stuffing, potatoes and vegetables. I never did find out how she had acquired a turkey, but that's Shanghai for you. So on Christmas Eve we got a morning train to Hangchow and reached the West Lake Hotel in time for lunch. It was cold, there had been some snow, and the scenery was picture postcard perfect, especially the nearby lake-side bamboo groves, which were covered with a thin layer of white. We were joined at the Hotel by Andrew and Maggie Watson, another British couple, who were teaching English at the Sian Foreign Languages Institute, so our Christmas group was expanding. As far as we could see, there were no Chinese guests staying at the

156

hotel, except for our colleague Old Yang, and we were the only foreign residents. On arrival and on our departure, the local public security office sent someone to the hotel, and he dutifully stamped all our visas for internal travel.

Andrew had a lovely anecdote about their life in the huge Friendship Guesthouse in Sian. One morning, having breakfast in the empty and cavernous dining-room, they saw a solitary male westerner sitting at a table in the far distance. This was a rare occurrence, so Andrew went over to say hello and introduce himself, and discovered that it was Andre Malraux, French Minister of Culture. Strangely enough, I had a similar experience there five years later in April 1971. Travelling with a small SACU tour group, we were staying at this Guesthouse in Sian. One evening, in the same barn-like dining room, we noticed another group of westerners around a table, far away in the otherwise deserted distance. Three of us went over to say hello, and to our surprise, we found it was the England table tennis team, and the Team Manager was Brian Merritt, who I knew because he had worked at the same factory as my father in Gloucester. 'Ping Pong' diplomacy had just broken out in China, with the arrival of the US table tennis team in Peking, and other teams had been invited too. I had known Brian in his younger days as an England international, when he would be practising endlessly with his fellow English international, Roy Morley, at the Gloucester Railway Carriage & Wagon Works Sports Club in Tuffley.

For Christmas Day lunch, Deirdre had a meeting with the hotel catering staff about cooking the turkey, and they put forward a small middle-aged man, as their expert chef on western cooking. We were satisfied to see him, as he looked old enough to have cooked for foreigners in pre-Liberation days. He also understood a little English, so he was bombarded with instructions on how long to roast our large turkey, and how to prepare the potatoes and vegetables. He blinked noticeably at our estimated roasting time of four to five hours; even Peking ducks didn't need that much time. Deirdre then repeated it all in Chinese for good luck. He was nodding furiously, and seemed to comprehend everything, and we left it at that, but he hadn't written anything down.

The next morning there was the usual Christmas Day excitement of presents for our sons, and early checking of the kitchen oven, the turkey and the cook. There was just time for Andrew and myself to take a short walk through the stunningly beautiful snow-covered bamboo groves nearby, and then we were all ready for Christmas Lunch. Everything was set out as we had requested, and the vegetable and Chinese dishes filled the table. But when the turkey was presented on the table, and we all chorused it as being 'piao.liang' (beautiful), Deirdre carefully chewed a sliver and pronounced it uncooked. She politely explained the problem to the little cook, and they disappeared back into the kitchen with the half cooked turkey. We all carried on and had a memorable Christmas lunch, albeit minus the turkey, which re-appeared later, well-roasted, for our evening meal. The hotel's electricity bill that day must have soared due to Deirdre's turkey roast.

On Boxing Day we visited the Ling Yin Temple of Buddhas, and saw at first hand the devastation caused by the Red Guards in previous months, with many shattered Buddha statues amongst the ruins. I was struck by a huge Buddha figure carved out of the hillside rock face, one of the few survivals of the Red Guards' violence, and there was in fact a stone mason working on it to smooth out any rough edges of damage. I cannot remember saying this myself, but in later years Old Yang told me of my comments on seeing the destruction: "Oh, the Red Guards can do anything they like. Absolutely lawless!" As we left the Temple, an extensive column of young demonstrators marched past, in a very relaxed atmosphere, and their slogans said that they were celebrating Chairman Mao's 73rd Birthday. They had Red Guard armbands on, but they weren't behaving in an aggressive or troublesome manner. So I warily took more photos.

Back to Shanghai and the Hunters had organised a large party for any passing foreigners in their guesthouse. As well as the Watsons, we were joined by Connaire and Ruth Kensit from Peking, who were also on a Christmas tour of China, and Ray and Sue Wiley, another couple working in Shanghai. Talitha Gerlach, an old resident of Shanghai was there too. It was a great evening and the main talking point, of course, was China and the Cultural Revolution, followed secondly by our imminent returns to home countries, which, by the way, all seemed based on another planet, and remote in the memory.

We were due to depart from Shanghai on the evening of 31 December 1966, and on the night before Neale and Deirdre took us out for a farewell dinner somewhere downtown. Another memorable meal and evening, where we drank warm Shaohsing [Shao.xing] [14] rice wine, and which we capped by going walkabout locally. That was a mistake. In some darkened street, we got into conversation with a group of older Red Guards, who thought we were from a national minority group, because of our foreign accents. So, bolstered by rice wine and our impending departure tomorrow, I unwisely bantered that we were Uyghurs[15]. Yet I was still in China, and this was not the time or place to banter. As we walked along we reached a well-light area, and they could see that our clothing was definitely not Uyghur-style, and also we weren't behaving in a subservient manner that minority people should show towards their Han[16] masters. They became suspicious of our origins, the atmosphere froze, and Neale and I had to do a lot of talking to get ourselves out of that fraught situation.

This was my second brush with Red Guards in Shanghai, and I had to produce my Institute badge, Chinese identity card and UK passport to satisfy them that we were genuine foreigners. For them, the Cultural Revolution was a momentous matter, and by creating that strained situation I had not shown them respect. It could have had very severe consequences for us, and it was time to leave China and go home.

On the evening of 31st December before we left the Guesthouse for the Airport, we went to the Office to pay our bill. Up to then all our accommodation charges in Peking had been settled by our Institute, and this was a new experience for me. I was quite irritated to find that the Guesthouse bill had increased by a small amount, and was above what I had been originally told. Probably it was some local tax charge that was added to every bill. My immediate response was to say we had no more Chinese money left, and I couldn't pay it. After two years of living under restrictive bureaucratic control in China, I finally snapped on my last day there, and refused to pay the small increment. Thereby causing some surprise to the Hunters and Old Yang.

We left on time to catch our evening PIA flight to Dacca, and they came to see us off at the Airport. Years later Old Yang told me that the accountant had had to accept my refusal to pay, and never asked him, as representative of our employers, to settle the outstanding amount. We took off late, in a relatively empty Boeing 707, and we were still in Chinese airspace when New Year 1967 arrived.

Chapter Notes

1. Liu Shaoji- Wikipedia online
2. Shanghai International Settlement- Wikipedia online
3. Francis Lister Hawks Pott- Wikipedia online
4. Shanghai Club Building- Wikipedia online
5. Former UK Consulate-General, Shanghai- Wikipedia online
6. Hans Koning- Wikipedia online (Hans Koningsberger)
7. Peace Hotel- Wikipedia online
8. Morris Cohen(adventurer)- Wikipedia online
9. The Hong Kong & Shanghai Banking Corporation- Wikipedia
10. Wing On- Wikipedia online
11. Erhu- Wikipedia online
12. Enver Hoxha- Wikipedia online
13. West Lake Hotel- Wikipedia online
14. Shaoxing wine- Wikipedia online
15. Uyghurs- Wikipedia online
16. Han chauvinism- Wikipedia online

24

SOME REFLECTIONS, WITH EUROPEAN CHARACTERISTICS

Fifty years have passed since I first arrived in Peking in 1965, and China has transformed herself into a significant world economic power today. I have a small booklet published in China in 1960 entitled 'Ten Great Years', with statistics covering the progress during the first decade up to 1958; the data fortunately stopped at that year, before the dreadful problems of the starvation years 1959-61. The subsequent, self-inflicted Cultural Revolution years of 1966-76 are labelled by Chinese people as the 'Ten Lost Years'. So the Chinese people had a stop-start existence for almost the first twenty-seven years of New China up to the death of Mao in 1976.

In 1965, to my fresh eyes, the central areas of Peking seemed, on the surface, to be quite traditional, with a thin veneer of socialism that was layered over everyday life, and that had, I suspected, lightly enveloped the old Confucian ways. The modern buildings stood out, because they were much higher and larger than the mass of old, two storey houses in the ancient alleys, hut'ung [hu.tong] [1], that spread out all over the centre of Peking. Wherever I went around the city, all the old buildings looked run-down, and in need of a coat of paint, repairs and renewal.

Little did I realise then, that beneath this modern mantle of socialism rested a much thicker seam of inherited bureaucratic authority, carried on the backs of the Chinese people. Still, it seems reasonable to argue that to govern such an enormous population in this huge country must demand an effective and extensive system of administration. This strict control of the population may appear repressive to western eyes, yet the Chinese people knew no alternative then, and was the price that they paid. As foreigners were virtually isolated from ordinary Chinese life, in the course of my two-year stay I could never get any feeling for the underlying values of the Chinese people, hidden away under this coating of socialism. With the differing practices of Confucianism and Maoism in the social admixture, I had no idea of the state of their moral compass or what was acceptable, and not acceptable in their society.

As I got to travel around by bicycle I gradually found that there were far more new buildings in the expanding suburbs to house the top research and educational institutes, as well as the factories necessary for China's scientific and industrial growth. Most of the old factories inherited in 1949 from foreign or Chinese ownership were still going strong; for example the Peking Iron & Steel Works[2], one of our organised visits in 1965, was slowly being modernised. After several factory visits, and without knowing anything about the industrial processes involved, I could see that there seemed to be a surplus of workers on the job. This might possibly be evidence of the practice of over-employment, which could be easily carried out in a state-controlled industry, in order to reduce the numbers of unemployed.

My superficial impressions were that this was a well-organised society, there was law and order, and things were under control. The limited traffic on the wide Chang An boulevard moved slowly, and the people on the streets all apparently ambled along at 'peasant pace'. It was not until we sometimes saw genuine peasants, as distinct to urban peasants, gawping and dawdling across the roads, oblivious to any passing traffic, that we understood something about the meaning of the word 'peasant'. At that time, everyone living in Peking, and other cities, had to have an official huk'ou [hu.kou][3] residential permit, so I will never quite know how those peasants managed to get into Peking city, but I'm sure that public security officers were soon on their case. The huk'ou residence system is a development of a centuries-old way of recording families and their places of abode. It was very convenient for the rulers of New China, who were able to use it as an instrument of social control over migration from the countryside into the urban areas. In recent decades it has been considerably weakened under the economic and commercial pressures of the expanding Chinese manufacturing base, and the consequent flow of humanity from the countryside to work in the towns.

Within eighteen months, my ingenuous view of a stable Chinese society was completely shattered by the chaos and turmoil of the Cultural Revolution in August 1966, and the breakdown in social order on the streets, as the Red Guards swept into action. Yet while the Red Guards were rampaging, policemen were still on traffic duty at major road junctions, unarmed soldiers were guarding the Friendship Store, and people were going about their daily lives. The People's Liberation Army (PLA) was the main authority left to contain the excesses of civil disturbances, and to maintain some semblance of order from then on until we departed, and right through to the end of this movement.

During autumn 1966 I saw diverse army uniforms on the streets, with none of the soldiers carrying weapons or showing any signs of their rank. In the early sixties Marshal Lin Piao had instigated a movement to politicise the army, and one spin-off effect had been an emphasis on equality rather than hierarchy, and this meant the removal of ranks from soldiers' uniforms. You could only get some idea of ranking from the age of the soldier and quality of clothing. I had not seen some of these uniforms before, such as the soldiers with warm headgear made from brown woollen fleeces, and I presumed that they were from the cold northern provinces of China. The movement of army divisions into the Peking area, to bolster or neutralise the local garrison, represented the struggle for power at the top, as members of the Politburo would have called on sympathetic Army Generals based throughout the provinces for political support. The Chinese Army had been directly involved in the politics of their country during the Chiang Kai-shek period, 1925-49, and were still there in the wings. Most foreigners, except for specialist China watchers, would have been completely unaware of these military implications, as was I.

Overt Han[4] chauvinism, and xenophobia against foreigners, did not clearly surface until 1967, culminating in the burning of part of the British Charge D'Affaires Office[5] in Peking in the summer of that year. Up to then the enclave of new foreign embassies in that area had been guarded by soldiers, but on this occasion they were rendered impotent by political orders. However, up to our departure in December 1966, I never had any fears for myself and family, as all foreigners were well protected in our Friendship Guesthouse. Unarmed PLA soldiers were always on guard duty at the imposing main gates, and also at the small, modest back entrance.

In 1965 China was a developing country with a struggling economy, and western powers, from their comparatively advanced standards of living, generally looked down on a China, as yet untested and unknown to the world, and with no economic clout. That summed up my attitude then. In fact, Britain was already exporting to China, and the previous year of 1964 had seen promising signs for Sino-British trade[6], and exports to China. Three large exhibitions of UK industrial and scientific products were held in Peking that year, and this is all recorded in Percy Timberlake's book *The 48 Group* (of British Traders with China), published in 1994 by the 48 Group Club. The list of participating UK companies at the 48 Group's British Mining & Construction Equipment Exhibition in 1964, is a dismal rollcall of Britain's lost engineering base. We are told that British manufacturing was in decline in the post-war period from 1945. This shrinkage accelerated in the 1980s, and was self-inflicted, helped in no small part by the then Conservative government's monetary policies. UK industry today seems to be the end-product of a whirlwind of misguided policies of successive post-war governments, all influenced by the dogma that the 'market' is the arbiter.

So Britain has a weakened industrialised economy, with a much reduced level of engineering and manufacturing products. Nowadays we are trying to expand our exports by sending groups of business people to Bei.jing, offering our services, luxury items and hi-tech. The rest of the world is doing the same thing too. It is all rather reminiscent of the old vassal states of antiquity sending missions to seek favours from and pay tribute to the Chinese Emperors in Peking. The Middle Kingdom [Zhong.Guo] is regaining some of the power and status that it enjoyed historically, but now its influence is worldwide, rather than limited geographically to the countries bordering Imperial China. One transformation emerging from this increased economic power is that China is now looking outward to invest some of its surplus funds overseas. In 2005 the Nanjing Automobile Corporation took over the Longbridge site of MG Rover, and then in 2013 Zhejiang Geely car manufacturers acquired Manganese Bronze, the makers of the iconic London taxi. For the first time, China is now investing worldwide.

All this time China has had to adjust to the rules and ways of doing international business, and carrying out diplomacy, as established by western powers before and during the supremacy of the Pax Britannica and Pax Americana. The main global institutions, such as the United Nations and associated bodies, World Bank, International Monetary Fund (IMF), World Health Organisaton(WHO) and World Trade Organisation(WTO), can all be seen as establishments created by the western world, and can be subject to western influence too. The Chinese may be probationers in learning the intricacies of the global ropes, but it is all part of the great race for them to acquire money, affluence and power. Their desire to be part of the world economic community was affirmed in 2001 when they joined the World Trade Organisation, WTO, which referees the rules of global trade and arbitrates on any disputes arising. And they are modernising their legal system to deal with the crucial requirements of international law on all aspects of business contracts and trade with the rest of the world. Another step forward was taken in 2015, when the Chinese ren.min.bi currency was accepted as a world reserve currency by the IMF.

The Chinese are obviously not happy to accept the American supremacy over world financial bodies, and they are starting to create parallel institutions, as alternatives to the old order. In 2014 China set up the Asia Infrastructure Investment Bank (AIIB), based in Bei.jing, which some commentators see as a rival to the World Bank, the IMF and Asian Development Bank. So the Chinese are flexing their financial muscles, and creating an investment bank under their own aegis, that will be independent of the USA. Any American criticism that questions the possible lower standards of governance of such a bank, is a direct attack on Chinese values and business ethics, as com-

162

pared to the 'superior' western canon of business law. Yet it was the activities of US and Western banks that caused the economic Banking Bubble of 2008.

Even in 1965, just after China had cut their ties with the Soviet Union, and they were struggling to build an industrial base and reconstruct their country, they had sent thousands of technicians to work overseas on projects in the developing world. China never asked other countries for direct help, and just wanted to trade on equal terms, to buy the technology and equipment that they needed to progress. Premier Chou En-lai had stated the basic principles of China's foreign policy at the Bandung Conference of Afro-Asian countries in 1955:

Mutual respect between countries
Mutual non-aggression
Mutual non-interference
Equality and mutual benefit
Peaceful co-existence

Of course the playing field, and international scene, have changed considerably since 1955, and we don't know how these principles are viewed in the corridors of power in 2015. One question of substance is how much the Chinese are attempting to put a distinguishing gloss on international law, or revising the rule books. This will surely happen in time, because the Chinese are definitely not a compliant people. They may be conformist within their own society, but liberated from those restraints, they can do business on the international stage, according to the rules and laws established by the western powers. And with supreme certainty of their superiority. On the rare occasions of meeting with any workers, peasants and soldiers during my stay, with or without a minder in tow, I was always struck by their stoic manner and air of cultural confidence, despite what I could see as their very low standard of living. I never found them undignified, or showing any traces of deference during our encounters.

China's economic policies since 1980, have allowed more freedom to private enterprise businesses and entrepreneurs, so that they can operate in parallel with state controlled industries. It has opened up a Pandora's Box of problems, which some foreign commentators attribute to weaknesses in the old socio-legal infrastructure, and to a lack of institutions. The financial progression has been so amazingly rapid that they have not had time to develop the needed institutions to cope with the emerging social realities arising from their success. As China copes with this new phenomenon of mass industrialisation, some Chinese factory workers, and their conditions of work, may be trapped in a 'developing country' time-capsule, roughly equivalent to the primitive attitudes in Victorian factories in nineteenth century Britain.

The Chinese government is having to deal with problems of factory conditions, land ownership, town planning, building standards and permits, the movement of people, legal rights and environmental issues, to name but a few. The old practice of sending memorials to the Emperor to rectify wrongs and settle disputes, is apparently still exercised by some Chinese, but now going to the leadership in Bei.jing. However China does not publicise anything about this anachronistic and feudal practice. Sadly, without the appropriate institutions being in place and working efficiently, and without an independent legal system[7], the laudable words of the 1954 Constitution of the People's Republic of China are of limited value to the ordinary Chinese person.

In a way, that constitution can be construed as a blueprint for a fairer and more equitable structure in Chinese society than existed in the maelstrom and upheavals of the early twentieth century up to 1949. But only under the strict control of the Chinese Communist Party, the self-proclaimed vanguard of the workers and peasants. Over the last thirty five years of dynamic economic growth, the legal statutes enshrined in the constitution seem to have been virtually overlooked, although there are now signs of the leadership revisiting the essential building block of 'rule of law'. Money, status and power are still the old 'institutions' that work and make things happen in China. Bribery, corruption and abuse of power are endemic. Communist cadres have too much power over those beneath them, and the Communist Party is only accountable to itself, and is above the law. Yang Ji.sheng, in his devastating book *Tombstone*, on the follies and famines of the three 'Bad Years', 1959-61, succinctly describes the attitude of Chinese officials as "a slave facing upwards and a dictator facing downwards". In recent years though, as economic standards have risen, the Party is beginning to have to pay more attention to public opinion and the people.

As a result of these changes, the Communist Party have finally put 'rule of law'[8] as a key theme for development at its Fourth Plenary session of the Eighteenth Communist Party meeting held in October 2014. After sixty five years of absolute power, it seems inconceivable that the Party is considering the promotion of new laws that could weaken its own power, so we should wait to see what sort of legal reality appears. The early indicators are that it will aim to make courts more impartial at local levels, and to penalise lesser officials who interfere in the judicial processes, while presumably leaving the top echelons of the Party still untouchable, and above the law. This issue is another reminder of the cross-cultural divides that occur when the Chinese decide to introduce a new concept into the social fabric of their country. In the past, for example, there had been misunderstandings between the two expressions 'rule of law' and 'rule by law', where the exact meaning is governed by the preposition used. No doubt, the 'rule of law' that will emerge in China, will be quite different, in form and content, to the 'rule of law' as defined and practised in Europe today.

The Chinese condemn the foreign 'semi-colonial' powers for creating a hundred years of humiliation for the Chinese people from 1842 to 1949, while apparently ignoring China's abject military weakness, inflexible conservatism, and intractable leadership in those times. The rulers of China up to 1911, during that period of national loss of face, were the Manchus[9] of the Ch'ing [Qing] dynasty from 1644 to 1911. They have now been relegated to the low status of a national minority group, and are of no significance today. Still, China could blame them, as well as the western colonialists, for all the sorrows that befell their country. There is little recognition that during Mao's period of power from 1949 to 1976, it was the Chinese people themselves who obediently inflicted suffering and pain on each other, at the behest of their leaders, and their policies. Just another medieval moment in China's long history.

Yet in Europe the Great War, 1914-18, was also medieval, when millions of young Western European men obediently inflicted terrible slaughter and inhumanities on each other, using the most advanced weaponry of the times. Perhaps the bloodshed and suffering of the Spanish civil war in the 1930s is a closer analogy to the Chinese experience. In such cases of intercultural censorious appraisal, it might be reasonable for each country to be judged within the context of its own historical development of morality and values, and not be measured by the standards of other cultures, especially ones that may occupy quite a different position on the spectrum of global ethics. Who can decide whether "One culture's 'bribe' is another culture's 'gift'"?

Never before in their history has such a large cross-section of the Chinese population become so affluent and wealthy, although the disparities between rich and poor are now huge. Looking at the extreme vagaries of their life over the past fifty years, the Chinese people moved on from the post-traumatic stress of the Cultural Revolution into building a socialist market economy and society, whereby some parts of the means of production could be in the hands of individuals, and not the state. That is, they were permitted to work towards a better life for themselves, and create wealth by their own endeavours.

China's economic power and enhanced status in the world implies moral obligations too, certainly in regard to the United Nations, and associated international responsibilities. Again, these moral obligations can be seen as derived from western cultures, with little input from oriental societies. China, in recent centuries, has never before been in such a situation of having to respond to global pressures caused by other faraway countries. One could argue that after having only thirty-five short years of economic progress, they will need to remain focused on their own needs and development, before taking on any external roles. Unless, of course, China's interests are under threat in some way.

In terms of 'exceptionalism'[10], many countries today may quietly regard themselves as special and separate to others. Western countries may think of themselves as 'exceptional', in terms of holding the high moral ground on human rights for the individual in their societies. On the other hand, China thinks of itself as a unique and distinctive civilisation, which is both 'exceptional' and superior. Whatever differences there may be between societies, China argues that countries are at differing stages of progression, and each one has evolved a culture-specific form. So it is inevitable that the Chinese way of doing things sometimes involves the addition of the term '…with Chinese characteristics', in order to emphasise their Chineseness and essence.

Chapter Notes
1. Hutong- Wikipedia online
2. Shougang Corporation- Wikipedia online
3. Hukou system- Wikipedia online
4. Han chauvinism- Wikipedia online
5. China-United Kingdom relations- Wikipedia online
6. CBBC- History- Wikipedia online
7. Law of the People's Republic of China- Wikipedia online
8. Rule of law- Wikipedia online
9. Manchu people- Wikipedia online
10. Exceptionalism- Wikipedia online

合 同

北京外国語学院（以下簡称聘方）茲聘請 曾鈴德・里理士・韓德 先生 女士（以下簡称受聘方）为

英 語教師，双方本着友好精神，同意签訂本合同。

一、聘期定为 二 年，自 1965 年 1 月 8 日至 1967 年 1 月 7 日止。

二、受聘方在受聘期間的工作任务为：

(1) 担任 英 語課堂教授、批改作业、指导課外活动和学年論文；

(2) 担任 英 語师資和研究生的培养工作；

(3) 編选 英 語教材以及其他有关 英 語方面的工作。

三、受聘方工作时間和工作的具体安排由双方根据上述任务共同商定。受聘方应遵守聘方的工作制度，按时完成工作任务并保证質量。聘方欢迎受聘方在工作中提出建議，并根据情况采纳，但受聘方应按聘方的决定进行工作。

四、聘方每月支付給受聘方工資人民币 律佰陸拾 元。

五、受聘方按照本合同附件所列各点，享受有关的生活待遇。

六、双方均不得无故提前結束聘期，如一方严重违反本合同规定时，经对方說明原因后有权在中途提出辞聘或解聘，自提出辞聘或解聘之日算起滿二个月后本合同即予失效。

七、本合同自聘期开始日生效。任何一方如要求延长聘期时，应在期滿前二个月向对方提出，由双方协商确定。双方未提出延长聘期或一方不同意延长聘期，本合同即按聘期滿后失效。

八、本合同在执行中如有未尽事項，由双方协商解决。

九、本合同用中文和 英 文两种文字写成，两种文本具有同等效力。

聘方代表

受聘方 R. A. Hunt

1966 年 3 月 日 北京

167

C O N T R A C T

    Foreign Languages Institute of Peking (hereinafter referred to as the first party) has engaged Mr. Reginald Charles Hunt (hereinafter referred to as the second party) as a teacher of

    English   , the two parties having in a spirit of friendship entered into the present agreement.

    I. The term of service is   two years, that is, from Jan. 8, 1965 to Jan. 7, 1967 .

    II. During his (her) term of service the second party will undertake work of the following character:

    (1) Class-room teaching of   English , correction of students' written work, and extra-curricular activity and term-paper guidance;

    (2) Training of teachers of   English   and research students, and

    (3) Compilation of   English   teaching material and similar work in the same language.

    III. Details concerning working hours and concrete tasks will be arranged by mutual consultation within the scope mentioned above. The second party undertakes to observe the school regulations and complete his (her) tasks according to schedule and on a high standard. The first party welcomes any suggestions that may come from the second party in the course of his (her) work and will take them into favourable consideration in so far as circumstances permit; on the other hand, the second party agrees that all work will be carried on in accordance with the decisions of the first party.

    IV. The second party will receive a monthly salary of   460   yuan (Chinese currency).

    V. Other particulars regarding the treatment that will be accorded the second party are stated in the appended articles.

-1-

VI. Neither party shall without sufficient cause or reason end the term of service herein agreed upon before it expires. Should one of the parties seriously violate the terms of this contract, then the other party, after dur explanation, would have the right to serve advance notice of contract termination, in which case the present contract ceases to be effective two months after such notice is given.

VII. The present contract comes into effect on the first day of the term of service herein stipulated. If either party wishes to extend the term of service, the other party shall be notified at least two months before it expires. If neither party makes a proposal for its renewal, or if one of the parties fails to agree, then the present contract ceases to be effective at the expiration of the stipulated term of service.

VIII. In the course of its execution, should any questions arise which are not covered by this contract, they should be settled by mutual agreement.

IX. The present contract is drawn up in Chinese and
_____English_____, the two versions being equally valid.

_____
(For the First Party)

_____
(Second Party)

Peking, ___March___,___1966___ .

-2-

169

Appendix B

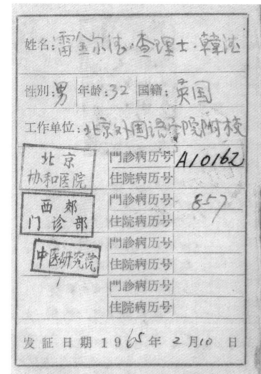

姓名: 雷金尔德·查理士·韩法

性别: 男 年龄: 32 国籍: 英国

工作单位: 北京外国语学院附校

北京 协和医院	门诊病历号	A10162
	住院病历号	
西郊 门诊部	门诊病历号	857
	住院病历号	
中医研究院	门诊病历号	
	住院病历号	
	门诊病历号	
	住院病历号	

发证日期 19 65 年 2 月 10 日

卫生部
医疗专用章

意 事 項

1. 就诊时必須携带此证;
2. 凭证可到左列医院诊治;
3. 如此证遗失, 請即报告
   发证单位, 补領医疗证;
4. 工作期滿回国时, 請交
   回此证。

Appendix C

Appendix D

REGULATION RE ACCOMMODATION

Experts living in the Guest House are asked to cooperate in the observance of the following principles affecting accommodation.

I. Allocation:
one person - one room;
two to three persons - two rooms;
four to five persons - three rooms;
six to seven persons - four rooms;

2. In general, the above allocations will be observed. If residents, however, require extra accommodation, the management will consider their claim on its merits provided additional accommodation is both necessary and available. Such additional accommodation will be changed to the guests' account.

3. Resident's visitors are not expected to stay in the Guest House overnight.

4. No cooking can be done in apartments in Building No. I, II and IV which have no kitchens and cooking is not allowed in the rooms.

5. Every room is adequately furnished. No extra furniture can be supplied.

6. Guests are suggested not to remove any furniture or fittings from their room; to lend or borrow such articles or pull articles of furniture apart. Compensation is expected when furniture or furnitions are damaged by residents.

7. Please do not put nails in the doors, window frames or walls; do not disfigure or paste things on the walls.

8. Some electric rings and irons are available for the use of residents free of charge in all the buildings.

9. Guests desiring to use their own electric rings must not

install more than one which should be between 600-800 watts. The use of higher powered electric rings liable to cause grave accidents.

10. Please do not change any electric fittings in your apartment nor replace the bulbs by more powerful ones; nor change the shades or bowls. Incase of absolute necessity, the agreement management should be sought in regard to all electric fittings. The cost of any changes in fittings should be met by the residents.

II. Guests are requested to answer that their children do not create noise by running about the corridors.

I2. In the interests of the general comfort of the residents, it is requested that no noisy eveningparties be held in private room and that the volume of all radios be kept reasonably low.

I3. Residents are asked not to keep dogs, cats, chicken or other livestock in their rooms.

I4. Guests needing the loundry or clean services are asked to hand in their goods at the service desks.

I5. Please lock your door when going out and put the key in the place provided at the service desk or hand them to the floor assistants.

Management of the Friendship

Guest House

Appendix E

午饭　　M E N U　　　8　　February　　　1976.

　　　　　　　　　　　LUNCH　　　　　　　　ALMUERZO
　　　　　　　　　　　-----　　　　　　　　--------

菜花汤　Beef soup with cauliflower
　　　　Sopa de carne con coliflor　　　-----------　.30

凌　　汤　Consomme with noodles
　　　　Consome con fideos　　　　　　-------------　.20

鸡肉豆芹捲　Pancake roll with chicken meat
　　　　Pastel relleno con pollo　　　----------　.80

牛肉饭　Beef rizotto
　　　　Carne con arroz　　　　　-----------------------　.45

法式猪排　Pork chops, French style
　　　　Chuletas de cerdo estilo Frances　　-----　.50

己式羊排土豆　Mutton chop with potatoes, Pakistan style
　　　　Chuletas de cordero con patatas estilo Pakistan
　　　　　　　　　　　　　　　　　　　　　　　.50
查素菜　Boiled vegetables
　　　　Verduras hervidas　　　-----------------　.15

布　　丁　Bread and apple pudding　　-------------　.30

　　　　　中烧　CHINESE FOOD　　COMIDA CHINA
　　　　　　　-----------　　-------------

古老肉　Sweet, sour pork
　　　　Cerdo con salsa agridulce　　-----------　.60

青椒牛肉　Slice beef with green pepper
　　　　Trozos de carne con pimiento verde　-----　.50

肉虎尤菜　Rape with pork
　　　　Colza con cerdo　　　-------------------------　.35

炆豆芽　Stir-fried bean sprouts
　　　　Brotes de soya semifritos　　----------　.15

饺子　Ravioli
　　　Raviole　　　------------------------------------　.02

酿鸡子　Cold stuffed eggs
　　　　Huevos relleno frio　　　-----------------　.25

茄子泥　Mashed aggplant
　　　　Berenjenas molidas　　　-----------------　.25

红鱼子　Red caviar
　　　　Caviar rojo　　　　-----------------------------　.50

174

Appendix F

Junior II Dictation and Punctuation exercise   April 1965

NOTE: Our Chinese colleagues would often ask us to write short passages or descriptions about the pupil's life and activities. I wrote the following exercises and passage about the two weeks physical labour that Junior II class carried out in April 1965, in the middle of our first term of teaching.

Dictation & Punctuation passage for Junior II:

on monday april 12th 1965 junior two started two weeks physical labour first they dug up the primary school playground with pickaxes and shovels there were several piles of earth some pupils shovelled the earth onto a handcart then two pupils pushed the handcart to the courtyard some pupils shovelled the earth on to a wheelbarrow then one pupil pushed the wheelbarrow to the courtyard

My Original Dictation Passage, which was deemed too difficult:

One day when I was walking across the courtyard I saw some junior two pupils pushing a handcart they were working hard during their physical labour as I walked towards the teachers dining room I saw quite a few pupils all working very hard some were using pickaxes and shovels to dig up the primary school playground others were digging a trench I asked teacher chiu will you dig up the basketball stands and she replied no when we have levelled the foundations we will lay a mixture of earth and lime and then we will pound the mixture to make a hard surface she said that after physical labour the pupils would review their work with me in english during the next week I visited them again and the work was almost finished some of the pupils were rolling the surface using a heavy stone roller two pupils were pulling and two were pushing.

My Description of Junior II Physical Labour in April 1965:

On Monday April 12th 1965 Junior II started their two weeks physical labour. Their task was to re-lay the playground of the Primary School. First of all the old surface soil was dug up using pickaxes and shovels and then carefully put into piles of earth. That soil was removed to a depth of about 4 inches, and the foundations were levelled. Next, all the piles of earth were sifted using large wire screens, and the fine earth was separated from the bricks and rubble, in the following way: The wire screens were firmly fixed almost upright by resting on two wooden poles and then the pupils shovelled the earth at the screen.

The bricks and rubble were not able to pass through the screen and rolled down into a specially prepared trench, while the fine earth easily passed through the screen. The pupils did this work very easily.

Then, any rubble and bricks that were not needed were taken away by the pupils on handcarts, in wheelbarrows or sometimes in pannier baskets. If the pupils used a handcart they would push it or pull it. If a wheelbarrow they would push it. If a basket, two pupils would balance the bamboo pole on their shoulders with the basket hanging from the middle of the pole.

After the playground foundations were levelled the next step was to prepare the surface mixture. It was made by mixing the fine earth with white lime and water, and it was a grey colour. When the mixture was ready the pupils carried it in pannier baskets and carefully laid it on the foundations. Some pupils were using large wooden rakes to level the surface. After it was levelled the surface was pounded by the pupils using heavy wooden blocks, and this was hard work. After the pounding the surface was watered and straw laid on top. Finally the surface was rolled with a heavy stone roller.

NOTE: In the early days one problem for me was that I didn't know the core foundation of English of the different classes. Only their Chinese teacher of English knew that. So my colleagues asked me to write material that was too advanced for the class level, and then they would modify it to the required language level for use as exercises. I had already simplified the preceding passage that I wrote for Junior II, but it was still too difficult and too structurally complex for their stage of English.

Appendix G

Essay by Senior 3 student in February 1965, before being corrected:

"We worked in the countryside for less than a month. It was a good chance to live with the poor and lower-middle peasants. We learned a lot from them. They were not only hard-working, but also had the happiness of the people at heart. They often said that they must produce more grain for the revolution. They also took good care of us. They let us live in the best houses but they themselves lived in the worst ones. Once a comrade got ill, they nursed him back to health.

There our main work was to dig the Peking-Miyun irrigation channel. All of us worked in real earnest. We were the first to bear hardships, the last to enjoy comforts. When we were tired we would think of the truth: "After all you are not a real revolutionary youth, if you are afraid of difficulties." On thinking of this, our courage screwed up at once. No matter how great the difficulties were, we could overcome them all. So everyday we finished the work ahead of time.

After work we always had a good time. Some studied Chairman Mao's works. Some read newspapers. Some sang songs. Some put things in rhymes. During physical labour , our life was full of happiness, because we created wealth with our own hands."

Author's note: This was one of the better essays among the Senior 3's efforts, and you can imagine my reaction, after only a couple of weeks teaching in Peking. He had to write something positive and inspiring about his manual work, without being critical in any way. It was written in correct Basic English, but it seemed stilted to me, except for the idiomatic mention of "our courage screwed up". Very short sentences were commonplace because they were safer to produce, and they followed the English language sentence order of Subject-Verb-Object e.g. "Some read newspapers". The students had a lot of reading material from their teachers written in this style, so they were faithfully re-producing the sentence format and structures that they had been taught. See the precise usage of 'after, also, always, because, but, during, often' throughout the essay. I realised that my main task in teaching English was to build up morale and encourage my students, rather than dwell on their errors.

Appendix H

SACRED HEART SCHOOL - PEKING

Name: *Timothy Hunt* Year: *Preparatory*

1965 - 66

	Reading	Dictation	Spelling	Arithmetic	Ethics	Writing	Drawing	Singing		Classwork Av.	Attendance	Application	Politeness	Discipline	Conduct Av.	Total Average	Class Rank	Parents' Signature
Sept.																		
Oct.																		
Nov.																		
Dec.																		
Jan.																		
Feb.																		
March	75		40	59		60	60	60		61	96	67	70	79	78	70	17	Hunt
April	75		40	62		62	61	60		62	96	68	70	70	74	68	19	Hunt
May	77		50	67		70	65	62		69	100	70	72	74	79	74	13	R.D. Hunt.
June	75		58	70		72	67	64		68	88	72	73	73	76	71	16	

Promoted to First Year

SACRED HEART SCHOOL PEKING

178

Appendix I

Talk for Foreigners - 28 April 1966

At very short notice, foreign experts in the Druzhba were invited to attend a large gathering of foreigners at the Old Wing of the Peking Hotel, on the morning of 28 April 1966. This was an unusual event, which occurred several weeks before the term 'cultural revolution' had entered the foreigners vocabulary, and we could not fathom the political motivation behind it. It was reported in *Peking Review* of 6 May 1966:

> *"May Day Receptions: Two days before May Day, there was a reception in Peking for the experts and their families from over 60 countries who are helping China in its socialist construction. Teng Hsiao-ping, General Secretary of the Central Committee of the Chinese Communist Party and Vice-Premier, and Po I-po, Alternate Member of the Political Bureau of the Party's Central Committee and Vice-Premier, attended. Both leading comrades proposed toasts and thanked the experts for their great help. They also expressed the hope that, through them, the mutual understanding and militant friendship between the Chinese people and the people of the world would be promoted."*

The ballroom seemed to be packed out with foreigners, and I vividly remember Teng speaking there, but not Po I-po. Regretfully, I do not have copies of transcripts of their speeches, and I have to rely solely on the account above, given in Peking Review. It was also the only time that I was able to visit the original wing of the Peking Hotel, the centre of foreign social life in old semi-colonial China before 1949.

Appendix J

List of possible places for a small group to visit

1. Museum of Peking Man
2. Coal mine - Opencast
                Underground
3. Peoples Daily
        Editorial and Printing departments
4. Radio station and Television studies
5. National Minorities Research Institute
6. Chinese Music Exhibition Hall
7. Chinese Music Research Institute
8. Conservatory of Music
9. Peking Academy of Ballet
10. Stadiums being built for GANEFO games.
11. Dairy Farm on Commune

The most convenient times for visiting would be
          Wednesday afternoon
          Friday   afternoon

R.C.Hunt
81231.

25.4.66

Appendix K

Peking No 2 Middle School- August 1966

'Declaration of War' wall-poster:

"The floodwaters of the Great Proletarian Cultural Revolution are now pounding the various positions of the bourgeoisie. The hotbeds of capitalism are no longer safe. "Ducktail" haircuts, "spiralling" hairdos, other queer hairstyles, cowboy jeans, tight-fitting shirts and blouses, various kinds of Hong Kong-style skirts and dresses, and obnoxious photographs and journals are now under heavy fire. We should not regard these matters lightly, because it is here that the gates to capitalist restoration are wide open. The former Peking Municipal Party Committee was deaf and blind to these things for 17 years, and even forbade any reforms. We must block all channels leading to capitalism, and we are not going to be soft on these things."

Appendix L

A Letter from Chairman Mao to the Red Guards of Tsinghua University Attached Middle School on 1ˢᵗ August 1966:

Red Guard Comrades of Tsinghua University Middle School:

I have received both the big-character posters which you sent on 28 July *[1966]*, as well as the letter which you sent to me, asking for an answer.   The two big-character posters which you wrote on 24 June *[1966]* and 4 July *[1966]* express your anger at, and denunciation of, all landlords, bourgeois, imperialists, revisionists and their running dogs who exploit and oppress the workers, peasants, revolutionary intellectuals and revolutionary parties and groupings.   You say it is right to rebel against reactionaries. I enthusiastically support you.

I also give enthusiastic support to the big-character poster of the Red Flag Combat Group of Peking University Middle School, which said that it is right to rebel against reactionaries, and to the very good revolutionary speech given by Comrade P'eng Hsiao -meng, representing their Red Flag Combat Group at the big meeting attended by all the teachers, students, administration and workers of Peking University on 25 July *[1966]*. Here I want to say that I myself, as well as my revolutionary comrades-in-arms all take the same attitude.

No matter where they are, in Peking or anywhere in China, I will give enthusiastic support to all who take an attitude similar to yours in the Cultural Revolution movement. Another thing, while supporting you, at the same time we ask you to pay attention to uniting with all who can be united with.   As for those who have committed serious mistakes; after their mistakes have been pointed out you should offer them a way out of their difficulties by giving them work to do, and enabling them to correct their mistakes and become new men.   Marx said that the proletariat must emancipate not only itself but all mankind. If it cannot emancipate all mankind then the proletariat itself will not be able to achieve final emancipation.   Will comrades please pay attention to this truth too!

Mao Tse-tung

Appendix M

<u>Copy of the original 4 Americans' DAZIBAO of 1966.</u>

WHY IS IT THAT FOREIGNERS WORKING HERE AT THE HEART OF
THE WORLD REVOLUTION ARE BEING PUSHED DOWN THE REVISIONIST ROAD?

What monsters are behind the treatment of foreigners working in China?

Why is it that foreigners regardless of class or attitude toward the
revolution, all get the same 'Five-don't-have-two-have' treatment?

The Five-Don't-Haves:-

    1) Physical labor
    2) Ideological remolding
    3) Contact with peasants and workers
    4) Class struggle
    5) Struggle for production

The Two-Haves:-

    1) Super-High living standards
    2) Special treatment

What kind of thinking is behind this treatment?

    It is NOT the thinking of Mao Tse-Tung!
    It is Krushchev's thinking!
    It is revisionist thinking!
    It is the thinking of exploiting classes!

What is the object, what is the result of this treatment?

    1) - to prevent foreigners who want to be revolutionaries from
        grasping Chairman Mao's thought!
    2) - to gradually soften up revolutionary foreigners living in
        China and push them down the revisionist road!
    3) - to prevent foreign children brought up in China from
        becoming revolutionaries!
    4) - to isolate foreign revolutionaries from their Chinese
        class brothers, to break down their mutual class love,
        to undermine proletarian internationalism!

We think this is not a question of a few individuals, but a question of
principle related to world revolution.

We resolutely oppose this kind of treatment!

      - We are determinded to become real revolutionaries!
      - We are determinded to become staunch fighters against
        revisionism!
      - We are determinded to steel ourselves for an all out
        struggle against U.S.Imperialism!
      - Our children must become staunch successors to the revolution;
        they must never be allowed to become revisionists!

THEREFORE WE REQUEST:—

1) That we be treated not like bourgeois experts but like
   class brothers.

2) That we be permitted and encouraged to join physical labor.

3) That we be given every assistance in our ideological remolding.

4) That we be permitted and encouraged to have intimate contact
   with workers and peasants.

5) That we be permitted and encouraged to join the three
   great revolutionary movements.

6) That our children be treated the same as Chinese children
   and have the same strict demands made on them.

7) That our living standards be the same as that of the Chinese
   personnel of the same category.

8) That special treatment be abolished.

— only in this way is there a chance for us to become
   revolutionaries of the kind called for by Chairman
   Mao-Tse-Tung!

LONG LIVE THE GREAT PROLETARIAN REVOLUTION!

LONG LIVE THE GREAT UNITY OF THE PEOPLE OF THE WORLD!

LONG LIVE THE GREAT INVINCIBLE THINKING OF MAO TSE-TUNG!

LONG LIVE THE GREAT LEADER OF THE CHINESE PEOPLE, THE
INTERNATIONAL PROLETARIAT, THE OPPRESSED PEOPLE AND OPPRESSED
NATIONS — COMRADE MAO TSE-TUNG!!!

Appendix N

THE CONSTITUTION OF THE COMMUNIST PARTY OF CHINA

Adopted by the Eighth National Congress of the Communist Party of China- 26 September 1956: Foreign Languages Press, Peking, 1965

EXTRACTS FROM THE GENERAL PROGRAMME, Pages 1-9

Paragraph 1:

The Communist Party of China is the vanguard of the Chinese working class, the highest form of its class organization.   The aim of the Party is the achievement of socialism and communism in China.

Paragraph 2:

The Communist Party of China takes Marxism-Leninism as its guide to action.   Only Marxism-Leninism correctly sets forth the laws of the development of society and correctly charts the path leading to the achievement of socialism and communism. The Party adheres to the Marxist-Leninist world outlook of dialectical and historical materialism, and opposes the world outlook of idealism and metaphysics. Marxism-Leninism is not a dogma but a guide to action.

Paragraph 3:

In the year 1949, after long years of revolutionary struggle and revolutionary wars, the Communist Party and the people of the whole country overthrew the rule of imperialism, feudalism and bureaucrat-capitalism and founded the People's Republic of China – a people's democratic dictatorship led by the working class and based on the alliance of workers and peasants. Following this, the Party led the masses of the people in accomplishing the task of the democratic revolution in most parts of the country and achieving great success in the struggle to establish a socialist society.

Final Paragraph on Page 9:

The Communist Party of China requires all its members to place the Party's interests above their own, to be diligent and unpretentious, to study and work hard, to unite the broad masses of the people, and to overcome all difficulties in order to build China into a great, mighty, prosperous and advanced socialist state, and on this basis to advance towards the achievement of the loftiest ideal of mankind—communism.

SHORT SELECTION OF BOOKS FOR READING & REFERENCE

Some books on China published before 1950:

Belden, Jack. *China Shakes the World,* New York, Simon & Schuster, 1949.

Russell, Bertrand. *The Problem of China*, London, George Allen & Unwin, 1922.

Smedley, Agnes. *China Fights Back*, London, Victor Gollanz, 1938.

Snow, Edgar. *Red Star over China*, London, Victor Gollanz, 1937.

Some books on China published from 1950-1979:

Clubb, O.Edmund. *Twentieth Century China*, New York, Columbia University Press, 1964.

Cranmer-Byng, J.L. *An Embassy to China* [Lord Macartney's Embassy, 1793], London, Longmans, 1962.

Fitzgerald, C.P. *The Birth of Communist China*, London, Penguin Books, 1964.

Fung,Yu-Lan. *A Short History of Chinese Philosophy* [Edited by Derk Bodde], New York, Macmillan Paperback, 1960.

Harrison, James P. *The Communists and Chinese Peasant Rebellions*, New York, Athenaeum, 1969.

Hibbert, Christopher. *The Dragon Wakes- China and the West, 1795-1911* London, Longman Group, 1970.

Hinton, William. *Hundred Day War- The Cultural Revolution at Tsinghua University*, New York, Monthly Review Press, 1972.

Karol, K.S. *China- The Other Communism*, London, Heinemann, 1967. [Photos by Marc Riboud]

Koningsberger, Hans. *Love and Hate in China*, New York, McGraw-Hill, 1966.

Kuan, Ta-tung. *The Socialist Transformation of Capitalist Industry and Commerce in China*, Peking, Foreign Languages Press, China Knowledge Series, 1960.

Ling, Ken. *Red Guard in Mao's China*, London, Macdonald, 1972.

Needham, Joseph. *Science & Civilisation in China, Volumes 1-27*, London, Cambridge University Press, 1954 to date.

Schram, Stuart. *Mao Tse-tung*, London, Penguin, 1966.

Snow, Edgar. *The Long Revolution*, London, Hutchinson,1973.

State Statistical Bureau, *Ten Great Years: Statistics of the Economic and Cultural Achievements of the People's Republic of China (1949-1958)*, Peking, Foreign Languages Press, 1960.

Treadgold, Donald. *The West in Russia and China-Religious & Secular Thought in Modern Times (Volume 2: China 1582-1949)*, London, Cambridge University Press, 1973.

Some books by foreigners who lived in China during 1950-1979:

Alley, Rewi. *At 90: Memoirs of my China Years*, Beijing, New World Press, 1986. [Includes catalogue of his writings]

Broyelle, Claudie & Jacques. & Tschirhart, Evelyne, *China: A Second Look*, Sussex, England, Harvester Press, 1980.

Chen, Jack. *Inside the Cultural Revolution*, London, Sheldon Press, 1976.

Collier, John & Elsie. *China's Socialist Revolution*, London, Stage 1, 1973.

Cradock, Percy. *Experiences of China*, London, John Murray, Paperback edition, 1999.

Crook, David & Isabel. *Revolution in a Chinese Village- Ten Mile Village*, London, Routledge, 1959.

Ginsberg, Sam. *My First Sixty Years in China*, Beijing, New World Press, 1982.

Gordon, Eric. *Freedom is a Word*, London, Hodder & Stoughton, 1971.

Grey, Anthony. *Hostage in Peking*, London, Michael Joseph, 1970.

Horn, Joshua. *Away with All Pests*, London, Paul Hamlyn, 1969.

Hunter, Neale. *Shanghai Journal*, New York, Praeger Publishers, 1969 & Oxford University Press, 1988.

Jenner, Delia. *Letters from Peking*, Oxford University Press, 1967.

Knight, Sophia. *Window on Shanghai- Letters from China, 1965-67*, London, Andre Deutsch, 1967.

Mackerras, Colin & Hunter, Neale. *China Observed*, [1965-67] Sphere Paperback, 1968.

Milton, David & Nancy. *The Wind Will Not Subside: Years in Revolutionary China 1964-1969*, New York, Pantheon Books, 1975.

Rittenberg, Sidney & Bennett, Amanda. *The Man Who Stayed Behind*, New York, Simon & Schuster, 1993.

Shapiro, Michael. *Changing China*, London, Lawrence & Wishart, 1958.

Smedley, Agnes. *The Great Road- The Life and Times of Chu Teh*, New York, Monthly Review Press, 1956.

Some books on China published after 1980:

Boyd, Julia. *A Dance with the Dragon- The Vanished World of Peking's Foreign Colony*, London, I. B. Tauris, 2012.

Brady, Anne-Marie. *Making the Foreign Serve China*, USA, Rowman & Littlefield, 2003.

Buchanan, Tom. *East Wind: China and the British Left, 1925-1976*, Oxford University Press, 2012.

Dikotter, Frank. *Mao's Great Famine 1958-62*, London, Bloomsbury, 2010.

Fairbank, John King. *The Great Chinese Revolution, 1800-1985*, London, Chatto & Windus, 1987.

Fairbank, John & Twitchett, Denis [Editors]. *The Cambridge History of China* [13 Volumes published to date] Cambridge University Press, 1979 to date.

Gittings, John. *China Changes Face*, London, Oxford University Press, 1989.

Hinton, William. *Shenfan*, London, Secker & Warburg, 1983.

Hofstede, Geert. *Culture and Organizations- Software of the Mind*, New York, McGraw-Hill, 1996.

Hollander, Paul. *Political Pilgrims- Travels of Western Intellectuals to the Soviet Union, China, and Cuba, 1928-78*, Oxford University Press, 1981.

Jung, Chang. *Wild Swans- Three Daughters of China*, New York, Simon & Schuster, 1991.

Heng, Liang. & Shapiro, Judith. *Son of the Revolution*, London, Chatto & Windus, 1983.

Timberlake, Percy. *The 48 Group*, London, The 48 Group Club, 1994.

Wilson, Dick. *Mao- The People's Emperor*, London, Futura Publications Ltd, 1980.

Yang, Ji.sheng. *Tombstone- The Untold Story of Mao's Great Famine* [1958-61] London, Allen Lane, 2012.

Zhong, Wen.xian [Editor]. *Mao Zedong: Biography, Assessment, Reminiscences*, Beijing, Foreign Languages Press, 1986.